ARRIVAL CITY

ARRIVAL CITY

HOW THE LARGEST MIGRATION IN HISTORY IS RESHAPING OUR WORLD

DOUG SAUNDERS

PANTHEON BOOKS, NEW YORK

Copyright © 2010 by Doug Saunders

All rights reserved. Published in the United States by Pantheon Books, a
division of Random House, Inc. Originally published in Great Britain by
William Heinemann, the Random House Group Ltd., London, in 2010.

Pantheon Books and colophon are registered trademarks of Random
House, Inc.

Library of Congress Cataloging-in-Publication Data

Saunders, Doug.
    Arrival city : how the largest migration in history is reshaping our
world / [Doug Saunders].
        p.   cm.
    Includes bibliographical references and index.
    ISBN 978-0-375-42549-3
    1. Rural-urban migration. 2. Cities and towns—Growth.
3. Immigrants—Social conditions. 4. Urbanization. I. Title.
HB1955.S38 2010   307.2'4—dc22   2010029651

www.pantheonbooks.com

Jacket design by Joe Montgomery

Printed in the United States of America
First United States Edition

2   4   6   8   9   7   5   3   1

CONTENTS

For Elizabeth Renzetti

THORNCLIFFE PARK

TOWER HAMLETS

HERNDON/WHEATON

PARLA

LOS ANGELES

PETARE

SANTA MARTA

JARDIM ANGELA

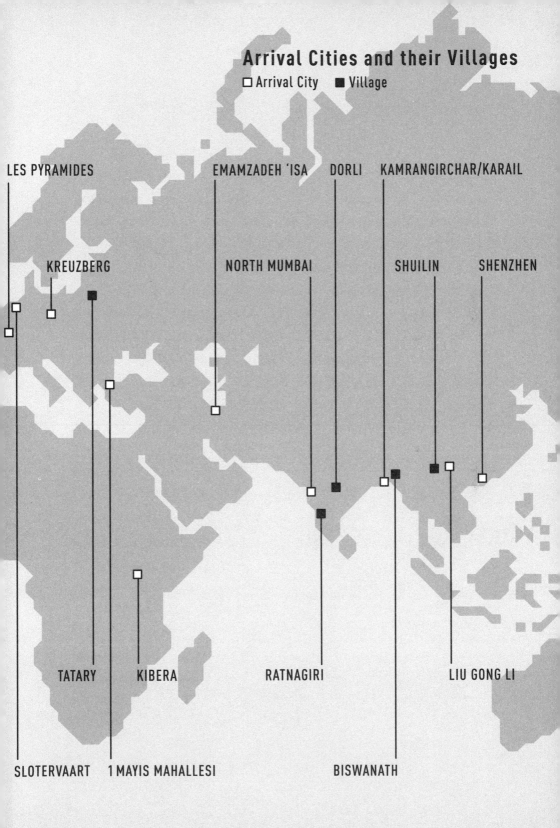

Arrival Cities and their Villages

□ Arrival City   ■ Village

LES PYRAMIDES

KREUZBERG

EMAMZADEH 'ISA   DORLI   KAMRANGIRCHAR/KARAIL

NORTH MUMBAI

SHUILIN

SHENZHEN

TATARY   KIBERA   RATNAGIRI   LIU GONG LI

SLOTERVAART   1 MAYIS MAHALLESI   BISWANATH

ARRIVAL CITY

PREFACE

THE PLACE WHERE EVERYTHING CHANGES

What will be remembered about the twenty-first century, more than anything else except perhaps the effects of a changing climate, is the great, and final, shift of human populations out of rural, agricultural life and into cities. We will end this century as a wholly urban species. This movement engages an unprecedented number of people—two or three billion humans, perhaps a third of the world's population—and will affect almost everyone in tangible ways. It will be the last human movement of this size and scope; in fact, the changes it makes to family life, from large agrarian families to small urban ones, will put an end to the major theme of human history, continuous population growth.

The last time humans made such a dramatic migration, in Europe and the New World between the late eighteenth and the early twentieth centuries, the direct effect was a complete reinvention of human thought, governance, technology, and welfare. Mass urbanization produced the French Revolution, the Industrial Revolution and, with them, the enormous social and political changes of the previous two centuries. Yet this narrative of human change was not to be found in the newspapers of the 1840s or the parliamentary debates of the early twentieth century; the city-bound migration and the rise of new, transitional urban enclaves was a story largely unknown to the people directly affected by it. And the catastrophes of mismanaged urbanization—the human miseries and revolutionary uprisings and wars—were often a direct result of this blindness: We failed to account for this influx of people, and in the process created urban communities of recent arrivals who became trapped, excluded, resentful. Much of the history of this age was the history of deracinated people, deprived of franchise, making urgent and sometimes violent attempts to gain a standing in the urban order.

If we make a similar mistake today and dismiss the great migration as a negligible effect, as a background noise or a fate of others that we can avoid in our own countries, we are in danger of suffering far larger explosions and ruptures. Some aspects of this great migration are already unfolding in front of us: the tensions over immigration in the United States, Europe and Australia; the political explosions in Iran, Venezuela, Mumbai, Amsterdam, the outskirts of Paris. But many of the changes and discontinuities are not being noticed at all. We do not understand this migration because we do not know how to look at it. We do not know where to look. We have no place, no name, for the locus of our new world.

In my journalistic travels, I developed the habit of introducing myself to new cities by riding subway and tram routes to the end of the line, or into the hidden interstices and inaccessible corners of the urban core, and examining the places that extended before me. These are always fascinating, bustling, unattractive, improvised, difficult places, full of new people and big plans. My trip to the edge was not always by choice: I have found myself drawn by news events to the northern reaches of Mumbai, the dusty edges of Tehran, the hillside folds of São Paulo and Mexico City, the smouldering apartment-block fringes of Paris and Amsterdam and Los Angeles. What I found in these places were people who had been born in villages, who had their minds and ambitions fixed on the symbolic center of the city, and who were engaged in a struggle of monumental scope to find a basic and lasting berth in the city for their children.

This ex-rural population, I found, was creating strikingly similar urban spaces all over the world: spaces whose physical appearance varied but whose basic set of functions, whose network of human relationships, was distinct and identifiable. And there was a contiguous, standardized pattern of institutions, customs, conflicts and frustrations being built and felt in these places across the poor expanses of the "developing" world and in the large, wealthy cities of the West. We need to devote far more attention to these places, for they are not just the sites of potential conflict and violence but also the neighborhoods where the transition from poverty occurs, where the next middle class is forged, where the next generation's dreams, movements, and governments are created. At a time when the effectiveness and basic purpose of foreign aid have become matters of deep and well-deserved skepticism, I believe that these transitional urban spaces offer a solution. It is here, rather than at the "macro" state or "micro" household level, that serious and sustained investments from governments and agencies are most likely to create lasting and incorruptible benefit.

In researching this book, I have visited about 20 such places, in an effort to find key examples of the changes that are transforming cities and villages in far more countries. This is not an atlas of arrival or a universal guide to the great migration. Equally fascinating developments are occurring in Lima, Lagos, Cairo, Karachi, Calcutta, Jakarta, Beijing, Marrakesh, Manila. Nor is this book without precedent. Scholars in migration studies, urban studies, sociology, geography, anthropology, and economics have documented the phenomena described here, and many of them have generously assisted me with my work.

But the larger message is lost to many citizens and leaders: the great migration of humans is manifesting itself in the creation of a special kind of urban place. These transitional spaces—arrival cities— are the places where the next great economic and cultural boom will be born or where the next great explosion of violence will occur. The difference depends on our ability to notice and our willingness to engage.

1

ON THE EDGE OF THE CITY

Liu Gong Li, China

It begins with a village. To an outsider, the village seems fixed, time-less, devoid of motion or change, isolated from the larger world. We consign it to nature. To those who might glance at its jumble of low buildings from a passing vehicle, the village seems a tranquil place of ordered, subtle beauty. We imagine a pleasant rhythm of life, free from the strains of modernity. Its small cluster of weathered shacks is nestled into the crest of a modest valley. A few animals move in their pens, children run along the edge of a field, a thin plume of smoke rises from one of the huts, an old man strolls in the patch of forest on the crest, a cloth sack on his back.

The man is named Xu Qin Quan, and he is searching for a cure. He walks down the ancient stone pathway alongside terraced fields toward the small glade on the valley floor, as members of his family have done for 10 generations. Here he finds the remedies he has known since childhood: the slender stalks of *ma huang*, for sweating away a cold; the leafy branches of *gou qi zi*, for mending the liver. He slices the stalks with his pocket knife, stacks them in his bag, and walks back to the crest. There, he stands for a while, looking at the eruptions of dust rising to the north, where a construction crew is turning the narrow, bumpy road into a broad, paved boulevard.

5

A journey north to Chongqing and back, once an all-day affair, will soon take no more than two hours. Mr. Xu watches the dust plumes turn the distant trees ochre. He considers the larger suffering, the pain that has racked their lives and killed their children and held them in decades of food panic followed by years of paralyzing tedium. That night, at a village meeting, he proffers the larger cure. After tonight, he says, we shall stop being a village.

It is 1995, and the village is called Liu Gong Li. Very little about its appearance, its families, or its thoroughly unmechanized cultivation of wheat and corn has changed in centuries. It got its name, which means "Six Kilometers," during the building of the Burma Road, when the great inland city of Chongqing was the eastern terminus. That name, for decades after the Second World War, was a fantasy, for the original bridge to the big city had been bombed, and the nearest replacement, many kilometers away, was impassable enough to make the journey economically pointless, even if the Communist Party had allowed it. The little village had no connection to any city or any market. It farmed for itself. The soil, and the rudimentary farming methods, never provided quite enough food for everyone. Every few years, the vicissitudes of weather and politics would produce a famine, and people would die, children would starve. In the terrible years of 1959 through 1961, the village lost a large portion of its population. Starvation ended two decades later, replaced by a scraping, passionless dependency on government subsidies. In Liu Gong Li, as in peasant villages around the world, nobody sees rural life as tranquil, or natural, or as anything but a monotonous, frightening gamble. In the final decade of the twentieth century, when China embraced a form of capitalism, the villages here were suddenly permitted to develop non-arable land for market purposes. So when Mr. Xu suggested his remedy, there was no dissension: All the land would be declared non-arable. From that moment, it stopped being a village and became a destination for villagers.

Fifteen years later, Liu Gong Li reveals itself as a specter at the side of a traffic-clotted four-lane boulevard a kilometer into the city:

Amid a forest of apartment towers there unfolds a glimmering mirage of gray and brown cubes cascading across hillsides as far as the eye can see, an utterly random crystal formation that has obliterated the landscape. Closer, the crystals materialize into houses and shops, jagged brick and concrete dwellings of two or three stories assembled by their occupants without plan or permission, cantilevered over one another, jutting at unlikely angles. Within 10 years of Mr. Xu's prescription, his village of 70 had gained more than 10,000 residents; within a dozen years, it had fused with neighboring ex-villages into a solid agglomeration of 120,000 people, few of whom officially reside here. It is no longer a distant village, or even a place on the far outskirts; it is a key and integral part of Chongqing, a city of some 10 million people packed in and around a skyscraper peninsula that resembles Manhattan in both its density of population and its intensity of activity. With more than 200,000 people a year being added to its population and 4 million unregistered migrants within its borders, it is very likely the world's fastest-growing city.*

That growth is largely driven by the multiplication of places like Liu Gong Li, self-built settlements of rural escapees, known in China simply as urban "villages" (*cun*), hundreds of which flourish around the city's perimeter, even if city authorities do not acknowledge their existence. Their streets and blocks are tightly organized by the villages and regions from which their residents come; residents refer to their urban neighbors who've arrived from their own rural regions as *tongxiang*—literally "homies." At least 40 million peasants join these urban enclaves across China each year, though a good number—perhaps half—end up returning to their rural village, out

---

* The title "fastest-growing city" has a number of legitimate claimants, including Dhaka and Lagos, because it has a number of meanings: it can be the place that adds the largest number of people every year (a measure that favors large cities), the place whose population increases by the largest proportion (a measure that favors small cities), or the place with the highest increase in its rate of growth. However, with a growth rate approaching 4 percent per year across its wider metropolitan district (whose population is 32 million), Chongqing qualifies by any measure.

of hardship, desperation, or personal taste. Those who stay tend to be deeply determined.

To an outsider, Liu Gong Li is a fetid slum. The old pathway into the valley is now a busy street overhung with a shambles of thrown-together houses, its dirt lane lined with phone shops, butchers, huge steaming woks full of pungent peppers at streetside eateries, merchants hawking clothes, tools, fast-spinning bobbins of thread, a cacophony of commerce spiraling away for two kilometers into dizzying back pathways and snaking staircases whose ungrounded perspectives resemble an upturned Escher engraving. Electrical and cable television lines fill the air; raw sewage spills from the concrete, runs down the sides of buildings, cascades along open gutters into a terrible stinking river beneath the concrete bridges at the foot of the valley. Garbage and waste are seemingly everywhere, accumulating in a small mountain behind the houses. A chaos of vehicles with two, three, and four wheels clots every lane. There is no space without people, without activity, and none to be seen with greenery. It might seem, from this vantage, that this is a hellish refuge for the destitute, a last-ditch landing pad for the failed outcasts of an enormous nation—a place for those on the way downward.

The true nature of places like Liu Gong Li becomes evident when you walk off the main lane into the rough dirt side streets that descend into the valley. Behind each window, each crude opening in the concrete, is a clatter of activity. On the crest of the valley, near the place where Mr. Xu made his big decision in 1995, you are drawn to a noisy cinder-block rectangle, jammed into a steep corner, exuding a pleasant cedar scent. It is the shop-cum-home of 39-year-old Wang Jian and his family. Four years before, Mr. Wang moved here from the village of Nan Chung, 80 kilometers away, with the money he had saved from two years of carpentry work, a total of 700 renminbi ($102).* He rented a tiny room, accumulated some scrap wood and iron and began building, by hand, traditional Chinese wooden

---

* All figures in this book are converted to United States dollars.

bathtubs, which have become popular with the new middle class. These took two days to make, and he sold them for a profit of R50 ($7.30) each. After a year, he had earned enough to get power tools and a bigger shop. He brought over his wife, his son, his son's wife, and their infant grandson. They all sleep, cook, wash, and eat in a windowless area in the back, behind a plastic curtain, in a space that is even more exposed and cramped than the dirt-floor hut they endured in the village.

But there is no talk of returning: This, filth and all, is the better life. "Here, you can turn your grandchildren into successful people if you find the right way to make a living—in the village you can only live," says Mr. Wang, in boisterous Sichuan dialect, as he bends an iron strap around a tub. "I'd say about a fifth of the people who've left my village have ended up starting their own businesses. And almost everybody has left the village—there are just old people left. It has become a hollow village."

Mr. Wang and his wife still send a third of their earnings back to the village, to support their two surviving retired parents, and the year before, he'd bought a small restaurant down the road in Liu Gong Li, for his son to run. Mr. Wang's margins are tiny, because the competition is intense: There are 12 other wood-bathtub factories in Chongqing, one of them also located in Liu Gong Li. "Mine has the highest output," he says, "but we're not necessarily the most profitable." So it will be years of saving, and hoping for the best in the bathtub trade, before they will be able to buy their own apartment, send their grandson to university, and get out of Liu Gong Li— although by then, if the dream comes true, Liu Gong Li might have evolved into the sort of place where they'd want to stay.

All down the valley, the gray cubism materializes into a quilt of tiny, officially non-existent industries hidden behind ramshackle concrete slum buildings. Down the street from the bathtub shop is an exceptionally noisy place where 20 employees are making metal security railings; a little farther, a shop making custom walk-in refrigerators; a powdered-paint blending shop; a place churning out computer-guided embroidery patterns on half a dozen massive machines; a factory making electric-motor windings; a sour-smelling place where barely teenaged workers hunched over heat-sealing machines make inflatable beach toys; similar family shops, of every description, making shop displays, vinyl-frame windows, extruded industrial air-conditioning ducts, cheap wood cabinetry, ornamental wooden bed frames, high-voltage transformers, computer-lathe-milled motorcycle parts, and stainless-steel restaurant range hoods. These factories, most of whose goods are destined for Asian consumers, were all launched during the previous dozen years by villagers who arrived here or by the former employees of the first wave of villagers.

In every unpainted concrete cube, it is the same rhythm of arrival, struggle, support, saving, planning, calculation. Everyone who lives in Liu Gong Li, and all 120,000 people in this strip of land, has arrived, since 1995, from a rural village. Everyone who remains here beyond a few months has decided to stay for the long haul, despite the filth and the crowding and the difficulty of life and even though their children are often left behind with family members back in the village, because they have decided that it is a better life. Most have endured extraordinarily long odysseys of self-denial and austere deprivation. Almost all send money, quite often almost all of their earnings, back to support the village and put some into savings for their children's education here in the city. All are engaged in a daily calculation that involves the unbearable burden of rural deprivation, the impossible expense of full-fledged urban life, and the broken pathway of opportunities that might someday form a bridge between the two.

In other words, the main function of this place is *arrival*. Liu Gong Li, like millions of other new and peripheral urban neighborhoods around the world, performs a specific set of functions. It is not merely a place for living and working, for sleeping and eating and shopping; it is, most importantly, a place of transition. Almost all of its significant activities, beyond mere survival, exist to bring villagers, and entire villages, into the urban sphere, into the center of social and economic life, into education and acculturation and belonging, into sustainable prosperity. The arrival city is both populated with people in transition—for it turns outsiders into central, "core" urbanites, with sustainable social, economic, and political futures in the city—and is itself a place in transition, for its streets, homes, and established families will either someday become part of the core city itself or will fail and decay into poverty or be destroyed.

The arrival city can be readily distinguished from other urban neighborhoods, not only by its rural-immigrant population, its improvised appearance and ever-changing nature, but also by the constant linkages it makes, from every street and every house and every workplace, in two directions. It is linked in a lasting and intensive way to its *originating villages*, constantly sending people and money and knowledge back and forth, making possible the next wave of migrations from the village, facilitating within the village the care of older generations and the education of younger ones, financing the improvement of the village. And it is linked in important and deeply engaged ways to the *established city*. Its political institutions, business relationships, social networks, and transactions are all footholds intended to give new village arrivals a purchase, however fragile, on the edge of the larger society, and to give them a place to push themselves, and their children, further into the center, into acceptability, into connectedness. Liu Gong Li makes many things, sells many things, and houses many people, but all with one overarching goal, one project that unites its mad range of activities. Liu Gong Li is an *arrival city*. Here, on the periphery, is the new center of the world.

At the crest of the valley, a short, steep walk up the curved gravel road from the factory-packed valley floor, is an especially dense conglomeration of concrete buildings. If you enter an alley behind a small restaurant, then cut through a labyrinth of tunnels and narrow passageways surrounded by high walls, you will reach a small gray courtyard. It is a tranquil spot amid the chaos of the slum, with low wooden stools surrounding a small table. The air is filled with the pungent smells of Sichuan cooking and the remote sounds of motors, babies crying, shouted commands, horns. Crouched near the table is an old man, dressed in the traditional green cloth jacket and beaten canvas shoes of a peasant, and a Nike baseball cap. Beside him is a conical bamboo hat filled with herbs he has gathered on a walk in a little-known green patch at the far end of the valley, behind the five-story garbage mountain that covers most of the old glade.

This is Xu Qin Quan, the cure-gatherer and village patriarch, still living in exactly the same spot at the center of Liu Gong Li. The shift to urban life has made him a wealthy man: from his rental earnings he has housed most of his family members in condominium apartments costing $75,000 each, or 10 years' earnings for a manager. He alone stays here, close to his medicinal trove. The "village" is still owned collectively by its original residents, and it is still legally a village. This means that none of the hundreds of dwellings here, other than this one, fully belong to their owners, even though many have purchased title deeds from the collective and buy and sell their houses for profit. The thriving property market has driven rents and unofficial land prices upward, giving the village-migrant "owners" a source of capital through rent, sublease, and property speculation—none of it official or taxed—which they often use to launch businesses. At any moment, the city authorities could bulldoze the whole district and either throw all 120,000 residents out or move them into apartment blocks with clean, official garment factories next door. China has done this to hundreds of such neighborhoods, disrupting the lives and economic relationships of families that have invested everything in this urban foothold. Liu Gong Li's founders are confident that they have at least a decade before this happens.

Officials from the Chongqing People's Congress tell me vaguely that they someday want to turn their entire megalopolis into a place without shantytown settlements, replacing them with neat workers' dormitories and private apartments built around industrial centers. But they also tell me that they want to urbanize as fast as possible, at a rate of growth that cannot possibly be absorbed without an exponential increase in these high-density, informal settlements. There may be several thousand housing towers under construction around Chongqing on any given day (all by private companies), but the budget for housing is dwarfed by the influx of people, and village arrivals are still officially excluded from housing unless they're able to earn enough money to afford it on the private market. The arrival city is not a temporary anomaly. In inland Chinese cities, these arrival-city "villages" have become intrinsic, if unacknowledged, parts of the city's growth plan, its economy and its way of life.

"My tenants are generally people who want very badly to become urban residents, but only a fraction will be able to do so," Mr. Xu tells me, as his daughters prepare a lavish meal for the June dragon-boat festival. "They often don't make enough money to save anything, and it's becoming too expensive for them. Unless things change here, a lot of them will have to move back. We all want to quit being peasants, and China wants us to become city-dwellers now, but they've made it so difficult to get there."

Indeed, a great many of Liu Gong Li's residents are like Wang Zhen Lei, 36, and her husband, Shu Wei Dong, 34, who spend their nights in a two-by-three-meter room, built of drywall sheets hung from thin wood joists half a meter below the poured-concrete ceiling of a couples' dormitory, which is home to a dozen similar chambers, the whole structure cantilevered precariously over a fetid stream. The sole window is barred and covered, except a 60-centimeter slit at the top; light comes from bare incandescent bulbs. Ten hours a day, and often on weekends, they sew garments at work tables in an adjoining concrete room, its walls coated in a shag of lint, equally barren except for a color TV showing a constant stream of Chinese soap operas. The factory, with 30 sewing tables, is owned by a man who moved from a distant village to Liu Gong Li in 1996, initially as a garment worker himself, and who pays his workers by the piece; they earn between $200 and $400 a month. The dormitory room is provided free (which is not the case in all factories). Mrs. Wang and Mr. Shu's life here consists of exactly 29 possessions, including four chopsticks and a mobile phone; they have never seen the great city of Chongqing beyond Liu Gong Li's streets. Each month, they keep $45 for food and $30 to cover expenses and send all the rest back to their village to support their daughter's secondary-school education and to feed their parents, who raise their daughter.

For 11 years, beginning in 1993, the two of them lived in more modern and somewhat less cryptlike worker dormitories in Shenzhen, the all-industrial city in the Pearl River Delta, 1,500 kilometers south. The garment factories there, which made goods for Western companies, had better working conditions and paid more. But they discovered a serious flaw: in Shenzhen, there was no prospect of arrival. No matter how much the couple saved, they could never afford an apartment, and the city offered them no option of purchasing a piece of shantytown housing, of the sort that dominates Liu Gong Li, because none exists in the planned city of Shenzhen. And they had no chance of seeing their beloved daughter, except once a year during Chinese New Year. There was, in short, no future. They moved north, in a painful bargain: they would have a family nearby, and maybe a future for their daughter and their parents in the city, in exchange for working most of the rest of their lives in a pit of lonely darkness.

Like so many people here, and around the world today, they have staked their entire lives on their daughter's education—something they know is not much better than an even bet. "We all want to have our kids stay in school and get into university so they don't have to work in a factory like this," Mrs. Wang says. "But if my daughter doesn't get in, I would accept the alternative, which is still better than the village—she works in this factory like we do."

For every 20 families like them in Liu Gong Li, there is one like Xian Guang Quan's clan. He and his wife arrived as illiterate peasants, spent years sleeping on open-air slabs on construction sites, moved into a concrete hut in Liu Gong Li, and saved. In 2007, they moved across the road into a 10-story apartment building, which was constructed by Mr. Xian, 46, and his crew. It's a rudimentary structure of unpainted red bricks with a raw-concrete staircase running up the center, but the Xian family have turned their apartment's spacious interior into something palatial: attractively tiled floors with big swathes of empty space, bright wallpaper, modernist chandeliers, a big orange sectional sofa, a large plasma TV and surround-sound system. Mr. Xian, a heavyset man with a balding pate and a permanent smile, spends his spare hours on shopping trips downtown or lengthy, smoke-filled, mah-jong games with his old village friends, a truly middle-class lifestyle, backed by a genuine middle-class income, that belies the six years he spent here, not long ago, exposed to the elements, with no money or possessions.

He came from the village of Shi Long, more than 100 kilometers away, in 1992, shortly after China's economy liberalized and the government began tolerating some peasant mobility. It was a move of desperation, from a farm where six of them slept in a tiny dirt-floor straw hut. Buildings were beginning to rise in Chongqing, replacing the ancient wood-gable houses with crude high-rises, and there was a demand for construction labor. He had only his hands, his wits, and his wife. She cooked for construction crews, and he worked, at first for 50 to 75 cents a day, plus meals of rice, which contained pork every five days, and the right to sleep on the site. They spent their nights wrapped in sheets on the foundations of buildings, joining hundreds of thousands of other homeless workers in the city.

They sent all of their income back to Shi Long and went years without seeing their daughter. They joined China's "floating population" of between 150 million and 200 million people. Under the country's rigid household-registration (*hukou*) system, people living in the city but holding village registration papers are not entitled to urban housing, welfare, medical care or access to schooling for their children in the city. After reforms to the *hukou* system at the beginning of the twenty-first century, it became possible for migrants to apply for urban *hukou*—but this is, in practice, virtually impossible and means giving up their village homes. Very few peasants are able to do this in the first generation, because China's primary-education, child-care, welfare, and unemployment-insurance systems are not even remotely sufficient to support the precarious life of a new city-dweller. So as many as a sixth of the Chinese population are neither villagers nor official urbanites.

Xian Guang Quan was determined to break into genuine urban life. In 1998, he organized 20 of his fellow village workers into a building crew and began operating as a company. They weren't registered or accredited to national standards, which would have required an urban *hukou*. The money became good, reaching the comfortable middle-class level of $15,000 a year and up to $30,000 in good years. Despite their financial security, Mr. Xian and his wife kept living in a tiny concrete hut they had bought in Liu Gong Li. "We could have lived in a better place when we first made our fortune in the late '90s, but we didn't want to take that risk," he told me. "First we had to put our daughter through school, set up our elders in the village with proper brick houses—we needed large amounts of money for future security in savings."

This need for poor village migrants to sacrifice much of their earnings to health, education, and emergency savings is exactly what has kept thousands of Liu Gong Li residents like Mrs. Wang trapped in an uncomfortable world that is neither urban nor rural, isolating them from their own children, preventing them from becoming full members of the country's economy. To mutual disadvantage, the Chinese state barely touches their lives. Mr. Xian broke through that barrier by hatching a plan. He gathered 14 of his most successful construction-worker friends, and they each pooled $15,000 to build three 10-story apartment buildings across the road from Liu Gong Li, in a settlement they gave a pleasant-sounding name that translates rather awkwardly to "Ethnic National New Village." One building would provide them with an income—they would rent its small apartments to "the farmers," as he calls the new village arrivals. The second would contain factory spaces for sale, as well as shopfronts on the ground level. And the third would contain 15 large condominiums for him and his partners. With this scheme, and 15 years of deprivation and saving, Mr. Xian and his mates were able to realize the dream of arrival.

It is rare, anywhere in the world, to find a family who grew up on a dirt floor and made it, in the same generation, into the middle-class world of mortgages and shopping malls. Many more people are like Pu Jun, 32, a slender and somewhat awkward man, who works in one of the scores of villager-owned factories at the bottom of the valley. This particular factory, unlike its neighbors, is quiet, neat, airy, and plunged into a perpetual darkness, which gives it the air of a minimalist cathedral; its 30 employees do the difficult work of refurbishing high-voltage transformers, intricate, toxin-filled devices the size of a car. Mr. Pu is a trained and experienced technician, educated in a trade school near his village in eastern Sichuan and seasoned in Shenzhen's factories, a background that should be a ticket to middle-class security.

Yet, when I met him in the factory one afternoon, he was in a mood of quiet anxiety, discreetly trying to absorb a blow that seemed to throw the whole venture into question. At the moment, he had $150 in his pocket, leaving him wondering how he'd find the remaining $15 for the month's rent. This from a man who had spent five years spending nothing on himself. He had been able to tell his two young children, only three months earlier, that they could look forward to living with him in the city by the end of the year.

But things had suddenly gone wrong. His father, 61, had come down with an illness that proved hard to diagnose and required constant medication. The anti-seizure pills, in a medical system that is far from free, now eat up a third of Mr. Pu's income, which is mainly devoted to supporting his children in the village. He had already endured a series of setbacks, including a disastrously failed attempt at shifting his village farm to fruit trees and the unplanned-for birth of his second child. And his marriage had collapsed. This last, in arrival cities around the world, is not uncommon: the transition to urban life places a terrible strain on marriages. But in Mr. Pu's case it was the end of this estrangement, just a few weeks earlier, that had cost more: his wife, who works as a dim sum server for $150 a month, had built up considerable debts trying to live on her own. "Now has become my worst time ever," he said plainly. "We lived apart, and when we live apart we fight, and we get to forget each other's common goals—we forgot that the goal is to build a future together. And suddenly I'm having to support three generations."

Now, if nothing else goes wrong, he expects it will be three more years before he will be able to live in the same house as his children, send them to school in the city, and end his family's peasant history forever. When work slows, he grasps the worn and creased photo of his son, Ming Lin, 6, and daughter, Dong, 4, and quietly whispers to them. He aches for their presence. "I hope the kids will under-stand someday—understand why we were away so much, under-stand why we were never there for them when they were learning about the world, and understand the sacrifice we made. I believe we can make it up to them. We want to provide them with a better future than we've experienced. For now," he says, using a Chinese phrase that is almost a mantra in the arrival city, "we will have to eat the bitterness."

The ex-villager enclave within the city, located on the periphery of our vision and beyond the tourist maps, has become the setting of the world's next chapter, driven by exertion and promise, battered by violence and death, strangled by neglect and misunderstanding. History is being written, and largely ignored, in places like Liu Gong Li, or in Clichy-sous-Bois, on the outskirts of Paris, or in Dharavi, the almost million-strong arrival city in Mumbai, or in the Latino arrival city of Compton, on the edge of Los Angeles—all places set-tled by people who have arrived from the village, all places that func-tion to propel people into the core life of the city and to send support back to the next wave of arrivals. Arrival cities are known around the world by many names: as the slums, *favelas*, *bustees*, *bidonvilles*, *ashwaiyyat*, shantytowns, *kampongs*, urban villages, *gecekondular*, and barrios of the developing world, but also as the immigrant neighborhoods, ethnic districts, *banlieues difficiles*, *Plattenbau* developments, Chinatowns, Little Indias, Hispanic quarters, urban slums, and migrant suburbs of wealthy countries, which are themselves each year absorbing two million people, mainly villagers, from the developing world.

I am coining the term "arrival city" to unite these places, because our conventional scholarly and bureaucratic language—"immigrant gateway," "community of primary settlement"—misrepresents them by disguising their dynamic nature, their transitory role. When we look at arrival cities, we tend to see them as fixed entities: an accumulation of inexpensive dwellings containing poor people, usually in less than salubrious conditions. In the language of urban planners and governments, these enclaves are too often defined as static appendages, cancerous growths on an otherwise healthy city. Their residents are seen, in the words of the former Brazilian president Fernando Henrique Cardoso, "as an ecologically defined group rather than as part of the social system."[1]

This leads to tragic urban-housing policies in the West, of the sort that made Paris erupt into riots in 2005, London in the 1980s, Amsterdam into murderous violence in the first decade of this century. It leads to even worse policies in the cities of Asia, Africa, and South America, to slum-clearance projects in which the futures of tens or hundreds of thousands of people are recklessly erased. Or, in an alternative version offered in popular books and movies, arrival cities are written off as contiguous extensions of a dystopian "planet of slums," a homogenous netherworld, in which the static poor are consigned to prisonlike neighborhoods guarded by hostile police, abused by exploitative corporations, and preyed upon by parasitic evangelical religions.[2] This is certainly the fate of many arrival cities after they have been deprived of their fluid structure or abandoned by the state. Yet, to see this as their normal condition is to ignore the arrival city's great success: it is, in the most successful parts of both the developing world and the Western world, the key instrument in creating a new middle class, abolishing the horrors of rural poverty and ending inequality.*

Rather than dismissing these neighborhoods as changeless entities or mere locations, we need to start seeing them as a set of functions. The first arrival-city function is the creation and maintenance of a *network*: a web of human relationships connecting village to arrival city to established city. These networks, aided by communications technology, money transfers, and more traditional family and village relationships, provide a sense of protection and security (always of primary importance in the arrival city); they generate a sense of leadership and political representation; they give the arrival-city enclave a self-identity. Second, the arrival city functions as an *entry mechanism*. It not only takes people in by providing cheap housing and assistance in finding entry-level jobs (through the networks), but it also makes possible the next wave of arrivals in a process known as chain migration: The arrival city sends cash and provides basic lines of credit to the village; it arranges jobs and marriages across international boundaries and sets up schemes to circumvent immigration restrictions. Third, the arrival city functions as an *urban establishment platform*: it provides informal resources that allow the village migrant, after saving and becoming part of the network, to purchase a house (through credit and informal or legal deeds), to start a small business (through loans, buildings, relationships), to reach out to the larger city for higher education, or to assume a position of political leadership. Fourth, the properly functioning arrival city provides a *social-mobility path* into either the middle class or the sustainable, permanently employed and propertied ranks of the upper-working class. These paths into the "core

---

* Inequality has declined with urbanization in those countries that allow their arrival cities to flourish. Brazil, Peru, and Malaysia have all seen inequality fall during their periods of urbanization. China, with its restricted arrival cities, has seen inequality increase. India, with chaotic urban policies, has seen no change. In all these cases, urbanization has sharply reduced poverty and improved the living standards of the poorest fifth of the population.

city" are provided through housing values and legalization, business success, higher-education opportunities for migrants or their children, employment opportunities in elite or "official" urban enterprises, or even through simple physical connections to the city and the upgrading of streets, plumbing, housing, and transit, allowing the arrival city's own rising real-estate values, and the opportunities provided by sale or rental income, to create an exit path. It has become popular in scholarly and government circles to describe such functions, vaguely, as "social capital." And that is, in short, what arrival cities are: repositories of social capital, machines for its creation and distribution. The aim here is to show exactly how this capital works in the larger economy of urban success.

An arrival city can be a single set of buildings entirely occupied by village migrants (like Liu Gong Li), or it can be a tight-knit network of people who constitute a minority, even as little as 10 percent of the population, in a deprived urban neighborhood (this is the case in most British arrival cities: Even ethnic enclaves such as Bradford and Bethnal Green have fewer than 50 percent migrants).

The modern arrival city is the product of the final great human migration. A third of the world's population is on the move this century, from village to city, a move that began in earnest shortly after the Second World War, when South American and Middle Eastern villagers left their homes to build new enclaves on the urban outskirts, and is entering its most intense phase now, with 150 to 200 million Chinese peasants "floating" between village and city, vast shifts under way in India and Bangladesh, and huge numbers of Africans and Southeast Asians joining the exodus. In 1950, 309 million people in the developing world lived in cities; by 2030, 3.9 billion will. As of 2008, exactly half the world's 6.7 billion people lived in villages, most of them in Africa and Asia, including almost all of the billion poorest people in the world, those whose families subsist on less than $1 a day. The wealthy nations of North America, Europe, Australasia, and Japan, which were largely peasant-populated as recently as the late nineteenth century, today are between 72 and 95 percent urban, figures that have not changed in decades. In most of these countries, less than 5 percent of the population is employed in agriculture; this is still enough to produce more export food than all the peasant-heavy countries of the developing world combined. At the moment, only 41 percent of Asians and 38 percent of Africans live in cities—leaving a population of villagers that is unproductive and unsustainable. They are on the land not because it is a better life but because they are trapped.

This is changing fast. Between 2007 and 2050, the world's cities will absorb an additional 3.1 billion people. The population of the world's countryside will stop growing around 2019 and by 2050 will have fallen by 600 million, despite much higher family sizes in rural areas, largely because of migration to the city. India's rural population, one of the last to stop growing, will peak in 2025 at 909 million and shrink to 743 million by 2050.[3] Each month, there are five million new city-dwellers created through migration or birth in Africa, Asia, and the Middle East. Between 2000 and 2030, the urban population of Asia and Africa will double, adding as many city-dwellers in one generation as these continents have accumulated during their entire histories. By the end of 2025, 60 percent of the world will live in cities; by 2050, more than 70 percent; and, by century's end, the entire world, even the poor nations of sub-Saharan Africa, will be at least three-quarters urban.[4] This point, when the entire world is as urban as the West is today, will mark an end point. Once humans urbanize, or migrate to more urban countries, they almost never return.* After this final half of humanity has moved to the cities, there will be migrations again, but never again a mass movement on this scale. Humanity will have reached a new and permanent equilibrium.

---

* There are exceptions. The post-communist years in Central and Eastern Europe saw urban-to-rural migrations as people fled the collapse of industrial pseudo-economies to the security of subsistence agriculture. Mao's China was essentially a huge experiment in re-ruralization. In a number of sub-Saharan African countries, the AIDS crisis and military conflicts have similarly led populations to leave the city for villages. There is every indication that these reverse transitions are temporary, lasting only as long as the root crisis.

This migration is, in any measurable sense, an improvement. There is no romance in village life. Rural living is the largest single killer of humans today, the greatest source of malnutrition, infant mortality, and reduced lifespans. According to the World Food Programme, three-quarters of the world's billion people living in hunger are peasant farmers. The rural village is also the predominant source of excessive population growth, with its need for large families to provide labor and stave off ruination. Urban incomes everywhere are higher, often by large multiples; access to education, health, water, and sanitation, as well as communications and culture, are always better in the city. The move to cities also reduces ecological damage and carbon emissions by decreasing distances and increasing shared technologies: Cities, in the words of one major study, "provide an opportunity to mitigate or even reverse the impact of global climate change as they provide the economies of scale that reduce per capita costs and demand for resources."[5] Mortal poverty is a rural phenomenon: Three-quarters of the world's poor, those with less than a dollar a day, live in rural areas. The dramatic declines in the number of very poor people in the world around the turn of this century, with 98 million people leaving poverty between 1998 and 2002 and the world poverty rate falling from 34 percent in 1999 to 25 percent in 2009, were caused entirely by urbanization: People made better livings when they moved to the city and sent funds back to the village. Urbanization doesn't just improve the lives of those who move to the city; it improves conditions in the countryside, too, by giving villages the finance they need to turn agriculture into a business with salaried jobs and stable incomes.

The arrival city is often barely urban in form or culture, but it should not be mistaken for a rural place. Urbanites tend to see the arrival city as a simple reproduction, within the city, of the structures and folkways of the village. "Look, on one side villages, on the other side buildings," the Indian-American writer Suketu Mehta hears his young son observe on first seeing the arrival-city enclaves nestled against apartment towers in Bandra, in northern Mumbai. The father reacts approvingly: "He has identified the slums for what they are: villages in the city."[6] People responded similarly to the realization that Los Angeles barrios are each directly linked to a Mexican or Central American village, and Chinese tend to view their "urban villages" as being, too literally, villages. But this view misinterprets the urban ambitions of the arrival city, its fast-changing nature and its role in redefining the nature of urban life. The culture of the arrival city is neither rural nor urban, though it incorporates elements of both—often in grotesquely distorted form—in its anxious effort to find a common source of security among its ambitious and highly insecure residents. It is a fallacy that people move in a straight line from backward, conservative rural customs to sophisticated, secular urban customs. The period in between, with its insecurities, its need for tight bonds and supportive institutions, its threats to the coherence of the family and the person, is often the time when new, hybrid, protective cultures are developed.

Because people fail to recognize the function arrival cities serve, and owing to their poverty and improvised form, they are often condemned as permanent and irredeemable slums. True, many arrival cities begin as slums, but not all slums are arrival cities. In fact, the most insalubrious and dismal slums are usually not sites of rural–urban transition. The infamous slums of East London in the nineteenth century, like Bethnal Green, were "flypaper" neighborhoods, which captured and trapped those who had fallen out the bottom of inner-city society, with few village migrants among their population.[7] This is the case today in many of the inner-city slums on the Pacific Coast of the United States and Canada, such as Vancouver's Downtown Eastside and San Francisco's Tenderloin. And, if the path to arrival becomes permanently blocked, arrival cities can become depressed and destitute after a generation or two. In sub-Saharan countries, like Chad, Ethiopia, and Niger, close to 100 percent of urban residents live in slums that have existed for decades, so the village-arrival function is sometimes swamped or forgotten (though even here it's not hard to find recent village arrivals and distinct arrival-city enclaves within the slum). The African American ghettos of the United States in the twentieth century began as classic arrival cities, as the U.S. post-slavery exodus known as the Great Migration sent hundreds of thousands of southern rural ex-slaves in an optimistic search for the center of American society. But their arrival cities failed—because property ownership was unattainable in urban districts owned by indifferent or intolerant outsiders, because arrival-city residents were excluded from the economic and political mainstream by racism and bad urban planning, and because of the absence of government support and institutions. They turned into something else, places of failed arrival—a threat that hangs over many arrival cities today.

Nor do all rural-urban migrations create arrival cities. Emergency migrations, caused by war or famine, lack careful investment and planning among villagers and the tightly woven networks of support and linkage that characterize normal village-arrival patterns. But they tend to be temporary, with most refugees returning to the village when the crisis is over (though some usually remain or begin patterns of seasonal migration, sowing the seeds for genuine arrival cities later). Some rural populations, like Filipinos in North America, do not form distinct urban enclaves because of the nature of their employment, typically in domestic service—though a "virtual" arrival-city function exists.

Nor are all people living in arrival cities poor. As these enclaves improve and develop their own migrant-rooted middle class, they become magnets for people moving out of the crowded inner city, and they develop their own prosperous middle classes. Many of the most desirable neighborhoods in New York, London, Paris, and Toronto began as arrival cities, and there are arrival cities that have become fully middle class in Rio de Janeiro, Istanbul, and other successful capitals of the developing world; if managed well, many of this generation's villager enclaves will end this way.

There is another, even more damaging popular myth about the arrival city, which holds its cluttered streets responsible for spiraling urban growth, overcrowding, and sprawl. People look at the new shantytowns covering the hillsides, the migrant neighborhoods being ploughed into forest, and they imagine that the tide of people from the countryside is creating unmanageable megacities. In fact, rural-to-urban migration, in spite of its huge scope, is not the major cause of urban growth. For each 60 million new city-dwellers in the developing world, 36 million are born to established city-dwellers. Only 24 million come from villages, and only half of these have actually migrated; the rest become urbanites because their village, like Liu Gong Li, has been incorporated into the city.[8] Arrival cities are not causing population growth; in fact, they are ending it. When villagers migrate to the city, their family size drops, on average, by at least one child per family, often to below the steady-population rate of 2.1 children. Without massive rural-to-urban migration, the world's population would be growing at a far faster pace.

This is a crucial point. Sometime around 2050, according to the most recent United Nations projections, the population of the world will stop growing. After peaking at nine billion, for the first time in history humans will stop being more numerous each year, and the prospect of a Malthusian population crisis will end.[9] This will be a direct product of urbanization: Because of migration, smaller urban families will outnumber large rural ones, and, in turn, the flow of money, knowledge, and educated return migrants from the arrival city back to the village will push down birth rates in rural areas. We have already seen this in quickly urbanized countries like Iran, where the "urbanization of the village" has sent both rural and urban birth rates down to negative territory. After urbanization is accomplished, average family sizes around the world will fall below 2.1 children, and the problems of crowding and competition for resources will be replaced with the much more sustainable (though still challenging) problems of non-growing population. The date of this transition is projected, in the most likely scenario, for 2050; the UN's less optimistic scenarios place the peak a decade later, and the peak population a billion higher. What makes the difference is the arrival city, which has accomplished the things that bring fertility rates down:

educating girls and women, improving health, and creating physical and financial security. The arrival city is a machine that transforms humans. It is also, if allowed to flourish, the instrument that will create a permanently sustainable world.

Tower Hamlets, London, U.K.

On a warm evening in 1995, the Tafader sisters escape the cramped and noisy confines of their tiny two-bedroom row house in Coverley Close, an enclosed brick square amid a forest of public-housing towers. Under the glow of the nearby office towers, they sit against the low wall alongside the 15 to 20 older children and teenagers who populate its 14 houses, their doors all open, talking late into the night in East London English laced with phrases from the piquant dialect of their parents' Bangladeshi village. The smaller children race about on the pavement, oblivious to the frequent din of police sirens and occasional explosions of violence on the busy road outside. Early in the evening, they'd organized a badminton game on the concrete court; now they sit and talk late into the evening, their parents largely absent in all-night jobs. Fine-featured, sharp-eyed Razeema, the oldest of the three girls and an outspoken leader of her siblings, baffles them all by talking at length of her family's village, which she has visited a few times on school holidays. "I want to move there someday, when I am finished school, and grow all my own food in the quiet countryside," she says, interrupting the talk of Madonna and Mariah Carey with her agrarian idylls. The other children laugh at this, as they do at her newfound habit of wearing a headscarf. "You're welcome to it," her sister Sulama, two years younger, tells her, laughing. "By the time you get there, everyone else in the village will have left to come here." Salma, the youngest, does admit that she dreams of living in the countryside, albeit in England, in a big house with no neighbors. For now, the little concrete square and the shops around it, owned by people they know, feel like a welcome cocoon to protect them from the two forces that press on their young consciences at every moment: the push of the traditional life of their family village, and the pull of the impenetrable and often unwelcoming city just outside their courtyard.*

The Tafader family's journey from a dirt floor to the center of British life, a passage whose main instrument of transformation was an infamous arrival city on the edge of the world's financial capital, took less than 40 years, though its challenges were in many ways tougher than those facing a Chinese peasant, the urban surroundings no less improvised and awkward, the odds of finding a place in a foreign city with an alien language seemingly far longer. In the 1960s, the entire clan lived, as it had for decades, in a cluster of wood shacks, without electricity or even a road, around a treed patch amid rice paddies, in a rural corner of Bangladesh. The family saved to send Yousef, at age 17, to England, in search of any work he could find. Like most arrivals, he drew on contacts from fellow villagers who had moved back and forth doing industrial and shipping-port work over the previous decades. By the time Yousef arrived, the British manufacturing economy had collapsed, so he settled for a near-slavery job as a house servant for a Pakistani family; they kept his passport locked away. All his earnings went back to the village. He managed to quit after almost a decade and followed tens of thousands of other post-industrial Bangladeshis in remaking the British food-service industry, opening a small curry restaurant on the cheapest patch of land he could afford in the depressed London of the 1970s. His restaurant savings allowed him to bring his wife over, to start a family in London, and to start saving to buy a house.

The tens of thousands of curry houses, almost all of them Bangladeshi-owned, may have become an ethnic cliché, as well as turning chicken tikka masala, an invention of a 1960s Bangladeshi arrival city in Scotland, into Britain's favorite dish, but it also proved a salvation. The easy ability to open a small business in

---

* At their request, I have slightly changed the Tafader family's names. Other names and places in this book are unaltered.

Britain, to get credit and purchase property and obtain restaurant licences without prejudice, allowed the Bangladeshis to avoid destitution and dependency, to accumulate capital and provide legitimate employment to new arrivals as British immigration laws toughened, and to build futures for their children over the hot tandoori ovens. Small businesses of this sort are at the heart of almost any successful arrival city, and their absence, or the presence of laws that keep immigrants from opening them, is often the factor that turns arrival cities into poverty traps.

The Tafaders are among the 300,000 Bangladeshi villagers who have migrated to Britain since the 1960s, at least 90 percent of whom have come directly from the remote, very poor, completely agricultural northeast district of Sylhet.* Almost half a million Bangladeshis and their British-born children now live in Britain, half of them in London, and half of these on the eastern edge of the City of London, in Tower Hamlets, where they form over a quarter of the population across the council and, in some wards, are a majority. Much of the function of the Tower Hamlets arrival city is devoted to the transfer of cash, information, and people: the high streets are jammed with money-wiring shops, Islamic finance offices, Bangladeshi travel agencies, Internet cafés, immigration consultancies, marriage-arrangement offices. All of these businesses, and many of the spare-time activities of the residents here, are devoted to establishing a homeostatic relationship between village and city. This is what arrival cities do.

Each year, rural Bangladesh receives almost $11 billion in remittances from migrants and their descendants living abroad, a sum equivalent to all of Bangladesh's export earnings, far larger and more effective than all the foreign aid coming into Bangladesh each year,

---

* This is the pattern of arrival cities everywhere: Nations do not migrate, but rather regions and villages do. About 80 percent of the Pakistanis in Britain are from the tiny, fully rural Bihar state. Most of the million Poles in Western Europe are from villages in Silesia and the southwest. Mexicans in the United States mostly emerge from a handful of rural regions.

the largest single chunk of it coming from the Bangladeshis of Tower Hamlets.[10] As in arrival cites all over the world, this flow serves two important functions: It transforms the constant tide of villagers into financially secure and culturally successful urbanites, and it transforms the village, through infusions of cash, into a more urban and cultured place, which can support itself. As the arrival city becomes older and more established, the remittances decline in amount and frequency, but even in 70-year-old arrival-city *favelas* in Brazil, sums are still sent back to the village every month—allowing the village to become a post-agricultural, economically secure place.

For the Tafader family, change came slowly. After living for 10 years in a dismal high-rise East London housing estate with overtly racist neighbors, their restaurant earnings gave them enough to buy a small house, also with two bedrooms, in Coverley Close, which was developed in the 1980s to fill a cleared-out slum backlot in what had been one of the squalid quarters made famous in Dickens. This placed the Tafader family in the most dense and ethnically concentrated pole in London's Banglatown, one of Europe's great arrival cities, spreading eastward from its symbolic edge in Brick Lane across the dense expanses of Spitalfields, Bethnal Green, Stepney, and West Ham and soon sending its more successful members into Essex, covering much of the eastern fringe of the city.

By that summer of 1995, it seemed as if Banglatown was collapsing on itself. Bloody clashes between neo-Nazi skinheads and Bangladeshi gangs filled the papers. Tower Hamlets was suffering a full-scale outbreak of tuberculosis, a disease mainly prevalent in developing-world slums. Studies found that a third of families there were living on less than £4,500 a year; two-thirds of children were poor enough to qualify for free school meals, neglected housing was literally crumbling in on families, and the borough ranked lowest in Britain for standard of living, health, and quality of education. Overcrowding was five times worse than the national average, with numerous reports of three children sharing a bed, and male unemployment was more than double the national rate.[11] Britain had come to view this arrival city as a social problem, an island of gang violence, religious extremism and backwardness, made infamous through clashes with racist skinheads, the riots and protests against *The Satanic Verses* and the Iraq War, the bristle of minarets supplanting the steeples and synagogues of its cockney past. The new arrival cities of Europe and North America have plumbing, sewage and Internet access, but they are sometimes as alien and threatening to their native populations as the slums of Asia are to their cities' established residents.

Over the next 15 years, as the second generation came of age and the first generation put its savings to work on education and housing, things changed dramatically in Tower Hamlets. Today, you can still come by on many evenings and find the Tafader sisters in front of their family's tiny house, talking with the neighbors. The oldest daughter, Razeema, 33, has moved out with her new husband, Asad, to live in a minuscule one-bedroom flat, but she drops by most evenings to do her laundry and visit her sisters. Except for their ages, it might still be 1995. The changes become apparent in the morning, when the girls leave for work. Razeema walks to the local government office, where she is a parent-outreach officer for the school board; 30-year-old Sulama takes the bus to a secondary school, where she is a math teacher; and 28-year-old Salma rides the Tube to Whitehall, where she has a government management job organizing a new identity-card program. Their brother Zahir, 32, has a steady job as a car salesman and leads a somewhat adolescent life of leisure and entertainment; their youngest brother, 26, is severely autistic and cared for by his aging parents. The wall of their tiny front room is covered with big photographs of the three girls in their university graduation robes. The Tafader girls have degrees in biology, education, and public administration; they speak with the rounded vowels of the educated middle class, leavened with East End inflections: in lighter moments, their sentences end with "innit." They consider themselves feminists and don't want children until they're much older, if at all, and one of them abandoned an early marriage because she found it demeaning, though they are also devout Muslims. Their headscarves are the norm in East London but a subject of ridicule in Bangladesh, whose mild practice of Islam tends to leave female heads uncovered. The adoption of Islamic practice is a second-generation trend, an example of the hybrid culture of transition common to arrival cities, something that offers these rootless children of arrival a source of security and identity as they enter mainstream society.

All around the close, the children who joined the sisters sitting against the wall in 1995 are following similar paths. Their neighbor, a man who looks far older than his 60 years, owns two adjoining houses, which he bought after a terrible ordeal. He came over alone in the late 1950s, saved for years to set up a garment sweatshop and employ several dozen Bangladeshi villagers, and then was bankrupted when that industry collapsed in the 1970s, forcing him to become a bricklayer and odd-job man, too poor to bring his family over. But his collection of East End London property proved his salvation, multiplying in value many times over and allowing him, after 30 lonely and health-destroying years, to bring his extended family over and live comfortably. Now his children, nephews, and nieces—more than 10 of whom have lived in these houses at one time or another—are doctors, teachers, civil servants, computer scientists. The children of the close are united in a set of aspirations: to be accepted in the center of British society, to own a house, and never to work in a curry restaurant. Almost all of them, especially the girls, have managed this.

What has made the children of this small street flourish and others flounder? It may partly be the street itself. "I think more than just luck. It's something to do with living in a close," says Salma Tafader. "We all know each other's names, our parents know each other from when we're babies, we all went to the same schools, did the same activities, the same camping trips. You looked out for each other." Around the world, it appears that a good part of the success or failure of an arrival city has to do with its physical form—the layout of streets and buildings, the transportation links to the economic and cultural core of the city, the direct access to the street from buildings, the proximity to schools, health centers and social services, the existence of a sufficiently high density of housing, the presence of parks and neutral public spaces, the ability to open a shop on the ground floor and add rooms to your dwelling.

Many Tower Hamlets Bangladeshis still live in the sort of housing the Tafaders escaped, the council-estate housing tower in a blank concrete square. Although many successful families come from such quarters, they say the physical design is holding them back. Laila Nura, 32, who lives in the Peabody Buildings in Bethnal Green, says, "I don't have any connection to jobs, I can't see a way to buy my house, and I have nothing that can let me start a small business—I was better off back in the village in Sylhet." The only reason she hasn't moved out is because her children are doing very well in school and applying for high-level jobs in computer programming.

The Bangladeshi arrival city of London may be portrayed, with some truth, as a place of crime, religious extremism, and ill health, but it has also functioned for its second generation as a great integration machine. The London-born Bangladeshis, the children of the curry-house owners and sweatshop workers, have marched into the center of British society. They perform better in school than less concentrated immigrant groups and considerably better than the local white English population. In Tower Hamlets, 46 percent of Bangladeshi students achieved passing grades in five General Certificate of Secondary Education courses, only slightly below the national average of 51 percent and far better than the 30 percent achieved by the borough's white students.[12] And once they finish their educations, they have a far easier time moving out of subsistence-level employment. Studies have shown that it is much easier for immigrants to start a small business in London than in other European cities, making it far more likely that the arrival city here will be a toehold rather than a trap.[13] The curry restaurant was the quintessential, and largely very successful, form of entrepreneurship for village arrivals, a self-built economic and cultural rescue package, but the second generation have turned their back on the food trade, with its crushingly hard work, high risk, and ethnic stereotypes, instead entering finance, government, education, and information technology, with a significant and increasingly visible number of arrival-city children in national politics, media, and academia. Most still send money back to the village, but increasingly only on holidays. There are now as many Bangladeshi Britons departing Tower Hamlets for middle-class districts of London each year as there are arriving from Sylheti villages. This neighborhood, in other words, is a functioning integration machine.[14]

So it is with some accuracy that one group of scholars referred to the East End as "the traditional waiting room for admission into British society."[15] Indeed, the greatest public worry about Tower Hamlets during the past decade has involved the white English working-class residents, who are falling so far behind the village-migrant families that they are becoming an isolated, dependent, and angry underclass—a big problem, but an inversion of the one facing arrival cities of continental Europe, where it is the migrants who are the lost underclass. Still, the arrival city has not worked for all the villagers here. Many end up trapped, working at dead-end jobs, living in housing-project estates, uneducated, barely literate, unable to grab hold of the wider society around them. While upward social mobility is the norm for immigrant enclaves in London, a significant part of the Bangladeshi population does not manage fully to arrive.[16]

Razeema's husband, Asad, a first cousin (her mother's sister's son), worries that this is his fate. He is a villager who learned little English before his family found him a bride in London—in large part because tightened immigration laws had made the arranged marriage a necessary tool for reuniting villages, even though it revived a conservative practice that had been nearly obsolete among Bangladeshis. He now works at that new East London institution, the fried-chicken takeout named after a southern U.S. state (with the word "halal" appended), working the fryer 10 hours a day. Like a number of young men here, he does not seem to have a place in either British or Bangladeshi culture. He is a sad byproduct of the arrival process, a result of policies that do not fully comprehend how these neighborhoods function.

Still, the London arrival city has functioned better than those in Berlin, Paris, or Amsterdam and offers considerable lessons for the Latino arrival-city enclaves in the United States. After the terrible educational failings of the 1980s and early '90s, there is now a robust and well-invested education system, with many special programs aimed at immigrants and dedicated teachers versed in arrival; all the Tafader sisters credit their state secondary school with giving them their advantage. There is genuine citizenship: 85 percent of arrival-city residents have U.K. citizenship, compared with 42 percent of Turks in Germany. And the difference is not just in legal citizenship but in de facto citizenship: Despite the screaming headlines in the tabloids, British society, especially in the big cities, increasingly sees the arrival city as a source of fellow citizens, not as an alien threat. In Britain, 82 percent of Bangladeshis say their ethnic and religious background does not affect their job prospects, compared with 54 percent of Turks in Germany.[17] The eastern side of Tower Hamlets, in Spitalfields and Brick Lane, has become a popular eating and gallery-going attraction for well-off Britons and a residential colony for artists, turning the arrival city, for the established urban population, into a destination rather than an isolated exile to be avoided.

For all that, the more successful members of Banglatown's second generation are eager to escape. For them, the work of the arrival city is done, and its support networks are no longer needed. "I think you can only take so much of Tower Hamlets before it does your head in," says Salma, the youngest and most successful of the Tafader girls. "I need a mix of people, not just Bangla." Razeema still dreams of leaving England—though as a successful professional. Sulama intends to stay in East London, buy a house, and help improve the community. This is the gauge of an arrival city: If people are flowing through it, transformed into full-fledged contributors to the life of the city whether they leave the arrival city or stay there, then it is working. To understand how this can be made to happen, it is worth taking a detailed look at the birth, life, success, failure, and death of the world's arrival cities.

2

OUTSIDE IN:
THE LIVES OF THE NEW CITY

THE BEGINNING: SMALL MOVES, LARGE MOVEMENTS
Kolhewadi, Ratnagiri, India

In Mumbai each June, the skinny young men pull themselves off concrete floors and sidewalk paving stones, out of tin-roofed *chawls* and plastic-sheet huts, all over the city's dense northern neighborhoods. They live, in the hundreds of thousands, on the arrival city's margins. Not yet full-fledged residents, they consider themselves citizens of their villages, and now, at the beginning of the largest rice harvest, they become villagers again. They converge upon the crowded platforms of Dadar Station, where they pull out long-saved piles of rupees for a third-class ticket, $1 each way, and board the Konkan Railway slow train, packing its benches, hanging their heads out its barred windows, as it creakily begins its eight-hour journey southward along the Arabian Sea into the bamboo forests and rice paddies of the rural south of Maharashtra state.

Sanjay Solkar, looking younger than his 20 years, hops off the train at Ratnagiri, just north of Goa, carrying a cotton bag with all his possessions: a sleeping sheet, a change of clothes, saffron prayer beads, some folded rupees. He is excited: After spending the past 11 months sleeping on the four-meter-square floor of a tea shop backroom beside a train station in northern Mumbai, he is returning home for the annual rice harvest and wedding season. His worn plastic flip-flops slap in the monsoon puddles as he runs to a friend's waiting motorcycle; they race along jungle roads into a fertile emptiness of deep red mud and dense green foliage. Though he has been in the city since he was 14, and will likely spend the rest of his life there, this is home.

If you want to experience the raw edge of the great migration, to see the first, formative steps in a movement that is transferring a third of humanity from the village to the city, you're more likely to find it by joining the tides moving in the other direction, on trains and boats and minibuses, back to the village at harvest time. It is in this return movement that the new urbanites are most unified, most likely to build the networks that lead to permanent arrival, most conscious of their political and economic centrality. Their arrival in the city is part of a rural process, governed at first by the seasons, in which single individuals build links for larger communities. Nowhere in the world, except in war zones, will you find rural families packing up en masse and moving at once to the city. It doesn't happen that way, much as it didn't when Europe and North America were urbanized by villagers in the nineteenth century. The world's population shifts cityward in a back-and-forth oscillation of single individuals and clusters of villagers, pushed and pulled by tides of agriculture and economy, climate and politics.

When the urban economy takes a plunge, as it did in the crisis that began in 2008, large populations of tentatively settled workers move back to their home villages. Recent years have seen large-scale return moves of Chinese peasants from the Pearl and Yangtze river deltas, of Poles in Britain and Ireland, of villagers in the cities of sub-Saharan Africa. But they leave the knowledge of urban life and the networks of attachment in place, along with the hundreds of thousands who do not return, having earned or married or acculturated themselves into the permanent population; these arrival-city pioneers remain in the city, linked to the village, waiting for the migration cycle to begin again. It is a reciprocal, dialectic movement, which urbanizes the village as much as it revitalizes the city. It serves as a sorting and selection mechanism, leaving the most ambitious and able in the city, with a large number—typically about half of all rural-to-urban migrants throughout history—returning to the village for good.

Sanjay jumps off the motorcycle and slips down the steep red-mud footpath to his tiny village of Kolhewadi, a cluster of mud-and-dung huts at the foot of a forested valley around a swollen river. It is, to both outsider and resident, a small, fertile paradise. Children strip off and dive into the river, bringing back plump fish; the trees yield mangoes and coconuts, and the rice harvest this year is good. Sanjay is welcomed warmly; it has been a year since his mother saw him, almost a decade and a-half since he first left home, at 11. His mother, Aruna, has prepared him a lunch of rice-flour rotis and bowls of curd topped with rock salt, followed by mangoes and jackfruit. The family cluster on the mud floor, leaning against sacks of rice, and hear his tales of the city.

His grandfather, Sitaram, now almost 70, realized in the 1950s that his family needed a source of cash—something they had never had, or needed, before. Drawn by newly laid roads, he was the first to make the 14-hour road journey, decades before the village was connected by railway, telephone, or electricity. "I was not getting much out of the farm," he says, "enough to live off but never quite enough to keep us from being hungry from time to time—we sometimes wouldn't eat when the crops were bad, so at first I wanted to use the money just to buy some cows." For the first time, these subsistence farmers had a need for cash. As well, their one-room house was becoming unhygienic and was slowly collapsing. And, once they learned of gas-cylinder cookstoves, they realized they needed one. Schools arrived in their village, and books became important. And so on. Sitaram's rice crop wouldn't generate cash: the cost of bringing such small harvests to market would be greater than the earnings. (This is true for many peasant farmers.) So he made the long journey up the road to Bombay. There, he found a job with a grain store and grocery shop, working from 7 a.m. till 9 p.m. He brought over his sister, who worked as a domestic servant, and they shared a *chawl*, or concrete-floored one-room slum house, in Vile Parle, in those days a busy arrival city on the northern fringe of the city. Like almost everyone in that district, they lived for their village, sending home packets by post each month, visiting the family every few years. In 1967, they built a new, sturdy home in the village, roofed with terracotta tiles they'd saved for three years to buy. They developed close ties with Bombay's established community. Sitaram went home to marry a village girl and then sometimes went half a dozen years without seeing her. He fathered a lone son, Dashrath, who has stayed in the village and harvested rice his whole life, keeping the peasant life organized while father and son provided increasingly important cash.

Everywhere in the developing world, this mounting oscillation of back-and-forth movement was how the great urban migration began. In the two decades after the Second World War, manufacturing economies in South America, the Middle East, Asia, and Africa bloomed and became labor-intensive, and a great wave of road building made it possible for isolated farmers to consider the possibility of working in the city between harvest periods. At the same time, peasants became aware of several new pressures: Agriculture began requiring purchased inputs, like feed and fertilizer; electricity and roads made vehicles and appliances desirable even to the poorest farmers; and, perhaps most important, telephone and radio began to spread word to isolated villages of a better urban income. At first, governments encouraged this rapid urbanization as a boon to industrial growth; there was a need to strip the overpopulated countryside of unproductive farmers and fill the factories with labor.

By the time Sanjay came along, the pattern had changed. He stayed in school until he was 16—an option that hadn't been available to his father. From the age of 11, though, he spent months working in Mumbai, at rudimentary jobs, and he knew all his life that he would be the family member required to move there. And his move to the city was aided by a political organization, the Hindu-nationalist Shiv Sena Party, which provided wells and roads in the village and help finding jobs in the city. After finishing school he landed a spot at the tea shop, where he works from dawn to dusk and sleeps, with his bag of possessions, with three other young men in the backroom. He is almost certain to become one of the 100,000 people who come from villages to settle for good in Mumbai every year, 92 percent of whom say they never want to go back, even if they find themselves unemployed.[1] Virtually all of them have moved directly from their village of birth to the big city, without a stop in between—this is the pattern today almost everywhere, not just for internal migration but for overseas moves, too. A number of Sanjay's village neighbors have made the move to Dubai, where they work on construction sites; everyone on those sites has come straight from a village somewhere. Newcomers to big cities, throughout history and around the world, are almost all rural people.

The meaning of a "job" has changed dramatically in places like Mumbai. Until the economic crises of the 1980s, the cities of the developing world were dominated by an elite core of lifelong jobs backed by a few low-paying service jobs. Now, this world has exploded into small constellations of permanent employees dwarfed by a galaxy of informal work: small, unlicensed shops or street-vending sites; services, including domestic work and transportation; or short-term work in building and small manufacturing. The informal economy, previously considered a parasitic irrelevance on the edge of the "main" industrial economy, now represents a quarter of all jobs in post-communist countries, a third in North Africa, half in Latin America, 70 percent in India, and more than 90 percent in the poorest African countries.[2] It is a form of labor that is often less secure and that offers none of the social-security benefits or long-term guarantees of industrial work—but, to its immense benefit, it is a form of work that is available to almost everyone who comes to the city. On the whole, it appears that the informal, self-employed economy, even though it is more chaotic and often untaxed, is providing better livelihoods for rural migrants than the old lifetime-job economy. Self-employment, the starting-point of the arrival city, has become the global norm.[3]

"In my grandfather's time, you got a job," says Sanjay. "Now, you get some work."

Sanjay is now the family's major source of cash income: He sends home 1,500 rupees a month ($32), three-quarters of his tea-shop salary. That pays for kerosene, wood, electricity, kitchen supplies, cattle feed, schoolbooks, medicine—all of which are considered necessities now. It keeps his two sisters in school. Over two years, he was able to save enough to build a cowshed, increasing the family's rural income. He visits once or twice a year, at harvest and holidays, heartsick for the place, and once a month he walks to the phone shop in his Mumbai neighborhood and calls the family, who visit a neighbor next door who has a land line. He is saving to buy a mobile phone, something that seven or eight people in their village already possess. In a world dominated by informal jobs and makeshift shops scattered all over the city, the mobile phone has become, like kerosene, almost a necessity of life for the very poor of the world.

Despite almost 60 years of urban life and work, the Solkar family remain subsistence peasant farmers, and proudly so. Mumbai labor has allowed them to increase the productivity of their tiny rice farm somewhat (though not to the point that they produce more than they can eat) and to have heat and light and schooling, a radio, and access to a nearby television. As the economist Deepa Narayan has observed, the rural poor of the developing world thrive by building "joint portfolios" of farming, business, and migration remittances, to hedge economic risk across several platforms.[4] The city begins as one among many tools, though its culture and customs soon "urbanize" the village. The men of Sanjay's family are, culturally, urbanites: they speak the Hindi-laced Marathi slang of Mumbai, talk of urban politics and Bollywood intrigues, have social networks in the village consisting of other sometime urbanites. But, despite decades on the fringe of the arrival city, none has considered moving permanently. Sanjay may well be the first. For there has been an imperceptible but important change between grandfather and grandson: Before, the work in the city was a begrudged way to support the village. Now, for Sanjay, the village has begun to serve as a supportive backstop and safety net for his emerging career in the city. Urban arrival has shifted into the foreground.

On his day off, Sanjay sails across Mumbai, clinging to the outside of the Suburban Railway train as it traverses the peninsula, enjoying the prospect of visiting someone from his village. The young migrants of Kolhewadi have not yet congealed together in a common neighborhood. Many of them, perhaps half, will end their lives back in the village. For most of his village neighbors, the move to Mumbai for work is an enormous shift into an alien world, one that will take them away from the village, except for rare visits, for a decade or more, often for life.

Many begin their urban careers like Archana Kelkar, a 16-year-old girl who spent her childhood down the road from Sanjay's family, in a one-room mud-and-dung hut with her parents, uncle, aunt, brother, and sister. Three years before, a mysterious crop disease had ravaged the Kolhewadi rice harvest. Archana, her sister, and her brother were the first Kelkars to make the trip northward on the Konkan Railway to find work in the city.

Today, Archana spends her nights curled on the polished marble living-room floor of a large middle-class apartment in Goregaon, a northwest Mumbai high-rise enclave. She is the live-in housemaid for a university-educated couple who work as composers in the Bollywood film industry; they have family roots in the same region of southern Maharashtra and found Archana through that network. Archana cooks, cleans, and maintains the house six days a week, sleeping across the room from the couple and waking before them to prepare their morning meal.

In exchange for this, Archana is paid exactly nothing. Like many middle-class Indian couples, her employers keep her, in a vestige of the caste system, on a promise to ensure her urban welfare, plus some funds sent to her family to support them between harvests, but, more importantly, on a guarantee that they will pay her dowry and other costs when she marries a village boy, likely at 18. Dowry fees are a constant and agonizing source of worry for peasant farmers, most acutely in India but to a lesser extent throughout the developing world.* A few decades ago, a small sum of cash and a cow may have sufficed, but the urban revolution has placed fast-mounting obligations of cash and treasure on parents of girls. Officially, the couple say they are saving Archana's salary earnings on her behalf, and she eagerly embraces this arrangement, though her form of employment still falls within most accepted definitions of slavery.

Given this, it might seem natural that Archana will return to the village when she marries and that her migration to Mumbai, like so many others', will have been strictly temporary and contingent. She yearns to go back. "I terribly miss the smell of bamboo forests and the music we sing together in the village," she tells me as she cleans the floor. Yet there is a powerful force pulling her toward permanent settlement in the city, whether she realizes it or not. That force is her 21-year-old brother Anant who has found his place in Mumbai.

I meet Anant at an air-conditioned pathology laboratory in Vile Parle, which, today, is a mix of tree-lined streets and dense slums near the Mumbai airport. His start in Mumbai was even more perilous than Sanjay's or his sister's: this extremely tall and thin young man arrived here at the same time as his sister and moved into a one-room *chawl* with his uncle, who had been in the city for 20 years and considers himself a permanent urbanite. After staying home with his uncle for a month, he finally found a job at a factory making springs, a hard physical job for the outrageously low wage of 1,200 rupees ($25) a month. Then he worked for an office-cleaning agency for four months, cleaning all night for 2,500 rupees a month, still not enough to give him any hope of living on his own. Then, one day, his luck changed, as it so often does for rural arrivals. Cleaning a

---

* Dowry payments have officially been illegal in India since 1961. This has not prevented them from becoming the largest single lifetime expenditure for many poor families. Often involving a motorcycle or amounts of gold and cash equivalent to a year's earnings, they are debilitating for farmers who are not otherwise reliant on cash and lead to dangerous debt crises.

gymnasium early one morning, he struck up a conversation with a wealthy Maharashtrian doctor and helped him with his weights. They developed a friendship in the weightlifting room, and soon Anant was hired as an assistant. His training wage is 3,000 rupees ($63) a month, allowing him to save, in the forbidding Mumbai shantytown property market, to purchase a real home in one of the better slums. He misses the rice and livestock of his home, he says, but he realizes now that the urban life will give his family options they never could have dreamed of before, and he hopes to move them all over for good someday.

The back-and-forth movements of people like Sanjay, Archana, and Anant have eluded most governments and scholars for decades. Even as the major cities of Latin America, Africa, and Asia became clotted with slums and other spontaneous arrival-city developments in the decades after the Second World War, the world was viewed as being divided sharply into the rural and the urban. Yes, there were rural laborers in the city, but they were seen as a temporary, transitory population. It was widely assumed by scholars and officials that villagers, even if they did spells of work in the city, would remain peasants forever. So there were rural policies and urban policies, and no attention was paid to the interface between them.[5]

In the 1970s, the British geographer Ronald Skeldon, studying the lives of villagers in Cuzco, Peru, and their trips to and from Lima, recognized a pattern. Back-and-forth migration was indeed occurring, often for many generations. But, eventually, there was something of a tipping point, a moment when the entire family, and sometimes the entire village, shifted its allegiances and investments to the city and ceased to rely on agriculture. This he called the "migration transition." Sometimes it took generations to occur, sometimes only years. The difference seemed to depend, above all else, on communication and education: people who had been to school, and had information coming from the city, tended to stop moving back and forth and make the transition sooner and more thoroughly.

And, at the core of this transition, Skeldon realized, was a certain kind of urban space: "The earliest migrants from any particular community tend to settle first in the center of Lima," he wrote. "Some years later, after they have become established in the city, they move out to the peripheral *barriadas*, or *pueblos jóvenes* (young towns). Once the links have been established between the peripheral settlement and the community of origin, migration tends to be direct to that settlement."[6] Those words form a precise definition of an arrival city.

At almost the same time, the American sociologist Charles Tilly was examining the history of rural-to-urban migration in Europe and North America and realizing that human migrations were of more than one type. Previously, it had been believed that the decision to migrate had been a matter of either "push factors," which thrust people out of the village through hardship and starvation, or "pull factors," which drew people to urban lives with tempting income opportunities. Tilly noted that, while these factors often apply, the decision to move rarely had anything to do with them. He recognized three major types of migration between village and city. There were *circular* migrations, like the Limousin stonemasons who migrated from their farms to the crowded arrival cities of central Paris every year for centuries to spend the winter season building the city, each year leaving a few men behind to settle permanently. There were *career* migrants, those who moved more or less permanently to the city to work for skilled trades, governments, armies. They didn't tend to be villagers and were proportionately few in number. And, his most significant discovery, there was the preponderance of *chain* migration, an activity that "moves sets of related individuals or households from one place to another via a set of social arrangements in which people at the destination provide aid, information and encouragement to new migrants."

Here he found the central mechanism behind the world's great population shift. The move was not a matter of pulling and pushing forces, or of passive victimization at the hands of economic structures (as another group of scholars had intimated); rather, it was the creation of a new culture between village and city. This is exactly the process by which seasonal migrants like Sanjay are pulled into the city and turned into urbanites. By turning from circular migrants into fixed agents who aid the future migration of others, they establish a more secure, village-owned urban base, and a set of informal institutions, which allows a larger, constant flow of villagers and makes a migration transition possible.

And chain migration, too, requires its own special sort of urban space, one that will host constant movement in both directions. Chain migrations, Tilly noted, "tend to produce a considerable proportion of experimental moves and a large backflow to the place of origin. At the destination, they also tend to produce durable clusters of people linked by common origin. At the extreme, the migrants form urban villages."[7] These "durable clusters" and "urban villages" are arrival cities, in their purest form. Once arrival cities are understood in this light, it becomes possible to see their importance for both urban and rural development. They are not mere slums housing the outcasts and failures of the urban society; nor are they temporary encampments for transient labor. They are the key mechanisms of the city's regeneration.

And what they produce, through this cycle of selection, are among the most inventive and resilient population groups in the world. Contrary to their popular image as the losers in a capitalist society, the individuals and families who make it into the slums and shantytowns are the winners of the rural-urban lottery, the best of the best from the villages, the most successful of a highly ambitious group. "The migrants from the villages come with very high expectations, often higher than those of the native-born city dwellers," says Patricia Mota Guedes, a Brazilian scholar who studies schools and social conditions in *favelas*. "They always have the choice to move out and go back to the village, and more than half of them do. Those who stay are the toughest and smartest ones, and they can take a lot of change." Or, as one Kenyan urban-planning administrator concluded, "slum dwellers are generally more robust than the rest of the urban population."[8]

THE BIRTH PANGS: AN ARRIVAL CITY TAKES SHAPE
Kamrangirchar, Dhaka, Bangladesh

First come the men with saws and machetes, clearing the swampy, low-lying land on the edge of town. Then come the families, carting piles of bricks and wood down mud pathways, staking out rudimentary foundations on the small plots they have purchased. Then come months of scavenging and hard work, as mud, sticks, stray boards, scraps of tin, and sheets of plastic are cobbled together by the family into the beginnings of a one-room house. Here, on the fast-expanding southwest corner of Dhaka, on the edge of an island that was swampy farmland a few years earlier, the houses are built up on bamboo stilts, East Asian style, so the inevitable floods won't wash them away. Just up the road, where the floods are only occasional, they are built from random collections of bricks and boards. The Bangladeshi capital is vying with Chongqing and Lagos as the fastest-growing and most migrant-filled city in the world, and its slum houses are packed together to an extraordinary density. All are spaced tight up against one another, in clusters around small courtyards known in Bangladesh as *bustees*, built by their owners. It is here where seasonal, temporary migration turns into permanent, tenacious settlement, and a new arrival city is born.

Next comes Jainal Abedin, a young man in a neatly pressed shirt, with a patient demeanour and a small toolbox, strolling along the pathway, entering every door. He is the new neighborhood's first link to the larger city. He greets the new families, collects their names, writes them in a vinyl-bound ledger book, passes along advice and gossip and news of threats to the neighborhood and opportunities for work. He listens to their financial troubles and collects small piles of money. He scrawls symbols on the outer walls of houses and makes promises.

Jainal is the cable-TV man. This makes him a powerful and influential figure in the new slum, in good part because his is the first and most reliable utility to be delivered, years or decades ahead of running water, postal services, and sewage.* All across the developing world, in South America and Asia and the Middle East, the cable guy has become a source of influence in the slum. In the vast slums of Mumbai, the cable-*wallah* is a mafioso figure, wielding, on behalf of shadowy gangs, the power to loan and to influence government, to save huts from demolition or condemn them to the bulldozer. In the *favelas* of Brazil, where the average slum family has 1.5 TVs, 14 percent have computers, and 7 percent have internet access, cable and satellite TV hookups are part of the social-control arsenal of the drug gang.[9] Jainal's powers are more diffuse; he purchased his territory when he was 18, with the help of his cable-installer father, hooked it up to the cable-TV trunk by hand and lays the cables in the ever-expanding shantytown himself. He works as a mild intermediary between business, property owners, tenants, and other less visible figures. He charges 200 taka, or $3, per month for a 30-channel package—a spectrum of Hindi musicals, Bengali melodramas, Persian Gulf newscasts, and English cricket matches, which glows from at least one TV in each *bustee*. To walk through the slum at night is to traverse pools of blue light and competing blasts of tinny music.

The roaring success of the cable-TV business in an overcrowded Asian slum packed with former farmers earning less than $1 a day might seem a bizarre and inexplicable anomaly. If so, it's because we so completely misunderstand the nature of the arrival city and its inhabitants. To the outside eye, this looks like a failed community relegated to the most horrid and repellent sort of houses: thick encrustations of unstable buildings elevated on stilts over open cesspits, separated by shadowy passageways less than a meter wide, crawling with livestock and untended children and reeking of waste. It is widely imagined, both by visiting Westerners and by established residents of cities like Dhaka, that such places must be the last refuge

---

* Here and in the slums of all but the most advanced countries, electricity is most often cannibalized from public power lines by the residents.

of failures, the human fallout of industrial society. But this is to dis-regard what the residents believe is the temporary nature of the filth and disorder, the investments they are making and the dynamics of a community that envisions itself becoming crisp, paved, lighted, legal, sanitary, and fully linked to the city as soon as possible. The 20,000 people in this corner of Dhaka, and most of the five million slum dwellers who make up 40 percent of the city's population, have fought and saved for years to get here, have made their urbanization a matter of constant planning, calculation, and strategizing.* This can be seen in the booming cable businesses (which now sometimes include Internet access as well), the thriving market in every sort of mobile-phone service, the complex network of credit sources, appli-ance and furniture stores that have stoked a rudimentary wave of consumerism—and, above all, in the well-organized property market that allowed the slum-dwellers to buy their tiny patches of land. The arrival-city slum is a place of upward mobility—or at least a calcu-lated grasp for the best hope of mobility. These are, in the words of a United Nations agency, not "slums of despair" but rather "slums of hope."[10]

Jainal Abedin knows this. He watches the back streets of Kamrangirchar transform themselves from tentative improvisa-tions into a permanent urban community. He first encounters the lone men and women who have been working and sleeping in the city for years, staking their claims on property, then the packages of cash going back to the village every month, then the rest of the family arriving. Many people move out after a few months. There are the frustrated ones who give up and return, the ones who move on to other, more central slums or to better neighborhoods. Poor people move house frequently, and arrival cities, in their early years,

---

* Of the 500,000 people who migrate to Dhaka every year, a sizable proportion are seasonal agricultural workers or work-seeking refugees from floods and other climate or food disasters; they pack into temporary shelters and pavement spaces. Almost all are temporary. Those who attain tenure on slum dwellings are more organized and less desperate, as they have been able to save to make the move.

are places of constant movement and change. Jainal keeps track of it all. "These are very poor people living on this street, they've come from Barisal district," he says of one fast-rising row of shacks, whose residents come from a swampy farming region 120 kilometers downriver to the south. "The men here are drivers, but they've saved a lot of money." This island is known for its drivers of pedal-rickshaws, the major form of public transportation in Dhaka. It is a physically ruinous job, known for early deaths and high rates of drug and alcohol addiction and AIDS, but also known as a quick way for poor arrivals to make decent money. The men often do it for a few years, then move on to lower-paying but more family-friendly jobs in industry or construction. The women, increasingly, find more remunerative work in Dhaka's booming garment industry. In Bangladesh, as in many other places, the arrival city is turning women into primary breadwinners, and they play a prominent and visible role in these communities.

Up the road, along Jainal's cable route, I meet Selina Akhter, an elegant and serious woman of 22, who arrived three weeks earlier from the Jhenaidah district, near the western border of Bangladesh and India. Her one-room house had been half-built by a couple from the north who had grown disillusioned and moved back before the doors and window had been filled in. Now, dressed in the bright, celebratory sari favoured by Bengali women, she is outfitting her family's space: a mattress, raised on a platform bed, with a few feet of floorboards for her three-year-old child, a small cooking area in the back with a single butane burner, and a storage loft above. She shares a small dirt courtyard and a larger outdoor cooking fire with five other families.

"There is far less space than in the village, but there is no question that life is better here," she tells me. "I knew as soon as I became a mother that I would have to come to Dhaka. We're alone here, we don't have any family around us, but one guy we know from our home village, we met him working in the city and he recommended we take this house here. It's the beginning of our family's new life."

Three years before, she gave birth to her first child, a healthy son. Children in her region do not fare well: it is subject to *monga*, a seasonal famine, mainly caused by poor farm investment and management, which leaves families without enough food in the winter months. This is compounded by frequent flooding of her farm by the nearby tributary of the Ganges, resulting in appallingly high child-mortality and chronic-illness rates. Whereas her parents had been forced to endure such conditions, Selina and her husband were determined not to watch their boy starve in the winter. Her husband found work in Dhaka as a painter, sleeping on the pavement at first. After three years, sending back enough money to buy rice in the winter, he had saved almost $700, enough to pay for a single-room hut in a slum *bustee*. They were drawn to this place by the well-formed social network of people from their village living on this street.

Her husband earns 3,500 taka ($50) a month painting houses, a typical arrival-city wage, just enough to eat two meals a day, send money back to the village, and pay the $15 monthly payment on the house. That's enough for their needs today, but they will need more to afford their intended future. Selina wants to start working in a garment plant to pay for a private secondary school for her son, if she can find a source of child care while she works. This may have to wait until she finds a primary school. And it is here that her plans collide with the reality of this side of Kamrangirchar, one of the reasons why slum houses here are more affordable: it is outside the municipal boundaries of Dhaka. That makes it ineligible for schools, water and sewage lines, and assistance. Everyone on this street, in this neighborhood, is gambling that this well-established mass of migrants will become a sufficiently powerful demographic and political force, so that Dhaka will be forced to incorporate it into the city's boundaries—a reasonable gamble, since the city has done so with several slum districts before. On the other hand, Dhaka has also demolished bigger and better-established slums than this one.

As everywhere, life is a bet on the future of the children. Arrival cities are places of generational deferral, in which entire lives are sacrificed, often in appalling conditions, for a child's better opportunity. "It's harder here than in the village, there's less time to relax, but now I can have dreams for my son," Selina says, carrying him to the lone water pump several hundred meters away, where she will painstakingly wash him under the tap. "I won't talk of them—dreams vanish when you look at them. But definitely I'll send him to school, I'll find a way."

Her determination will serve her well. But in a hostile city in a world that does not really understand the arrival city, her challenges have just begun.

Arrival cities are built on the logic of the bootstrap: as a rural outsider without a real urban income, you cannot possibly afford to live in the city, but in order to escape being a rural outsider, you must first have a place to live in the city. This paradox has two solutions. First, you rely on your network of fellow villagers to find you a temporary berth in the city. Then, you organize and find a way to set up a house at a fraction of urban cost, by seeking out the property that is least desired or largely abandoned by urbanites, places that are too remote or inaccessible or ill-served by transport and utilities, or those that are, for geographic or climatic or health reasons, considered uninhabitable: the cliffsides of Rio de Janeiro and Caracas, the sewage-filled lagoons of east Asia, the verges of garbage dumps and railway tracks and international airports, the fetid riverside floodplains of many, many cities.

In the earliest decades of the great arrival-city boom, from the 1940s to the 1970s, the predominant way to acquire land was by squatting. Rural migrants, usually in organized groups that had met in inner-city flophouse enclaves, would simply take over a plot of unoccupied land, cut roadways and build houses there, and hope for the best. The land was usually government-owned or held by unknown or poorly registered parties. By the end of this period, the "land invasion" had become a well-organized institution in Latin America, and the practice had spread across the Middle East and Africa and into some parts of Asia. Land invasions were seen as transitory, tempo-rary phenomena. By the 1980s, many of these "invaded" enclaves, even those that had been repeatedly bulldozed, had evolved into full-fledged cities, with hundreds of thousands of inhabitants, legitimate governments of their own, and influential middle classes and internal economies. The Dharavi slum of Mumbai (800,000 people), Orangi in Karachi (500,000), Ashaiman in Ghana (100,000), Villa el Salvador in Peru (300,000), and the self-built Asian outskirts of Istanbul (over 1,000,000) all began as rudimentary squatter enclaves but are now successful, full-scale urban economies, each containing hundreds of migrant-owned factories and producing sizable economic output.

But the land invasion has become a much rarer activity, for good reasons. First, land nowadays tends to be private, with clear owners, as opposed to the socialized ownership or ambiguous land titles that blanketed the developing world in the early days. Second, rural migrants, almost universally, do not want ambiguity in their pos-session of the land beneath their feet: They want clear ownership, or at least secure and guaranteed tenure, as much as middle-class homeowners do. As a result, the majority of slum huts in places like Kamrangirchar are subject to ownership and often to mortgage competition, speculation on their future value, and all the other financial trappings of home ownership It may not be formal or registered ownership, or have legal weight, but it is central to the lives of arrival-city residents. "Regardless of the type of land use or the quality of homes produced, irregular housing is advertised, sold and rented in an operating market," one group of scholars concluded in a survey of slum housing. "Access to land in urban peripheries, and even in the more consolidated informal settle-ments, is nowadays obtained predominantly through market trans-actions." Despite its image, arrival-city housing is never free or even cheap. The price of a square meter of land is very often higher in the slum than in a prosperous, middle class neighborhood (but it is divided into far smaller parcels than would ever be allowed in better-off quarters). And slum-dwellers usually pay the highest prices for commodities like water and fuel, because they must be delivered by truck and are usually controlled by local oligopolies.[11] Arrival is an expensive investment.

Selina Akhter and her neighbors have not invested their entire life savings and energies in the arrival city only to see it remain a pungent slum. At the moment, though, having a roof over her head, a basic (if distant) source of water, a network of security, and some means of getting to work are the best she can manage. The next few years, and the decisions of Bangladesh's various governments and agencies, will determine whether this corner of Kamrangirchar will follow a path that leaves it stuck, isolated, and increasingly desperate, violent, and poor or one that transforms it into an increasingly permanent and established urban community, contributing to the economic life of Bangladesh and generating a stable middle class who will ensure the future vitality and security of the city.

Because arrival cities are so widely misunderstood and distrusted—dismissed as static "slums" rather than places of dynamic change—governments have devoted much of the past 60 years to attempting to prevent their formation. It didn't begin this way. In the two decades after the Second World War, squatter enclaves were tolerated. Industrial growth was occurring at such a pace that seemingly endless supplies of rural migrants were needed to fill labor shortages, and countries realized the value of urbanization. Then, as urban economies became increasingly informal, starting in the late 1960s, and manufacturing economies were no longer always the main destination for rural migrants, governments and international organizations developed an obsession with "over-urbanization." This coincided with a romanticized, idealized view of the peasant life popular in Marxist economies and in many corners of academia.

The result was policies that attempted to prevent the great migration, by discouraging, redirecting, or blocking villagers from entering major cities. These policies rarely worked. Authoritarian countries had the most success: the most dramatic and far-reaching such policy was China's *hukou* household-registration system, which prevented any urbanization until the 1980s (though it did not prevent countless millions of peasants from establishing footholds in the city, allowing the rapid creation of arrival cities when more liberal policies arrived). Other authoritarian states, such as South Africa's apartheid regime and Chile's Pinochet government, also physically blocked migration. It is worth noting that countries rarely experience economic growth while banning or restricting rural-urban migration: without urbanization, the economy stagnates, and people often starve.

Other strategies proved equally ineffective and damaging. Indonesia forced 600,000 families to move from villages on the central island of Java to more remote regions, partly to establish political control and partly to prevent urbanization. This did nothing to prevent Jakarta from rapidly urbanizing and may actually have accelerated the urban shift. Other large-scale attempts to settle populations in other regions of the country to avoid cities—in Sri Lanka, Malaysia, Vietnam, Tanzania, Brazil, and the Andean countries of South America—did nothing to slow or decrease urbanization and often did great damage to the economy and to the lives of millions of people. Arrival cities continued to form, but because of these policies they couldn't thrive or make the transition into formal and comfortable urban neighbourhoods. Studies of Dar es Salaam, Tanzania, and Jakarta, Indonesia, found that migration-control laws made life much worse for the poor while creating deep layers of corruption, since migration meant bribing officials; this, in turn, increased the criminality of the arrival city.[12]

Brazil's military government probably went the furthest in trying to prevent arrival cities from forming. They tried everything: initiating programs to mass-move northeastern peasants into the Amazon basin; constructing intermediate destination cities, including the new capital of Brasilia; giving grants to bolster existing medium-sized centers; outlawing all internal migration; establishing roadblocks and checkpoints to stop movement; and redirecting the entire state budget to facilitate "the rationalization and spatial distribution of population," whatever that meant. None of this stopped slums from forming in the major cities of Rio de Janeiro and São Paulo and at the most rapid rate in the world. The violence and squalor of these *favelas* masked the fact that nobody was moving back because their material conditions were better and their prospects more hopeful.

The first person who managed to see through the myths of the arrival city was the anthropologist Janice Perlman, who spent the 1960s within the *favelas* of Rio de Janeiro, engaged in the then-fashionable study of "marginality," in this case among peasant migrants. She had expected to find migrants "arriving lonely and rootless from the countryside, unprepared and unable to adapt fully to urban life, and perpetually anxious to return to their villages. In defense, they isolate themselves in parochial ruralistic enclaves." Instead, she discovered, in her landmark 1976 study, *The Myth of Marginality*, "Careful examination reveals a more complex reality . . . Beneath the apparent squalor is a community characterized by careful planning in the use of limited housing space and innovative construction techniques on hillsides considered too steep for building by urban developers. Dotting the area are permanent brick structures that represent the accumulated savings of families who have been building little by little, brick by brick." These supposedly marginal places, Perlman concluded, are "communities striving for elevation," built by "dynamic, honest, capable people who could develop their neighborhoods on their own initiative if given the chance . . . Over time the *favela* will evolve naturally into a productive neighborhood, fully integrated into the city." She warned, however, that these dynamic neighborhoods were becoming trapped: "In short, *they have the aspirations of the bourgeoisie, the perseverance of pioneers, and the values of patriots,*" she concluded. "What they do *not* have is an opportunity to fulfill their aspirations."[13]

Her ideas, and those of like-minded South American scholars, slowly caught the attention of the Brazilian leadership, notably the economist Fernando Henrique Cardoso, who was to become president in 1995. In the late 1980s, Brazil embarked on its first proper study of the phenomenon and realized that not only was urban migration creating improved urban lives for the former peasants but that *favela* residents, after 10 years in the city, ended up having better economic and social standing, on average, than native-born residents of the city.[14] In other words, the unimpeded arrival city was a more effective form of development than any known economic, social, or population-control policy.

By the end of the twentieth century, many economists and some governments realized that rural-urban migration, far from being a problem for poor countries, was the key to their economic futures. In fact, the largest study of the issue to date, by the World Bank in 2009, concluded that the most effective route to poverty reduction and economic growth is to encourage the highest possible urban population density and the growth of the largest cities through migration—as long as the urban areas where rural migrants arrive are given intensive investment and infrastructure development by governments.[15] This was the first full-scale acknowledgment that arrival cities are at the center of the world's future. But in many places, official attitudes continue to lag far behind this larger understanding. As recently as 2005, almost three-quarters of developing-world governments told researchers that they felt they should restrict rural-urban migration.[16]

ARRESTED DEVELOPMENT: A CITY WITHOUT ARRIVAL
Shenzhen, China

At 16 years of age, Jiang Si Fei traveled alone from her mountain village in Guangxi Province to the city of Shenzhen, found a job in an electronics factory, and fell in love. He was a shy man, six years her senior, working at another assembly table on her shift. His name was Hua Chang Zhan, and he had come from even farther inland, in Hunan Province. In a city where everyone is from somewhere else, most people are young, and childless, and working lives are often lonely and friendless, and the two became inseparable. Two years later, their factory went out of business, and they found themselves trawling the labor halls and job centers of Shenzhen together, searching for the perfect opportunity: a factory paying at least 1,800 yuan ($263) a month that had two positions open.

Given this, you might think that Fei and Zhan would be looking for a place to live together. But, despite their dreams of marrying and having a family someday, cohabitation is beyond even considering. "We are both looking for housing right now," Fei told me as she pored over listings, "but we'd prefer to live in separate dorms, the smaller ones with four to six other workers in the room, because it's so much cheaper and more convenient to do so. If we tried to get an apartment, we would never save any money." This is true: If they were to live together and thus move out of bunk-bed dorms, they would destroy any financial possibility of having a future in the city, or a home in some other city. Despite the length and commitment of their relationship, they can both name the number of times they have been alone in a room together. They both enjoy the lively bustle and high wages of Shenzhen and would love to find a way to move here permanently, but they've realized it is almost impossible to put down roots in any lasting way. Aside from the impossible housing costs, the city's regulations make it very difficult to raise a child here if you're from a village elsewhere, no matter how long you've worked here. Although the city was theoretically the first in China to abolish the rigid *hukou* requirements for citizenship, in practice, it grants this residence status only to skilled, educated, or wealthy workers. In a city of 14 million, only 2.1 million, or 15 percent, have a Shenzhen *hukou*, which entitles their children to education in the city.* Fei and Zhan have no hope of getting one. Their future, and their family, will have to take place somewhere else. Millions of other workers have come to the same conclusion.

---

* Workers in Shenzhen are granted the lesser residence card, which does not carry housing or education benefits. In 2009, Shenzhen introduced a system allowing residence-card holders to apply for a *hukou* after five years in the city, but there is little sign that low-wage workers have been able to take advantage of this.

Shenzhen, on the southern mainland of China across the Deep Bay from Hong Kong, is the world's largest purpose-built arrival city. As recently as 1980, it was a fishing village of 25,000 people; then Chairman Deng Xiaoping declared it the first Special Economic Zone, exempt from restrictions on movements of workers and freely allowed to practice capitalism, and it quickly swelled into an industrial hub whose population, by the end of the twentieth century, was officially almost nine million but more likely in excess of 14 million, owing to the masses of semi-permanent village migrants from all over China who pack its workers' dormitories. It spawned a thriving middle class, a leading high-tech sector, and one of the best universities in China. It's the place where iPods and Nikes are made, along with much of the Western world's clothing and electronics.

And yet, Shenzhen today is, by most measures, a failed arrival city. After its explosion of success in the 1990s, something went wrong. Despite its having the highest per capita income and urban living standard in China, workers have been flooding out of the city for years, most often headed to inland cities closer to their home villages, where the wages are half those in Shenzhen and it's possible to live in "urban village" slums, like Liu Gong Li. After the 2008 New Year holiday, during which half the workforce traditionally take a vacation in their home villages, Shenzhen officials were shocked to discover that two million workers had failed to return; 18 percent of the city's migrant workforce had decided to leave for good, despite large labor shortages: by the end of 2007, Shenzhen had 700,000 unfilled jobs.[17] City officials raised the minimum wage from 450 to 750 to 900 yuan ($132) per month, but it did little to attract workers back. In 2010, when hundreds of thousands more failed to return, Shenzhen announced plans to raise it yet again, to 1,100 per month, after facing labor shortages of more than 20 percent. Again, the promise had little noticeable effect. Officials were left bewildered. Some speculated that China's competitiveness in low-wage manufacturing was doomed, but few had good explanations.

You don't have to spend long among Shenzhen's migrant workers to realize the problem. There are millions of workers here who have bought apartments in dense tower blocks, moved their families in and settled down—but almost all of them are skilled tradesmen, technicians, managers, or people with post-secondary education. For ordinary factory workers, this dream is unaffordable. Nor is it possible to open a rudimentary shop or start-up factory, as migrants do in arrival cities elsewhere. In other Chinese cities, including Beijing and Chongqing, former villagers congeal into self-built "villages" of thousands or tens of thousands of people mainly from the same region—like Liu Gong Li. There they can get a crude but livable first home and build a small shop, restaurant, or even a start-up factory in its ground floor, as arrival-city residents do around the world.

But these self-built neighborhoods no longer exist in Shenzhen. In 2008, I tried to visit one of the last of these "villages," known as Min Le ("Happy People Village"), on the city's northwest edge, only to find a narrow, bulldozed patch of land with construction crews building more densely packed apartment towers. The sparc, small apartments were affordable to workers earning 5,000 yuan ($732) a month or more, far beyond the reach of a factory worker. The workers from this "village" had lost their shops and homes and moved back to their real villages. This pattern adds up to a serious crisis in Shenzhen, which is losing its workers by the millions to the slum-packed inland cities, causing it to raise its minimum wages and, in turn, lose its garment-manufacturing economy to lower-wage cities, like Dhaka.

After the crisis reached a peak with the mass departure of workers in 2008, one of China's most esteemed historians and urban-affairs experts staged a provocative intervention that startled Shenzhen's governing authorities. In a speech to an audience of Shenzhen officials, Qin Hui declared that the city could solve its problems only by encouraging the development of shantytown slums. "It is no shame for big cities to have such areas. On the contrary, Shenzhen and other cities should take initiatives to [permit] cheap residential areas for low-income residents including migrant workers who want to stay in the cities where they work," he told the audience of dignitaries.

"To protect the rights of these people, we should respect their freedom to build houses in some designated areas, and improve their living conditions . . . By building those areas, big cities could show more consideration for low-income residents, and provide them with more welfare." He spoke of the dangerous "sexual tension" caused by 140 million migrant workers being separated all year from their 180 million family members and claimed that 50 percent of male migrant workers were not the natural fathers of their children. And he chided the officials for their hypocrisy: They "enjoy the services of migrant workers" yet "want all migrants to return to their villages after [the cities have] exploited their precious youth." China, he said, should end a shameful era in which "rural migrants neither had the liberty to build houses nor could enjoy city welfare."[18]

Around the world, scholars and officials are beginning to realize that rural-migrant neighborhoods are crucial to a city's future, not a problem to be eliminated. The past decade has seen a dramatic change in official opinions. Still, the demolition of arrival-city slums is all too common a practice in such cities as Mumbai and Manila. These bulldozings destroy the economic and social functioning of the arrival city. Even in cases where evicted slum-dwellers are given rudimentary apartments in tower blocks—a common practice in Asia and South America—it is no longer possible for them to create shops, restaurants, and factories to suit the community's needs or to form organic networks to link village to city. The people become dependent, and their communities get stuck.

As recently as 2005, Mumbai launched an aggressive drive to demolish shantytowns, which occupy 14 percent of the city's land area and house 60 percent of its 12 million people. More than 67,000 homes were bulldozed, their families thrown into streets and fields. While some of the slums had been built on dangerous land, on the verges of railway tracks and airports or in national parks, this was explicitly a demolition aimed at the core purpose of the arrival city. Mumbai official Vijay Kalam Patil explained to reporters: "We want to put the fear of the consequences of unfettered migration into these people. We have to restrain them from coming to Mumbai."[19]

Of course, it did not work. Within a year, almost all of the slums had been rebuilt. The same thing happened when Beijing, as part of its 1999 beautification campaign, demolished 2.6 million square meters of "urban village" housing, restaurants, markets, and stores built by migrants: they quickly returned. For the most part, governments have realized the folly of such acts. Slum-demolition campaigns get a lot of media attention—deservedly, given the misery they create—but they are relatively rare today: A few hundred thousand people are affected each year in Asia and Africa, out of the billion who live in slums. While overbearing urban planners will always exist, the larger logic of the city is inescapable: New people create new economies, and those economies develop best when those people, no matter how poor, are able to stage their arrival in an organic, self-generated, bottom-up fashion. The city wants to have migrants. It does not want to meet the fate of Shenzhen, a wound that will not heal, a place nobody can call home.

ARRIVAL POSTPONED: THE STUCK CITY
Kibera, Nairobi, Kenya

Eunice Orembo, her four sons, and her daughter spend their mornings and nights in a single room, ten by seven meters, its walls made from a slurry of red mud, stones, and garbage, packed flat and dried onto a lattice of tree branches lashed to wooden poles; these mud walls hold up a roof made of sheets of corrugated metal. Their home is a tight but welcoming space, with three small windows, colorful fabric and plastic sheets to cover the mud walls, a gas cooker, a CD player, a TV, some chairs, some bare fluorescent-tube lights, a shelf of textbooks, and some attractive decorations with a traditional lion motif. Eunice has hung sheets to divide the interior into two rooms. Her sons, aged 14 to 21, sleep on one side; she and her 5-year-old daughter sleep and cook on the other. These are very close quarters, penned in by great waves of noise, stench, frightening darkness, and criminal violence from outside.

This wattle-and-daub shack is perched amid a lake of similar houses jammed close together across a two-kilometer expanse, separated by narrow alleyways of mud, garbage, and slurries of human waste, a labyrinthine, pungent cluster of almost unimaginably high population density built on hillocks of refuse near the heart of Nairobi. This is the Kianda neighborhood in the Kibera slum, whose inhabitants, numbering close to a million, are perhaps the largest and most infamous slum community in sub-Saharan Africa, subject to disease infestations and bursts of political and gang violence on a terrifying scale. At the end of 2007, Kibera exploded into months of murderous political violence, in which members of the Luo tribe drove Kikuyus out of their neighborhoods, making this an even more ethnically segregated, and dangerous, place.

Kibera, like most African slums, is a true arrival city. Though it has existed here for 90 years, created when Kenya's colonial administration granted some parkland to the homeless Nubian veterans of the First World War, in the post-colonial decades it has become a vital instrument of urbanization, propelling entire villages and districts into the city. Despite its horrid conditions, it does provide a vital stream of cash to the troubled villages of Kenya and its neighboring countries, and it also succeeds in turning people into urbanites. "I am a Nairobi resident now, I speak the language and I know how to be a woman here," says Eunice, who grew up farming maize, cassava, and potatoes in the dry northwest of Kenya. There, her entire family lived in a grass hut and usually ate only one meal of porridge a day. As knowledge of the city spread and successive famines decimated their village, she and her husband soon realized that their only chance of keeping their children alive was to build a link to the city, 400 kilometers away.

First, in 1996, her husband went; he stayed a few months, but before he could find a job an unnamed disease killed him—not a rare occurrence among rural-migrant men in the African city. Eunice and her sons agreed she should make the move herself, in 2001, using a network of established people from her district within Kibera to find a landlord willing to rent her a hut. "We wanted to try to live again, to see if life could change," she recalls. The move provided her with a welcome escape from the tribal customs of the village, where she would have been required to marry her husband's brother after her husband's death. In the city, she was freed from the restrictive dress codes of the village, and from religion. She relished the chance to earn her own money and went to work as a housekeeper in one of the middle-class houses outside the slum (which is wrapped around Nairobi's main golf course). Over the next few years, she was able to bring her children, and now they are determined to make the city their home and their future, despite its many depredations. "The only way I will return to the village," Eunice says, "is inside a casket."

It would be a grotesque understatement to say that the Orembo family live in inadequate housing. To get water, Eunice must walk 75 meters and pay to fill up a plastic container from a hose supplied by one of the slum's "water mafias," at rates up to 20 times those paid by the city's wealthier homes (a price discrepancy that is typical of slums everywhere). She also pays 150 shillings ($2) a month for the privilege of lining up for half an hour to use crude municipal toilets, 50 meters away; the only alternative is the alarmingly popular "flying toilet," in which a plastic bag filled with waste is flung out the window at night, contributing to Kibera's mountain of stench. Getting into the proper city, less than a kilometer away, is damningly difficult, an odyssey of perilous and unhygienic lanes leading to a shortage of bridges and trains. There are almost no spaces in which someone like Eunice could open a small business (and she very much wants to do so), and most of these spaces are controlled by criminal gangs or ethnic mafias. There are very few free schools here, and the fees can be prohibitive: Eunice had to pull her youngest son out of school because she couldn't afford the fee. This, and the lack of decent employment opportunities for males, leads to thousands of idle young men on the street who turn to theft, drug dealing, or the brewing and selling of homemade liquor to get by, a social stew that prevents Kibera from developing into a successful arrival city.

For the privilege of living here, Eunice pays a landlord $17 a month, around half her typical monthly income. The landlord, who rents out hundreds of huts, does not own the land himself; it is municipal land, and his claim to ownership is as ephemeral and insecure as are Eunice's chances of owning her own property. This lack of secure tenure, more than anything, has contributed to the failure of places like Kibera: If you can't own your house, it is very hard to rise above your circumstances.[20]

The solution, in theory at least, is just over the hill. Within sight of Eunice's shack, rising along the horizon, is a growing cluster of neat, gray, high-rise buildings, with red roofs and small concrete balconies, the site of an expansive slum-redevelopment project, to which Kibera's residents are, theoretically, to be moved into stable, sanitary, fully-owned apartment housing. It is a project initiated by UN-HABITAT, the United Nations human-settlements agency, whose world headquarters happen to be within walking distance of Kibera. That such a redevelopment project could only be launched three decades after the U.N. set up shop here is telling. That Eunice Orembo believes that she will never live in these houses is even more telling.

The project, called KENSUP, is typical of slum-redevelopment projects taking place in such cities as São Paulo, Istanbul, and Beijing. It is, in some ways, reminiscent of similar efforts, popularly known as "the projects," that transformed the inner cities of the United States between the 1950s and 1970s: The inhabitants of the chosen neighborhood (this project is starting with the one next to Eunice's, known as Soweto) are moved into a "decanting site" for months or years as their old shacks are demolished and replaced with apartment buildings with plumbing, sewage, and electricity; they are typically given title deeds on these apartments, with a small mortgage to be paid off at rates similar to their previous rent payments. This is an improvement on the previous method employed by Kenya and many other countries: the mass demolition of slums and expulsion of their residents, justified by the twin mythologies that slum-dwellers are a cause of urban poverty and that the presence of an unmolested slum will encourage further migration. These bulldozings (which continue at a lower intensity today) had the effect of destroying small-business networks, demolishing capital that had been saved for lifetimes, and scattering people into hundreds of smaller, more precarious slums or into homelessness. So, in 2000, when Kenya's government acknowledged that slum dwellings ought to be improved rather than eliminated, it was a revolutionary change.

The problem with so many of these rehousing projects is that governments fail to realize that better housing will always have higher commercial value, and that people in slums, as much as anyone in the middle class, view their housing as a source of equity. Slum-dwellers around the world are continually and obsessively interested in the property values of their dwellings, for the real-estate market is one of the most effective levers for escaping poverty. There is nothing quite as empowering as having a full, legal title deed on your property: Ownership gives slum-dwellers legitimacy and rights they'd never possessed before. One of those rights is the right to sell the property. If the apartments were not much larger than a slum hut and had communal plumbing, they would be traded among other arrival-city residents. But the apartments in the KENSUP project, as in many such initiatives, have been built to Kenya's legal housing standards, designed for the middle class, which require two fully habitable rooms, making them effectively a three-room apartment whose value far exceeds that of slum housing. Slum-dwellers quickly realize that there are two ways to extract this value: either by renting two of the rooms to other families and living in the third (thus ending up with a smaller and less private house than the original slum shack) or "selling" it to a middle-class family (using a gray-market "secret" deed to circumvent slum-development rules against such transactions). The gains from such a sale can be enough to put your children through university or start a small business—even though it means moving back into a slum shack. As a result, slum-redevelopment projects have a way of turning into middle-class enclaves on the edge of the slum.

This problem is compounded by another. The arrival city is far more than a pile of housing. Its residents are connected in complex networks and use the space as a source of upward mobility by operating businesses and informal enterprises there. "The slums are commonly referred to as large open-air markets," writes the South African urban planner Marie Huchzermeyer in her study of the Kibera project. "One cannot accurately foresee from outside how an intervention will impact on communities, households and individuals, their income generation and their access to basic services."[21] Projects like KENSUP are generally housing-only facilities: they do not typically provide any space in or near the house to operate a shop, a workshop, or a small factory; there are no physical opportunities to expand the residence or to convert part of it to commercial use; and, crucially, there is no access to the street and to passing pedestrians, who might be able to do business with the tenant. As with the U.S. public-housing "projects" or the *banlieue* towers of France, housing without business space can lock tenants into permanent dependency.

Eunice Orembo has no faith in this housing project. She doesn't believe she will ever have the power to get an "upgraded" apartment, and she believes the upgrading process would ruin the small gains she has made since 2001. "Neighbors are important," she says. "When you have a good understanding and relationship with them, they can keep you alive. Building that connection is very important, friends are very important here." Shunning efforts to improve her housing immediately, she is instead putting all her extra money into getting her sons educated. Emmanuel, 21, is studying dressmaking, and 19-year-old John is training in hairdressing; even now, both young men have ambitions to earn their family's way out of the slum. "The children see things differently from me because they see that their house is not like the other homes in the city," Eunice says. "It may be possible to move into better housing someday because my kids are in college and will make us enough money to buy a decent house someday—I'm counting on them."

REFORM: TEETERING ON THE PRECIPICE
Santa Marta, Rio de Janeiro, Brazil

Devanil de Souza, Jr., a lanky young man with a short-cropped afro and a shy smile, has spent all 12 years of his life looking straight down upon the bustling streets of Rio de Janeiro's Copacabana neighborhood from a great height. The sole window of his family's tiny wood-and-tin house peers over a sheer cliff to the prosperous commercial district below, only a few hundred meters from the bottom of his cliffside community. But Devanil can count the number of times he has set foot there, in the *asfalto*, the proper "asphalt" city of Rio. As soon as he could walk, he learned the rules for leaving the Santa Marta *favela*, a tight-packed accumulation of 10,000 people covering a steep hillside. First, he had to walk down the 788 steps and across countless precarious pathways, a 55-story descent that took him past piles of garbage, grotto shrines, cliff-face bars, and hundreds of ramshackle houses cantilevered over the steep cliff. He would then encounter the *traficantes*, young members of the Comando Vermelho (Red Command) drug army that controlled every aspect of life in the *favela* and tell them that he intended to go into town; they would inform the teenagers who stood guard at the *favela's* street entrance, with 9-mm pistols pressed against their legs, to let the child pass without being shot. On the way out, he would run the gauntlet of the "crack line," a stretch of street lined with tables covered in bricks of cocaine, sold wholesale to dealers, guarded by 15-year-old boys with assault rifles. On the way back in, the armed teenagers would inspect his bags, to make sure he hadn't bought cylinders of cooking gas or other crucial supplies in the city, rather than paying the gang a 30 percent markup.

After that, he faced the steep climb home. It was not a journey he enjoyed taking.

At first glance, Devanil's life fits into a standard narrative surrounding Brazil's *favelas*, or self-built slums, one popularized in movies like *City of God* and endless magazine and television reports, which portray them as places of perpetual violence and depredation, populated by a lost and victimized underclass. It is a more severe and violent version of the story that surrounds migrant-dominated urban enclaves everywhere. But this vision of the *favela* as a fixed commodity, a fallen and immutable population of "the poor" living at the bottom end of "the system," to be dealt with as victims, misses the larger story of the arrival city, the journey being taken by the families who have built and propelled it. The violence and deprivation are an interruption on that journey, an unnatural and sometimes terminal incursion. People here are not "marginal" but rather central actors in the economy, momentarily locating themselves on the sidelines to attain a higher goal.

Devanil's father was born in Paraíba state in the far northeast of Brazil, where his parents had worked as sugar-cane harvesters, an extremely poor life in a wooden shack with no security. They came here in the 1970s, part of a human wave moving into Rio, which swelled Santa Marta, a 1930s hillside shack settlement, into a full-scale arrival city, a chaotic, vertical mass of teetering mud, wood, and tin shacks on an otherwise uninhabitably steep and inaccessible tongue of land, filled with families whose adults worked in the tourist-packed city below as porters, doormen, cleaners, and hotel staff. Despite its tough conditions and the mudslides that killed several residents every few years, Santa Marta functioned well as an arrival city: until the end of the 1970s, it sent thousands of people each decade out of its truly squalid confines into more comfortable, sometimes even middle-class, surroundings. It was governed by an effective neighborhood council, which won it electricity, water, and some sewage lines in the 1980s and seemed to promise pathways to proper citizenship.

Then, as Brazil's economy teetered into bankruptcy and its military government imploded in the 1980s, people stopped moving in and out, the *favela* grew more isolated from the city, and, as the Brazilian state withered away, the narcotic gangs took over. They governed totally and violently, usurping the community council. The Comando Vermelho became the sole source of employment for males, a dangerous life, which sent alarming numbers of Santa Marta's youth to their graves before the age of 21. Still, almost nobody in Santa Marta considered returning to the village, even though this would have been easy. They had a sense of secure ownership of the land beneath their shacks and a better living than their rural cousins. In exchange, Santa Marta's people effectively led a segregated existence within a violent narcotics factory. Unlike thriving arrival cities throughout the developing world, the gang-controlled *favelas* of Brazil lack the busy hodge-podge of shops and small businesses on the ground floors of houses; with the exception of drinking establishments, Santa Marta was almost devoid of commerce, or non-drug opportunities for work. Devanil's father was sucked into this vortex, and Devanil felt certain that he would be holding a pistol by the time he was 14.

At the end of 2008, this all changed, dramatically and violently. Shortly before Christmas, Devanil found himself cowering on the dirt floor of his house one night, his mother screaming in fear, as hundreds of heavily armored military police invaded his *favela* in a commando raid, charging up the 788 steps, firing hundreds of rounds from assault rifles and machine guns, shooting and arresting all members of the drug gang and many bystanders. In itself, this was merely a hyper-intense version of the military-police raids that occurred almost every year. What happened next was different, though. Five weeks later, President Luiz Inácio Lula da Silva visited Santa Marta and delivered a speech declaring it his test-bed for *favela* transformation: "We are working in a way that the state is present in the day-to-day life of poor people . . . In the past it was only the police intervening with lots of brutality . . . [now] we have the biggest investment program of shanty-town urbanization, basic sanitation and house building that Brazil has ever had."[22] The president opened a funicular railway providing transportation to the top of the *favela*, a modern daycare facility, a technical college providing training in job skills, a lighted football pitch at the top of the mountain (the first recreational program the slum had ever seen). Government workers installed a street-lighting system, a WiFi network, and a garbage-collection system and began a large-scale program to rebuild all the houses in solid brick designs with proper sanitation and mudslide-proof foundations. The police force, rather than raiding and leaving, set up a fortress at the top of the hill and moved in permanently, practicing something they called "community-based policing," albeit a version that involved assault rifles and full body armor. All at once, in a community that had never seen any face of government except in the form of police raids, the physical benefits of the state were delivered. This is the sort of program that Kenya's government couldn't afford to attempt in the Kibera slum: It upgrades all the slum homes, and the infrastructure around them, to developed-world standards, without moving anyone out.

Less visible but more significant were changes imposed on the fabric of Santa Marta in early 2009. In effect, this was a shock-and-awe effort by Lula's government to do in a few months what functioning arrival cities accomplish over decades: a full integration into the life of the city. First, a crew of statisticians and cartographers moved into the slum, setting up shop in the new training college at the base of the mountain. They conducted a detailed census and made a map showing each property, its physical condition, and its needs. Then Santa Marta residents were given two things they had never possessed before: a birth certificate and a street address. Together, these made them official citizens, able to receive benefits and work in the legitimate economy, and also to pay taxes and electrical bills (both were the subject of shocked complaints from *favela* residents, who had never paid for such things, and in some cases could not afford them). A high wall was built on the far side of the *favela*, to delineate its existing boundary and provide clear property-ownership deeds to those who lived there.* The labor secretariat set up an office that linked *favela* residents with factories and businesses in Rio looking for work. "Mainly what we're doing here is building trust in the state," says Vera Lucia Nascimento, the project's chief social worker. "People had only ever worked informally, selling whatever they could on the streets and throwing their garbage out the window. We've had to come in and give them ways to be real, formal citizens and organize their lives. With real ID and addresses, so much more is possible. Without that, the only way the state is represented in the *favela* is through police raids. Now it's all about education, small business, jobs. They come to feel like part of the city."

Among the residents here, there is great fear and suspicion of the new government presence: fear, mainly, that they'll be gone in a few months and the Red Command will move back in. But there is also a palpable pride—in a community that previously had invested whatever small scrap of pride it could muster in its flamboyant and funky contribution to Carnival. Devanil no longer talks gloomily about a future as a *traficante*; rather, he boasts that his mother "works for the training college at the bottom of the hill." She has a job cleaning floors at the center, but mere presence in this building is a badge of legitimacy and a foothold in the broader city, which the people of Santa Marta have spent two decades struggling to gain.

The Santa Marta intervention is a token project, of course—one of a few dozen *favelas* being transformed, in this expensive and resource-intensive fashion, out of the many hundreds of such neighborhoods across Rio, many of them even more deprived. But it stands a good chance of succeeding, because it draws on the fundamental dynamics of the arrival city. If an impediment can be removed,

---

* This somewhat excessive "eco-wall," so called because it was also built to protect forests outside, became the subject of protests and media stories in 2009, after an activist group repeated a rumor that it was built to prevent people from migrating to Rio and setting up *favelas*. This never made much sense: The area beyond the wall has never been desirable for housing, and mass rural migration in Brazil is largely finished.

if the state can provide the basic fruits of the city to its residents, then an arrival city will take care of itself, like a river freed from an ice dam: its residents know what to do, they have been trying to do it for years, and they and their children will become part of the city. The practice known as "slum upgrading" has been taking place across the developing world for two decades now, with great success, but unfortunately only in limited, tokenistic locations. It is expensive to install infrastructure after a neighborhood has been fully built, though not as expensive as the criminal and political explosions that will result without it. Small interventions, like installing street lights or subsidizing a private bus service into the slum, can make an enormous difference, turning these neighborhoods into desirable and productive places. So, too, can full property ownership and political citizenship, even if this means paying taxes.

Brazil's urban poor are at the far end of an arrival process that is just beginning on other continents. South America is the first place in the world to have experienced the great postwar rural-to-urban migration, a full four decades ahead of most of Asia and Africa. By the early 1950s, 40 percent of its population was living in cities, a higher proportion than in Asia and Africa today. Over the next five decades, this number doubled, so that South America is now the first fully urbanized place in the developing world: Its migration is now practically complete. Brazil went from being 45 percent urban in the 1960s to 75 percent in the 1980s—almost as urban as Europe. This explains why living standards and average incomes of the Latin American poor are an order of magnitude better than those elsewhere in the developing world.

The Brazilian experience illustrates what can happen when arrival cities are ignored or misunderstood by governments. But given the chance, Brazil's *favelas* have often functioned successfully, transforming millions of desperately poor people into employed and integrated urbanites. In recent years, they have given rise to a sizable and successful "new" middle class that includes President Lula himself, who grew up in a São Paulo slum. Lula is among the first generation of politicians, including Turkish prime minister Recep Tayyip Erdoğan, to be products of the arrival city and to build their political constituency from its ex-migrant residents.

But Brazil, with its hundreds of high-population slums still controlled by narco-gangs, also offers a cautionary tale. Its governments spent decades trying to prevent, remove, isolate or ignore the arrival city, and its inevitable dynamics bit back: If left to its own devices and deprived of access to the larger political system, the arrival city will generate a defensive politics of its own. In Brazil, it took the form of the drug gang. In Mumbai, it is Hindu nationalism. In the arrival cities of Europe, Islamic extremism. The arrival city wants to be normal, wants to be included. If it is given the resources to do so, it will flourish; without them, it is likely to explode. The arrival city is not a static, fixed place. Rather, it is a dynamic location headed on a trajectory. It is within our power to decide where that trajectory leads.

3

ARRIVING AT THE TOP OF THE PYRAMID

THE GREAT AMERICAN ARRIVAL CITY
Los Angeles, California

The Salvadoran village of El Palón is little more than a narrow strip of farm shacks scattered along a dirt road, surrounded by small plots of dry grazing land and patches of forest. Much of it still does not have electricity or running water; its few score residents live off the vegetables and livestock they're able to farm, plus a diet of tortillas, rice, and beans. Children start working at age six, joining the family for long treks to take part in the seasonal coffee harvest, and life is a search for sparse sources of non-farm income and a calculated avoidance of the region's periodic bursts of violence. "We spent our time there in survival mode," says Mario Martinez, who grew up there in the conflict-ridden 1980s.

The area around the intersection of South Redondo and West Adams boulevards in Los Angeles could not be mistaken for a village, although it is tightly and intricately linked to El Palón. It is a grid of narrow bungalows with miniature front lawns, interrupted by blocks of industrial and commercial buildings on the main boulevards, all in the shadow of the elevated Santa Monica Freeway. Known to the city government as West Adams and to many Angelenos as a northern corner of South Central,* it is a gray, baking-hot, car-packed neigh-borhood, unleavened by any sort of park or green space, one of the most densely populated districts in the city. It is also one of the poorest.[1] Historically, it was an African American ghetto that had a reputation as a crime-ridden no-go zone among white Angelenos. It had no economy, its boulevard's only signs advertising heavily guarded liquor stores and check-cashing shops. In 1992, it exploded in violence, the Rodney King riots leading dozens of its buildings to be set aflame and scores more to be looted. Men stood on its tiny front lawns and outside its barren shopfronts with shotguns, des-perately defending their rented spaces and swearing to move away as soon as they could.

Yet this corner, almost two decades after the riots, has become something else altogether. Its tiny bungalows nowadays tend to be freshly painted and well maintained, with neat gardens and flower-beds surrounded by new wrought-iron fences in the front and thriv-ing vegetable patches in the back. Its boulevards are now more active and colorful, with many more shops, small industries, and lively markets and eateries, decorated with exuberant, colorful signs and displays. This will never be a beautiful neighborhood and is not a completely safe one, but it has become a much neater, happier, more optimistic one. It is now populated mainly with villagers: Six out of 10 people living here today were born in a Latin American village, often the same one as their neighbors.[2] The monthly trips to Western Union made by the Salvadorans living here are almost cer-tainly the largest source of cash income in El Palón; these packages of hundreds of dollars have changed the appearance and quality of the Salvadoran village's housing and given it electricity and televi-sion. Members of the Salvadoran enclave on West Adams have helped each other migrate here, find rental apartments, get jobs, save

* The L.A. government and the *Los Angeles Times* now call this neighborhood West Adams, but to many Angelenos this name connotes a more prosperous neighborhood of attractive nineteenth-century houses near the University of Southern California. Nobody living here seems to agree on the neighborhood's name.

money, set up small businesses, hire additional employees, and buy houses. This village-linked network and hundreds of others just like it, which connect adjoining streets and blocks to remote peasant districts in Honduras, Guatemala, El Salvador, and Mexico, have turned southern and south-central Los Angeles into a quilt of arrival cities. This rough-and-tumble parcel of city blocks not only turns Central American villages into better places, it also very efficiently turns their sons and daughters into functioning Americans.

It was in 1991, a few months before the riots turned this neighborhood into a storm of smoke and gunfire, that Mario Martinez made the journey from El Palón to Los Angeles. His two aunts, Victoria and Marta, had come in the early 1980s to escape the violence in the village. Victoria had done well for herself doing menial jobs and saved enough money to pay to have Mario brought into the country by an immigration agent. Mario, almost penniless, moved into her house in Inglewood (which also was hit hard in the rioting). In a troubled and depressed city, he joined a perpetual mass of brown-skinned men who worked as casual day laborers, doing odd jobs in building, moving, whatever he could find. The more established among his fellow Salvadoran villagers soon found him jobs in their shops and factories and rented him apartments. He sent money to his parents and siblings back in El Palón and saved enough to bring his teenaged daughter (from a short-lived relationship in El Salvador) into the United States.

In the late 1990s, he found a job at a Korean-owned shop that made neon signs. He proved a natural at the crafts of neon-bending, plastic-forming, and typography and was not bad at sales. The Koreans took well to him and tutored him in the business; he saved some money, fell in love with Bibi, a Guatemalan woman from the neighborhood, married, and settled into the backyard apartment of a subdivided bungalow just north of Adams Boulevard, owned by a successful Salvadoran friend. After a few years working at the shop, he strolled home one warm evening and was struck by the realization that the streets around him were now lined with crude storefronts of restaurants, small factories, import-goods shops, and upstart businesses, all owned by fellow Latin Americans. His fellow villagers, he discovered, were badly in need of signs.

So he scraped together $1,500 and, in 2000, rented the cheapest storefront he could find on a riot-damaged intersection a half-dozen blocks from his house and hung out a bright-colored banner announcing "JM Plastic & Sign Co.—Custom Design—Banners—Magnetics." He had no bank loan or business plan, only credit extended to him by vendors and materials suppliers, most of them Central American arrivals themselves. He was helped by a city post-riot reconstruction scheme, which eased zoning and business-incorporation rules, making it cheaper and easier to set up a small firm. He bought a second-hand computer for $150 and started making the rounds of Latin American storefronts.

They were innumerable. In the decade after Los Angeles burned, swaths of the city's core turned from poor neighborhoods, populated by black tenants who rented from absentee white landlords, into Latino arrival cities, whose residents struggled to buy their ghetto homes. Such notoriously dysfunctional neighborhoods as South Central, Crenshaw, Watts, and Compton turned into Spanish-speaking enclaves populated by new village arrivals who were even poorer than the previous black occupants. But there was a difference in perspective and strategy. While poor black Angelenos were struggling to escape their neighborhood as fast as they could and move into the suburbs, as the white working class had done a generation before, the Spanish-speaking arrivals were struggling to dig in, buy their homes, and set up shop.

This is partly a difference of culture—whereas white and black Americans aspire to have a big front lawn outside the city, Latin Americans, when they get some money, prefer to set up stakes in the urban core. But it is also a function of the arrival city. As villagers building networks of personal and economic support to create pathways into the city's central economy, Central Americans are not just getting by and searching for work but building full and coherent arrival cities. They did so in the 1990s to an extraordinary degree, turning most of the inner core of the city, plus all of its east and most of its southeast, into an arrival-city expanse. Anyone who was in L.A. at the time of the riots would not recognize the city today. Florence and Normandie, the district in South Central L.A. that had been the flashpoint of the 1992 riots, saw its Latino-born population rise from 25 percent in 1990 to 45.4 percent in 2000 and even higher in the next decade, a home-buying influx that allowed its existing city-wary residents to move to the better-off black suburbs, causing the black population of Florence and Normandie to fall by a third, from 76 percent to 53 percent.[3] The colonization of L.A.'s core by Central American arrivals added the demographic influence of these neighborhoods to the established Latino barrios of East L.A. and downtown and to Spanish-tongued neighborhoods, like Rampart and Silverlake, all of which had been overtaken by ex-villagers in the 1970s and '80s and had come to develop prosperous middle classes. There were, Mario Martinez discovered, a lot of people looking for signs.

Today, Mario still runs his sign-making shop out of the tiny storefront at the corner of Adams and Hauser boulevards. But this dusty and barren corridor has turned into a busy place, packed with small factories and shops, its sidewalks alive with constant activity. "I chose the location of my business based on what I could afford, which was hardly anything," he says, "but now I can't even contemplate leaving this location—it's in the middle of everything." His shop is surrounded by those of other successful former villagers: a plumbing-supply shop, a tile-making shop and ceramics workshop, a computer technician's office, a large artisanal bakery, a display-case manufacturer who teams up with him. Mario has expanded, in a quiet way. He spent $8,000 on a large-format printer, which creates full-color photographic signs that are popular with restaurants and markets here. He has two full-time assistants plus his wife, Bibi, who quit her job with The Salvation Army to work with him. Their village-upstart shopfront business has gained prominence through networks of

Latinos who have led him to some impressive contracts: Mattel, the toy company, hired him to build a series of illuminated display signs for collections, at $3,000 a case. The business boom came with an expanding family: Mario and Bibi now have a seven-year-old son, Jonathan, who is culturally more American than anyone in his parents' generation around him. While he speaks Spanish at home, he has never been to El Salvador and knows little of its culture.

What happened to Mario Martinez and his L.A. neighborhood is being echoed across the Western world, in the outskirts, the low-rent suburbs, the housing-project districts, and the abandoned inner-city enclaves of North America's and Europe's cities. The final great wave of rural–urban migration, as it moves the final half of humanity from village to city, is transforming the cities of the wealthy West as much as it is changing the urban fabric of Asia, South America, and Africa. Most Westerners do not understand that what is taking place in their cities is a process of rural-to-urban migration. The incomes and absolute poverty levels are different, but the frustrations, opportunities, remedies, and dangers are exactly the same.

In the *banlieue* outskirts of Paris or the apartment-block immigrant quarters of Amsterdam and Berlin, in the Bangladeshi East End of London or in Pakistani Bradford, in the barrios of Los Angeles and New York or the immigrant suburbs of Washington and Atlanta and Sydney, the people renting the apartments and buying the houses and running the shops are mainly former villagers. The act of sending regular payments back to the rural village is central to the economies of all these neighborhoods. And the Los Angeles arrival city does this at a scale unlike almost anywhere else in the Western world. At least half a dozen L.A. banks specialize in providing mortgages, denominated in U.S. dollars in minuscule sums, so that Central American migrants can buy homes in their original villages. It is a booming transnational property trade, driven by a population who aspire to entrepreneurship, education, and home ownership.

Los Angeles stands out as the premier arrival-city cluster of the United States, with almost half its population born in other countries (and predominantly in rural areas), a position equalled in North America only by Toronto, which plays a similar role in Canada. Los Angeles is described by demographers as a "gateway city," which is to say that it is a broadly successful arrival city: its poor neighborhoods send out successful middle-class and upper-working-class migrants to wealthier neighborhoods at rates similar to their intake of poor villagers. People move *through* its neighborhoods: L.A. flushes out at least a third of its population each decade, becoming an entirely new city in each generation. A major study of the city's immigrants shows that they arrive very poor, with poverty rates approaching 25 percent, but that these rates fall sharply, especially during the first decade of residence, generally to less than 10 percent.[4] Nevertheless, the neighborhoods themselves often stay poor or even get poorer. Since about 1990, poverty rates in immigrant-dominated neighborhoods have remained at about 20 percent, despite these gains in the migrant population's fortunes.

This, as the Los Angeles sociologist Dowell Myers has explained, is actually a result of the American arrival city's success: Because it is constantly sending its educated second generation into more prosperous neighborhoods and taking in waves of new villagers, in a constantly reiterated cycle of "arrival, upward mobility, and exodus," the neighborhood itself appears poorer than it really is. "At a given point in time, measurement of residents' characteristics includes the most disadvantaged newcomers to a city but not the more advantaged 'graduates' from the place," Myers says. "When the influx of disadvantaged newcomers is growing or when the departure of upwardly mobile residents is increasing, the city's average economic status will decline over time. This leads to an odd paradox: The downward trend for the place is the opposite indicator of the upward trend enjoyed by the residents themselves."[5] This paradox has created a sense among outsiders that the city's immigrant districts are poorer or more desperate than they really are, which leads to a misunderstanding of the forms of government investment they really need—a serious policy problem in many migrant-based cities around the world. Rather than getting the tools of ownership, education, security, business creation, and connection to the wider economy, they are too often treated as destitute places that need non-solutions, such as social workers, public-housing blocks, and urban-planned redevelopments.

Yet, it is clear to anyone who visits them that these neighborhoods are not on a downward spiral, but rather are becoming platforms for personal, family, and village transformation. The amount of investment in these urban tracts is formidable. In the 1990s, home ownership levels among Latino immigrants in the city reached 45.3 percent, a particularly amazing figure given the comparatively high prices of L.A. property and the very low neighborhood incomes. The university completion rate among the Latino-born of L.A. almost doubled, from 9.5 percent in 1970 to 18.8 percent in 2000.[6] Mike Davis, the Los Angeles historian given to apocalyptic visions of failed and oppressed slums of Latin America, became ecstatic at the effect of Latinization on the slums of his own city: "Tired, sad little homes undergo miraculous revivifications: their peeling facades repainted, sagging roofs and porches rebuilt, and yellowing lawns replanted in cacti and azaleas. Cumulatively the sweat equity of 75,000 or so Mexican and Salvadorean homeowners has become an unexcelled constructive force (the opposite of white flight) working to restore debilitated neighborhoods to trim respectability . . . they also have a genius for transforming dead urban spaces into convivial social spaces."[7]

By the middle of this century's first decade, the rapid investment and mobility of the Central American arrival city had become the dominant force in L.A.'s politics and economy. On one hand, the demand for inner-city home ownership by Central American villagers created a boom in home-sale revenues for older African American families, whose homes had held little value in the three decades after the Watts riots of 1965 but who suddenly found a steady demand for their homes. This, in turn, caused the black outer suburbs to see a rise in demand, ownership, and investment and a new start for many black families who had been trapped in a cycle of tenancy, underemployment, and dependency for decades.

At the same time, the new arrival cities developed their own very effective political structures, adding to the networks of Latino organization in the more established barrios, which had been slowly gaining influence for decades. This culminated in the election of Mayor Antonio Villaraigosa, a product of the East Los Angeles Latino immigrant power network and the first arrival-city child to end up running one of America's major cities. His father had been a poor Mexican villager who had crossed the U.S. border in the 1950s in an early post-war wave of rural-to-urban migration, settling in City Terrace, one of the first fully functioning arrival cities of East Los Angeles. Villaraigosa rose through the economic, educational, and political networks in the arrival city of East L.A. to become a favored vehicle for the political aspirations of the new inner-city arrivals, an emblem of the new political dominance of the village-born. He joins such figures as Brazilian president Luiz Inácio Lula da Silva and Turkish prime minister Recep Tayyip Erdoğan, leaders of arrival-city movements who have risen to occupy the highest offices.

Inside the Adams Boulevard neighborhood, Mario's sign business has given him tens of thousands of dollars in savings, even after sending large sums back to El Palón to keep his parents and siblings aloft and spending a small fortune to get his daughter naturalized in the United States. So Mario and Bibi have decided, at long last, to try to buy a house. They are determined to stay in this block, surrounded by fellow arrivals, building up the neighborhood. The only thing unusual in this is that Mario has waited so long to become a home-owner: For the greater part of two decades, he has been a tenant in the apartments and backyard houses of other migrants, who entered the property market with far less money than he has now.

The reason has everything to do with the changing U.S. approach to immigration. Because he arrived from El Salvador after 1990, he was ineligible for naturalization under a federal law (the 1987 NACARA Law) that granted amnesty to about 200,000 people who arrived from conflict-ridden Central American countries. Despite being a successful businessman, the husband of a naturalized immigrant, and the father of a young American citizen, he has not yet found a way to become a legal American himself (he is currently pursuing an asylum request, based on the still-simmering conflict in his village). In the past, the United States has granted amnesties to large numbers of illegal migrants, transforming them from informal, non-taxpaying underground workers into legitimate citizens who can invest in their society. Tens of thousands, if not hundreds of thousands, of other Angelenos are in similar positions: afraid or unable to put their earnings into their communities, trapped in a netherworld of half-arrival, despite being active in the economy. This ambiguous approach to citizenship can have damaging effects on arrival cities, turning them from opportunities into threats.

THE ARRIVAL CITY IN THE POST-MIGRATION NATION

The presence of a Central American peasant, like Mario Martinez, in Los Angeles, or a family of Bangladeshi villagers, like the Tafaders, in the East End of London, strikes many people as an aberration, an artifact of the past or a political mistake. In this age of border controls, high-technology information economies, and selective immigration policies, we often think there should be no reason to have large masses of the developing world's rural poor forming enclaves in the cities of the West. In many western European countries, in Canada, the United States, and Australia, governments respond to the arrival city not by making it function better but by trying to pretend that village-origin migration won't happen or can be permanently stopped or filtered out.

This is a perilous mistake. The great wave of rural–urban migration that will transform the developing world in this century will also be the main source of major, century-long migration flows from the world's South and East to the cities of the West. The flow may be slowed or stopped in certain countries for limited periods, but the larger arrival is economically and politically inevitable. It is already happening. Today there are more rural migrants in the cities of North America, Europe, and Australia than there have been at any time since the early twentieth century. Every year, more than five million people move from the largely rural developing world into the urbanized West.

The arrival city is a major phenomenon in the West, and its citizens are the same people who occupy the arrival cities of the developing world. About 150 million foreign-born people live in the wealthy quarter of the world, accounting for about 8 percent of Europe's population, 13 percent of North America's, and 19 percent of Australia's. They tend to be rural-born. The largest group of immigrants in Europe and the United States come from villages or regional cities in rural areas of the developing world and have migrated more or less directly to large cities. While it is not possible to quantify the rural-urban breakdown of immigrants (officials from the Population Division of the United Nations Department of Economic and Social Affairs tell me they would desperately like to have such statistics, but they are prohibitively difficult to collect), we anecdotally know that the rural-born make up the largest group of new arrivals in western Europe and the United States and of foreign-born citizens in Canada and Australia. Most migrants to the United States are Latin Americans, who overwhelmingly migrate from villages. They account for 18 million people, or 6 percent of the population; with their offspring, they number 40 million, or 14 percent of the population. In the European Union, there are legally 4.5 million people from North Africa, three million from the rest of Africa, five million from the Middle East and Turkey, 2.5 million from South America, and 1.7 million from the Indian subcontinent; most of these groups tend strongly to come from rural places.

Internal European Union migration also has a large village-to-city component. The largest group of migrants from Poland, Romania, and the Baltic states in western European cities are those who come from rural areas. Europe is also home to between five and 10 million migrants who live and work without proper authorization, most of whom come from rural areas in adjoining regions of Africa, the Middle East, and Eastern Europe. There are exceptions to the rural–urban pattern on both the sending and the receiving side: Places like Colombia and Egypt have sent out sizable populations of urbanites during troubled times, and the United States and Canada, in recent years, have seen a boom in Latin American and Caribbean rural-to-rural migration, in which Central American peasants come to work on farms. But these are notable precisely because they are exceptions. When people move across oceans and international boundaries—a far more difficult and permanent enterprise than moving within one's own country—the destination of choice is usually a city. And in the list of cities whose populations can claim more than a million foreign-born people, most are located in the wealthy and fully urbanized quarter of the world: Melbourne, Sydney, Singapore, Hong Kong, Dubai, Riyadh, Mecca, Medina, Moscow, Paris, London, Toronto, New York, Washington, Miami, Chicago, Dallas, Houston, San Francisco, and Los Angeles.[8]

Our debates about immigration are too often concerned with questions of what should happen, what ought to be allowed; we devote far too little to planning for what will occur. It is perfectly reasonable for governments to limit or stop immigration, or to restrict it to a limited group of skills, for political or economic reasons, during periods of high unemployment or out of a public sense of cultural disharmony or simple crowding. But we should recognize that such measures will not be permanent, that Western countries will continue taking in unskilled immigrants in the long term, and that, no matter what is done, a sizable proportion of these immigrants will be the sort of people who form arrival cities. Countries like Canada and Australia, which have managed to restrict the number of rural-origin migrants temporarily, will not be able to do so for much longer, and probably will not want to. The villager will be a feature of the Western city throughout this century.

There are two important reasons for this. The first is economic: the countries of the West will experience severe labor shortages during this decade and throughout the century, in both skilled and, importantly, unskilled fields. This shortage is caused by shrinking family sizes leading to a fast-aging population. Most Western nations have seen their reproduction rates slip below 2.1 children per family, the level needed to keep the native-born population stable, so the proportion of pension-earning, government-service-consuming seniors in the population is increasing. This itself is an expensive problem, which is most easily solved by bringing in new working-age immigrants whose taxes can cover spiraling state expenses. Alternatively, governments can raise taxes, cut services, or raise retirement ages, but, without immigration, the standards of living will decrease and governments will be unable to afford crucial services and policies.* As it is, the fiscal cost of paying for the credit-crunch bailouts of 2008 and 2009 is expected to consume between 2 and 4 percent of the GDP in Britain and the United States for more than a decade. So, while immigration is not a mandatory solution to labor shortages, the combination of cash-starved governments and higher demographic costs will make it the least painful and most voter-friendly solution.

According to a 2009 study by the University of Southern California's Marshall School of Business, the United States will require 35 million more workers than its working-age population can provide by 2030, Japan another 17 million by 2050, the European Union 80 million by 2050. Canada, even if it continues to take in

---

* The one country that has successfully avoided migration, despite labor shortages and an aging population, is Japan. The lack of immigrants has resulted in a declining standard of living, a price Japanese leaders still say they are willing to pay. However, Japan has never had substantial immigration, so there is no existing arrival-city population to propel further demand.

250,000 to 300,000 immigrants a year, will be short a million workers by the end of this decade.[9] Even the high levels of unemployment that struck the West after the 2008 credit crisis only temporarily mitigated this long-term demographic problem. During the worst months of the downturn, there were substantial labor shortages in many countries. Australian business leaders were calling for a rapid increase of immigration in late 2009 to fill hundreds of thousands of semi-skilled vacancies in Victoria and Western Australia and warning that the shortage would increase to 1.6 million workers during the decade ahead.[10] In Canada, 14 percent of businesses at the end of 2009 were reporting "shortage of un/semi-skilled labor" as their main business constraint (skilled labor shortages affected 29 percent of businesses), despite rising unemployment rates.[11] A return to economic growth will push the United States and Europe into similar labor shortages, and immigration will be the only easy way out.

The second reason why village-origin migration will continue is political. Immigrants, and their children and grandchildren, become citizens and voters and politicians and cabinet ministers and leaders, united across parties and ideologies by the overweening issue of having access to their families and fellow villagers. The sociologist Christian Joppke, in a study titled "Why Liberal States Accept Unwanted Immigration," noted that the only countries that have managed to control levels of immigration have been those with authoritarian governments—communist, fascist, autocratic. Everywhere else in the world, on every continent over a period of decades, he documented "the gap between restrictionist policy goals and expansionist outcomes," meaning that almost all policy efforts to restrict or end immigration had failed because the purported subjects of the laws were already active citizens, using the arrival city as a platform for its own self-preservation.[12]

During all the periods in which such countries as the United States, Germany, and France have supposedly had zero-immigration laws, millions of low-skill migrants have entered those countries, using arrival-city-based networks to create paths of entry. Walls and policing regimes have done little to reduce the numbers. In most cases, governments come to realize that millions of potential tax-payers are living below the radar, earning incomes but not paying taxes, and creating gray-market families and awkward legal para-doxes as their deracinated children come of age; the result is usually a mass amnesty. The United States has granted post-facto citizenship to millions of illegal immigrants in recent decades (most recently in the early 1990s); similar amnesties, involving hundreds of thousands of undocumented migrants, have been granted in Spain, Italy, France, Britain, and Germany. More such amnesties are almost cer-tain in the future.

A typical example is the U.S. Immigration Reform and Control Act, or IRCA, which began in 1986 as a congressional effort to stop, once and for all, the movement of Latin American villagers across the southern border. And yet, by the time it was passed, pressure from the Chamber of Commerce and agriculture lobbies had trans-formed it into a mass amnesty that provided legal citizenship to almost three million "illegals," combined with a new program allow-ing low-skill migrants to enter under a guest-worker program demanded by agricultural industries in the western states. This guest-worker program eventually led to its own mass amnesty. An effort in the next decade by the conservative House of Representatives, led by Newt Gingrich, to reverse the effects of the IRCA, this time backed by widespread public pressure against "illegals," had a similar result: The 1990s saw more immigration to the United States from Latin America than in any other decade in U.S. history, a surge of legal and illegal migration totalling 31 million people. The economy needed people, and it got them.

When they do recognize that labor shortages will be a long-term reality, many countries have tried a second option: weeding out the less educated, less skilled, and, generally, rural-origin immigrants from the stream. Australia and Canada were the first to do this, intro-ducing "points-based" immigration systems, in which only those appli-cants who score the highest for linguistic aptitude, post-secondary education, specialized skills, or pledged investment savings are admitted entry. This has indeed created a more middle-class, acculturated group of immigrants, but it has sidestepped a serious problem. Labor shortages often tend to be in low-skilled and semi-skilled areas (such as trades) unsuited to these elite, highly educated immigrants. At the height of the crash in 2009, the sectors reporting serious labor shortages in Europe and North America included household services, agriculture, transportation, construction, tourism, catering services, and frontline social services. The world shortage of welders has already reached 200,000, and the shortage of semi-skilled manufacturing workers is expected to hit 14 million by 2020.[13]

Not only will many countries be forced to admit large numbers of low-skilled and semi-skilled immigrants, but they will soon have to compete for them. Demographics are fast reducing the global supply of labor in all categories: eastern and central Europe have sub-replacement birth rates that will cut off the supply of workers, and, as of 2010, China was experiencing large-scale labor shortages in all areas. India's rapid economic growth and fast-shrinking fertility rate mean that it will cease to be a reliable supply of workers. China has already initiated programs to import workers from sub-Saharan Africa and the Indian subcontinent, putting it in competition with the Gulf states and the West for workers. Rather than trying to stem a flood, North American and European countries may well find themselves engaged in active recruitment.

To bring in only urban, university-educated elites to fill these vacancies is a waste both of human potential and of foreign policy, since the immigrants often get their degrees at universities in their own countries that have been funded by foreign governments to help create medical, legal, and technical knowledge in the developing world. If the products of these programs all become hotel desk clerks and roofers in Western cities, the entire aid agenda is wasted.

This is exactly what is happening in Canada, Australia, and other countries that have emulated their points systems (as Britain began doing in 2005). In Canada, in 2008, an extraordinary 60.1 percent of immigrants with university degrees were working in occupations that required an apprenticeship or less—1.5 times the over-qualification rate of Canadian-born workers.[14] A significant number simply weren't fitting into an economy that needed physical skills, not professions. Of "chronically poor" immigrants in Canada, 41 percent have university degrees.[15] In other words, countries like Canada have been bringing in the wrong sorts of workers for a generation.

So it is a source of both social frustration and economic relief that these countries have all discovered that large numbers of villagers are still managing to enter and settle legally, forming arrival-city enclaves. For the fact is that a "skilled" migrant is often a single, village-born urbanite from the developing world who brings an entire network of spouses and relatives from the root village or foreign arrival city. Canada, with one of the toughest points-system programs, is a typical example. Officially, 57 percent of its 250,000 annual immigrants are "economic class"—mainly highly skilled workers and "business immigrants" willing to invest hundreds of thousands of dollars. But in 2005, of the 133,746 immigrants in this category, only 55,179 were principal applicants—that is, those with the skills or money. The remaining 78,567 were their children, spouses, parents, or other dependants, who in many cases do not speak the language and are drawn from villages. And an additional 62,246 immigrants every year—more than the total of points-based entrants—were "family class" immigrants: parents, spouses, and other relatives of settled immigrants who are brought over from the home country to reunite families; anecdotally, a high percentage of these have rural backgrounds. (Another 39,832 immigrants were refugees or other humanitarian cases, themselves often rural.) The result is that only 23 percent of Canada's immigrants are those who are selected through the points system,[16] the rest hewing much closer to the arrival city.

Even larger proportions of village-born relatives enter other countries. In the United States, 39 percent of immigration is "nondiscretionary" (that is, family-reunification class); in the United Kingdom, 49 percent; in France, 83 percent.[17] This is just as well, given

the actual employment needs of these countries. The Canadian government was surprised to discover that the uneducated relatives of
points migrants are faring better economically than the original
migrants themselves: High-skilled primary immigrants are 18 percent
more likely to fall into low-income poverty than their low-skilled
family-class counterparts.[18]

As the cultural conflicts of immigration became acute in the early
twenty-first century and arrival cities became focal points of religious
and political hostility, governments began trying to crack down on
family-reunification immigration as a way to keep villagers out.
Britain, France, Canada, the Netherlands, and Germany tried to
restrict family-class entrants. None of it worked for more than a brief
period. France's attempts, launched by President Nicolas Sarkozy as
a 2007 election pledge, were among the toughest, requiring DNA
tests to prove that applicants were immediate blood relatives. Within
two years, the attempt had been abandoned; Immigration Minister
Eric Besson declared the idea "stupid."

Such restrictions failed partly for the economic and political reasons described above, but also for a third reason: When immigrants
are brought over without their networks of relatives and village
neighbors, they are more likely to become isolated and unsocialized,
to fall into criminality or social conservatism. This happens when
family-reunification migration is restricted or when countries rely on
temporary guest-worker programs to attract low-skilled workers
without their families, as Germany did in the 1970s and Canada and
Australia are attempting today.

When settlement of families is restricted, arrival cities and their
supportive networks are unable to take shape, and behavior changes.
A study by Dennis Broeders and Godfried Engbersen at Erasmus
University, in Rotterdam, examined immigrants forbidden to bring
over relatives: Without family networks to support them, the migrants
were forced into a "dependence on informal, and increasingly criminal,
networks and institutions."[19] Arranged marriages, often to a cousin
from a distant village whom the primary-immigrant spouse hadn't

met, became commonplace, even when the migrants are from countries such as Bangladesh or Turkey, where these practices are dying out. So, in the West, successful attempts to prevent the arrival city from forming have actually created waves of religious conservatism, sexual oppression, and organized crime. Such practices are the products not of arrival but of failed arrival: When we invest in the arrival city and give it a chance to flourish, it acts as an antidote to such extremes.

THE SUBURBANIZATION OF ARRIVAL
Herndon, Virginia, and Wheaton, Maryland

At the traffic-light intersection of two four-lane roads on the far outskirts of the U.S. capital, nineteen brown-skinned men, some young and some old, variously stand, sit, and lean against a low brick wall in the entrance to the parking lot of a vacant Pentecostal church. The Salvadoran, Honduran, and Mexican men stand out as the only signs of non-vehicular activity in this long expanse of gas stations, mini-malls, and one-story government buildings. For long minutes they are motionless. Then a mini-van slows, some words are exchanged in rudimentary English, and two of them get in. It is a moving job, what appears to be a home foreclosure, a half-day's work at $10 an hour. Twenty minutes later, the remaining men hunch beneath shrubs and walls as a police car passes: Standing and looking for day work, a rite of passage for new arrival-city residents and a vital source of start-up income, is now illegal and dangerous in Herndon, Virginia.

As recently as 1980, the suburban town of Herndon was 96 percent white and English-speaking, a lower-middle-class bedroom enclave close to the light-industrial jobs around Washington Dulles International Airport. Like so many American suburbs, it changed its character and function almost overnight. By 2000, it was only 47 percent white, more than a quarter Hispanic and 14 percent Asian, the site of an explosion of arrival. The aviation-industry workers had moved out of the apartment blocks in its center, using expanding mortgage markets to buy homes in suburbs even farther out. Word spread to the dense Latino enclaves of D.C., and to the villages of Central America, of the low-rent and comparatively pleasant apartments and small homes of Herndon and the ample service-industry work nearby. Networks of assistance took shape: small shops, Spanish-speaking churches, social clubs. More people moved, helped one another get set up, and became known to the area's employers as a good source of labor. At the beginning of the twenty-first century, Herndon was shocked to discover that it had become a full-fledged arrival city.

The shift of immigrant arrival to the suburbs is a new and dramatic phenomenon in North America and Australia. As of 2005, for the first time more immigrants were living in the suburbs than in the central cities of the United States, with immigrants settling in the burbs outnumbering downtown arrivals by almost two to one. This trend has transformed the suburbs. Racial and ethnic minorities now represent a third of the population of America's suburbs, up from 19 percent in 1990.[20] Almost half of all Hispanic Americans now live in the suburbs.[21] Scholars call these "melting-pot suburbs" or "ethnoburbs." Although much attention has gone to Asian migrants to the suburbs, who arrive with skills, savings, and high levels of cultural capital, they are actually outnumbered by the suburb-bound Central Americans and Mexicans, who, in their first stages of arrival, have filled construction, landscaping, and service-industry jobs in the fast-expanding suburban fringe. Much of the suburban settlement has to do with family and village networks, which establish chain-migration footholds in an affordable suburb, rapidly turning a small group of workers into a large and concentrated influx; one Washington-area official calls this "the cousin syndrome." Economists have also observed an immigration-driven pricing mechanism with a suburbanizing effect, in which first-wave migrants arrive in the urban core in such great numbers that they drive up arrival-city rents and drive down immigrant wages, making the inner-ring suburbs appear more appealing, in wages and rent, to the next wave of villagers to arrive.[22]

This pattern is even more sharply defined in the largest cities of Canada. In Toronto, which receives 40 percent of the country's 300,000 annual immigrants, a 2008 study found that almost all of them were settling in the suburbs—a complete reversal of the pattern of the 1970s, when most migrants settled in the downtown core—with wealthier urban–urban migrants from the Indian subcontinent and China settling in the outer suburbs and village-born migrants from Africa, Latin America, and Asia settling in inner-ring arrival cities such as Victoria Park, Thorncliffe Park, and southern Etobicoke. This new settlement had much to do with the gentrification of urban-core neighborhoods, which turned the inner suburbs into the last low-rent enclave. As Robert Murdie of the University of Toronto's Centre for Urban and Community Studies has found, this has the deleterious effect of increasing the isolation and segregation of immigrants in a city that had been famous for its integration.[23]

The sudden transformation of suburbs into arrival cities is often a shock to the established population. It can reawaken a dormant suburb, bringing new entrepreneurial economies, cultures, and attractions. Or it can anger the established "white" residents, many of whom had long associated immigration with the faraway urban core (and some of whom had fled that core, in an earlier generation, to escape immigrants and minorities). In Herndon, the result was a political explosion of statewide proportions. It began, rather humbly, with men standing on the street and looking for work.

In the early 1990s, when Herndon's arrival city was only beginning to take shape, the newly arrived men would gather at the corner of Elden Street and Alabama Drive, near apartment complexes where many of them lived, to look for cash work. There was a constant demand for hourly, daily, and weekly labor, so most did not stand in vain. After a decade and a half, this exposed and unprotected setting had become a social and humanitarian worry, so, in 2005, the Herndon town council, led by Mayor Michael O'Reilly, voted to create an indoor day-labor center, using county funds and staff from a local church non-profit agency. This initiative attracted anti-immigration forces, such as the vigilante group the Minutemen, which opened a chapter in Herndon. They claimed that it was unacceptable to use taxpayer money to assist illegal immigrants. The proposed center then became the focus of an ugly election for Virginia governor in 2005, in which Republican candidate Jerry Kilgore built much of his campaign around his opposition to Herndon's approach, making the town a conservative emblem of wrongheaded state support for undocumented migrants. (He lost by a narrow margin.)

Then, months after the center opened in a former police station on a two-year funding contract, the people of Herndon responded by voting Mayor O'Reilly out of office by a wide margin in a single-issue campaign devoted to the center and replacing him with Stephen J. DeBenedittis on a radical anti-immigrant policy. Not only did he shut down the center in 2007, driving laborers back onto the streets, but he enrolled the town police in a federal program to train local officers to enforce immigration laws. He also enforced a zoning ordinance, aimed at Latinos, which mandated eviction if more than four "unrelated people" shared a residence. It got about 200 non-compliance complaints a year.

Yet this backlash was ignoring the most significant effect of the Herndon migrant boom. Those men on the street, many of them undocumented and very poor, were only the poorest and least well-connected of the Central American villagers arriving here. Most did much better. Within a decade of the first immigrants' arrival, 53 percent of the foreign-born in Herndon were home owners, a rate approaching the 62 percent average for the native-born population of the Washington area. The upward social mobility of the migrants was striking. Nevertheless, the backlash had an effect: Latino-owned businesses had trouble getting started, and large numbers of immigrants departed when the economy slumped in 2008. Herndon's economy suffered.

———

There is another way to respond when your suburb becomes an arrival city. On the other side of Washington, the northeastern suburbs of Montgomery County, Maryland, experienced an equally dramatic transformation in the 1980s and '90s: The suburb of Wheaton, at the very end of Washington's Metrorail line, went from being 90 percent white in the 1970s to 40 percent immigrant in 2000, just like Herndon. Led by Salvadorans, its arrival-city communities include Vietnamese, Jamaicans, Filipinos, Peruvians, Mexicans, and other Central Americans.

But unlike in Herndon, the voters and officials of Montgomery County saw the villagers not as a threat but as an opportunity to revitalize their fading town center. They built and embraced a day-labor center and launched a branding campaign to make Wheaton known across the capital region for its multi-ethnic cultures, festivals, and foods, under the banner "deliciously habit-forming." Zoning rules and business offices were used to encourage and help immigrant entrepreneurs set up restaurants, markets, and colorful shops, which were promoted in city-sponsored advertisements. A county official in Wheaton described the suburb's self-image as "accommodating and capitalizing on the immigration trend" by promoting its "funky, ethnic mix that makes it feel like a true urban environment without the urban problems."[24]

This sort of promotion, which did indeed revitalize Wheaton's core, would not have been possible without the community's agreement to invest in the arrival-city process. There was an understanding among officials not only that the influx of ex-villagers was inevitable but that it would go much better if money was spent on making it work right. Arrival cities do not automatically thrive on their own; they often need investment. In Wheaton, it took the form of a parallel social-services system aimed at the arrival city, including a full-service primary-care medical service, known as Proyecto Salud, offered to immigrants through a public-private partnership, and a well-staffed career center with multilingual staff offering computer training, legal aid, and language classes. The results have been striking: The region is booming with immigrant-owned small businesses, and it has an immigrant home-ownership rate of 62 percent, almost identical to Washington's "white" level and the highest in the capital area.

Of course, it was the spread of easy home ownership that led to the economic collapse of 2008, and black and Latino home owners had the highest rates of foreclosure. The ethnic suburbs were hit hard. Not only did some better-off Latinos lose their houses but the poorer new arrivals, who were often dependent on the building and property-maintenance industries for their livelihoods, found themselves without their main source of employment. The downturn, however, did not affect the basic logic of the arrival city. Latin American migrants sharply reduced their flow of remittances to villages in late 2008 and in 2009, but there was no return migration. It appears that the Latinos moved downmarket temporarily, relying on arrival-city networks of support. Interestingly, the proportion of Latino immigrants among homeowners in the United States did not fall between 2008 and 2009: The foreclosures were balanced by purchases by more successful migrants. Nevertheless, it was an extremely difficult time in the outer suburbs of Washington. In Herndon, the result was a great outflux of migrants to lower-rent neighborhoods, amid a bitter public mood that welcomed their departure.

In Montgomery County, something different happened. Citizens and officials, realizing that the immigrants were their main source of wealth creation, banded together to find ways to help them stay. In Gaithersburg, Maryland, a suburban town on the northern end of the county with an immigrant mix similar to Wheaton's, a coalition of officials, citizens, and activists developed a "door-knocking" campaign to save village-born immigrants from eviction. The idea, one official explained, was to "go to immigrants' homes, engage them through friendly door-knocking campaigns, speak their language, check on problems they face, let them know about neighborhood gatherings, help them tap available government and non-profit services . . . ask immigrant families about skills they might possess that may help their neighbors." The campaign was backed with a network of financial and business support services that, while not inexpensive to the taxpayers of this prosperous town, was seen as a wise investment. Uma Ahluwalia, Montgomery County's health and human services director, explained the logic to local reporters: A family evicted from their home in a foreclosure will need to be put up in a motel, at a cost to taxpayers of $110 a night for 40 to 60 nights; in comparison, some short-term rental or mortgage assistance is a bargain.[25] And, the officials believe, the benefits of keeping economically active immigrants around, and keeping their businesses intact, reach to the core of the suburb's success.

Montgomery County represents one of two paths that the arrival city can follow into the urban outskirts. Everywhere in the world, it is a choice between building a community's future or setting the stage for its demise. Without an investment now, before the next wave arrives, that choice will be made by circumstances. Without attention to their new populations, the suburbs will turn into the cruel and violent places of our irrational fears.

4
THE URBANIZATION OF THE VILLAGE

THE VILLAGE TRAP
Tatary, Poland

When school ends each afternoon, 17-year-old Gosia Storczynski abandons her friends in a quick flurry of Polish-English slang, mounts her bicycle, and makes the four-kilometer journey to a lonely field on the edge of her village. There, she covers her auburn hair in a kerchief and meets her father, a big, grizzled man who has arrived in a horse-drawn wooden cart. She takes a 10-liter pail from the cart, heads to the center of a field, squats beneath a grazing heifer with the pail between her knees, and begins the exhausting two-hour job of milking the family herd, entirely by hand, and hauling the heavy buckets home. Each afternoon, the effort is repeated; each morning, Gosia rises at dawn for more farm chores. Hers is the life of a peasant, timeless, exhausting, governed by the rhythms of nature.

But Gosia is, as she is well aware, a member of Europe's final generation of peasants. It is she, and several million fellow young subsistence farmers who cover the continent's eastern flank, who will put an end to this millennia-old institution. Indeed, she is one of the westernmost members of a worldwide generation who are declaring an end to the peasant life, sooner in Europe, within decades in Asia, and almost certainly by the end of the century in Africa.*

Gosia, like peasants almost everywhere today, has found her life governed less by the fruits of farming and the market for food than by the push and pull of the arrival city. Gosia's father, 53-year-old Marek, is the hereditary owner of these 16 hectares on the eastern edge of Poland, near the city of Białystok and the border of Belarus. That makes his farm large by local standards (and tiny almost anywhere else in Europe), but much of his land is unfarmable: Forest, meadow, and ravine account for more than half. Only seven hectares are arable, which makes this almost an average-sized Polish farm, not really large enough to provide a full income. Farms on this edge of the Western world are almost as small as those in the far more fertile wetlands of Asia: 60 percent of Poland's farms are smaller than five hectares; more than a third are less than one hectare. This is strictly peasant farming: Over 44 percent of Poland's farms produce solely or mainly for their own consumption, and another 10 percent produce nothing at all.[1] Poland's four million farmers are the largest remaining peasant population in Europe. They do have the advantage, vis-à-vis their fellow peasants in the post-communist East and in China, of being clear and outright owners of their land: During the communist era, Poland collectivized only its largest farms, leaving 80 percent of the land in the hands of small-hold peasants.

Poland's peasant farms are an enormously ineffective way to use farmland. Despite employing almost a fifth of the population, agriculture accounts for only 4.7 percent of Poland's economy—and almost all of this comes from only 5 percent of the farms, the largest ones. It is a waste of economic opportunity: Paid agricultural labor accounts for only 3 percent of Poland's rural workforce, a fifth of which is unemployed. Productive commercial agriculture

* For our purposes, peasant farming is defined as family-based agriculture in which the family is the main, and usually the only, source of labor, and in which the farm's output serves mainly to provide for the family's immediate nutritional and financial needs.

would employ far more. And it is a huge waste of land. Average European farms produce almost five times as much food per hectare as Polish farms do.[2]

As with much of the world's peasant agriculture, the Storczynski farm is economically unsustainable. Two hectares are used to graze the cows; the remaining five grow wheat, oats, and barley to feed the family and the cows; there is also a family vegetable patch. The milk, despite all the effort, earns payments of only about 800 zloty ($280) a month. After expenses, notably fertilizer, Marek pockets less than half of this. It's not enough to live on, even when added to his subsidies from the Polish government and the European Union, which together give him about 400 zloty ($140) per hectare farmed each year. But he receives a far larger income from his oldest daughter, Magda, 23, who is studying nursing in Warsaw and sends money back from her part-time work. Without these urban contributions, the family would have to abandon the farm. Indeed, they plan to do so—as soon as Marek is old enough to begin receiving his government pension, which has been the sole purpose of maintaining this farm since the 1990s.

"All I want is to get my pension, then the girls will wrap it up," Marek told me as he and his daughter hauled the sloshing milk pails to the wooden cart. "If you want to succeed in agriculture you need a big farm, and this isn't it. I'm 53, so I've got seven years left, and that's it. Everybody here is waiting for their pension. That's the future: People have to leave. I don't want my daughters living in Poland, after my family's been here forever. It's time to leave."

But for now they, along with four million other Polish peasants, are caught in a carefully maintained equilibrium that prevents them from moving off the land. The system of pensions and payments has managed to keep Poland's small farms from congealing into commercially viable enterprises—and, until the great explosion of westward migration in 2004, it prevented those four million peasants from giving up farming and moving to the city. Poland has pursued an expensive rural policy designed to prevent movement to the arrival city.

Poland's anti-urban effort was launched shortly after the collapse of communism in 1990. At its heart is a pension system, the Farmers' Social Security Fund, known by its acronym, KRUS. Like many agricultural-support programs across the developing world, the KRUS is grounded politically in a romantic attachment to the ideal of family farming and the aesthetics of the farm, and economically in a hard-nosed desire to prevent cities from being swarmed with migrants. In Poland and many other societies, beginning with post-revolutionary France and continuing in places like India today, the maintenance of the peasantry has been a substitute for a larger vision of social progress.

During its awkward post-communist transition decade, Poland's peasant population actually increased by 5 percent in a stunning wave of urban-to-rural migration. Before 1989, the cities had been packed with state-owned factories that produced goods with no market and little economic role, except to keep a restive people employed and away from Solidarity protests. As government debt, hyperinflation, and the end of communism forced the state to close those factories, hundreds of thousands of people fled to their ancestral villages to seek the security of an agricultural pension.

During a decade when two-thirds of Poland's three million unemployed were living in urban areas and there were severe housing shortages in Warsaw, this return to the village seemed wise. The KRUS was, in this sense, a shrewd program: It gave Poland some of the social protections of a full-fledged welfare state, without the high fiscal price of covering the full cost of living. Because the peasant farm itself provided some of the recipient's basic food needs and made rent subsidies unnecessary, Poland could keep its transition-shocked population at bay at reasonable cost.

The KRUS is available to men at age 60, if they have worked at least 30 years on the farm and agree upon retirement to give away all land except the one hectare surrounding their house—although the land can be, and almost always is, transferred to an immediate family member, so the farms rarely get consolidated into more viable enterprises. It pays reasonably well by rural Polish standards: 650 zloty ($178) a month, enough to sustain a family, especially if husband and wife are both receiving it.* It's an expensive program, accounting for 4 percent of Poland's entire economy in the early 2000s.[3] While it was intended to create larger farms, its main effect was to keep an entire generation of peasants on the land until they turned 60, without any incentive to improve agriculture or create entrepreneurial ventures, either on the farm or in the city. "The [KRUS] system," one study concluded, "is really a non-means-tested social welfare program, which provides no incentive for surplus labor to shift into non-agricultural employment."[4]

For a decade and a half, Warsaw and Wrocław and Gdansk remained without arrival cities, and without the bursts of economic activity that go with them. An entire generation, millions of productive and creative people, remained trapped on non-farming farms, relegated to a perpetual agrarian past. Then, in 2004, Poland gained membership in the European Union and became attached to the larger world—a world that included major cities, on the other end of Europe, that were built for arrival. Overnight, the economic logic of the Polish farm changed.

After the Storczynski daughters finish school and move out of Poland, their family's farm might end up looking like the nearby farm of 55-year-old Marian Snarski. His ramshackle collection of buildings on poor, sandy soil hardly seems to be functioning as an agriculture enterprise. The farm subsidies barely cover the cost of fertilizer, and Mr. Snarski has only his elderly wife and his teenaged daughter to work the fields. Yet a look at the family's balance sheets reveals the new face of peasant farming. Farm income and subsidies from the EU and Poland provide only a couple of hundred dollars a month. But both of these are dwarfed by the packages of cash the Snarskis receive every month from their two daughters, aged 19 and 27, who

---

* Slightly less generous sums are available to women who have worked 25 years, and a reduced pension for men who have worked 55 years and agree to hand their farm to someone under 40.

have domestic-service jobs in Britain. By sending perhaps $400 a month, the girls have become the main source of income for the Snarski family.

If Poland's policies were partially designed to prevent a flood of farmers from creating arrival cities in Warsaw and Gdansk, they ended up building a valuable pool of workers who flooded into the arrival cities of western Europe as soon as such mobility became possible. In the three years after Poland won its EU membership in 2004, between a million and two million citizens—most of them young, most of them villagers—left to work in the major cities of Britain and Ireland, as waiters, construction workers, domestic servants, child-care workers, drivers, shopkeepers, and factory hands. Entire districts of London became Polish arrival cities: One spread outward from the older Polish enclave of Hammersmith and Ealing in the west; another in the northern boroughs of Haringey and Enfield, in which dozens of shopfronts on every high street are now lettered entirely in Polish and defunct Anglican churches have converted into Polish-language Roman Catholic congregations. The mechanisms of the arrival city are highly visible here: Aid, marriage, housing provision, remittance-sending are all organized by specialized Polish services. Overnight, Poles became a dominant and generally popular and well-received British and Irish minority. Many Poles said they would stay temporarily, then move back; others married, started businesses, and began setting down roots. The rush of productive urbanization that Poland had long staved off was taking place on a dramatic scale somewhere else.

Together, these young villagers sent home more than $11 billion a year, amounting to 2.5 percent of Poland's entire economy, more than almost any other industry.[5] This foreign-remittance money, combined with Polish government pensions and other government payments, has become overwhelmingly the main source of farm income. As of 2004, only 27 percent of Poland's rural inhabitants earned their basic income from agriculture; the rest, in effect, were collecting payments from cities. The chip fryers and toilet cleaners of London and Dublin replaced the government of Poland as the main guarantor of peasant rural livelihood.

Poland, from EU accession in 2004 until the economic crisis of 2008, was deprived of skilled workers. Almost anyone with a trade, from plumbers and bricklayers to surgeons and MRI technicians, had left for the West. The economic logic of the farm changed dramatically. Back when KRUS was the major source of farm income, it made sense to keep a small-hold farm in the family for generations. Now, there is no reason for another generation to stay on the land. Marian Snarski expects his farm to come to an end with his death; at some point before that, he will take EU afforestation grants and return all his land to forest in exchange for a few hundred dollars a year. Gosia Storczynski has an even more popular ambition: She wants to sell her father's land to a larger, commercial farm, one with paid agricultural workers and proper land management.

The buyer of the land may end up being Krysztof Chlebowicz, the mayor of the adjoining village of Tykocin.* His main political role, as he sees it, is to help his constituents abandon peasant farming and to help those who remain consolidate their farms into commercial ventures. He plans to be one of them: In 1991–92, right after communism ended, he worked illegally in New York City and saved enough money to expand his five-hectare plot to 25 hectares; now he is using EU grants to buy up an additional seven hectares. "I am quite sure that only half the 1.5 million farms in Poland are actual farms," he says. "The rest are just farmers waiting for their pensions—I'd say half of them now. I'd say that in five to 10 years it will drop to a quarter. In a natural way, the more enterprising farms are taking over the smaller and less productive ones. I'm a great example of this."

---

* Tykocin, population 1,800, is better known for the pogrom of August 1941, during which local Poles, aided by occupying German soldiers, rounded up and killed 3,400 Jews, 73 percent of the town's population. Though residents are loath to discuss it, this is likely one of the reasons why its farms are somewhat larger than the regional average.

The economic crisis that began in 2008 sent hundreds of thousands of Poles back eastward, returning home with savings, connections, and skills. Most of them returned not to their family villages but to the major cities and industrial regions of Poland. The Poles and eastern Europeans of the 2000s have made what scholars call a "J-turn": They used migration to urbanize themselves in the cities of the Atlantic, then returned not to the village but to the major cities of their own countries, bringing savings and entrepreneurial knowledge with them. Their arrival ended the drought of skilled labor in Poland, and these arrival-city returnees contributed to economic revivals in Gdansk, Warsaw, and the "Polish silicon valley" of Wrocław, Cracow, and Upper Silesia. The Polish capital was by now experiencing genuine urban sprawl, and former rural areas around Warsaw's perimeter were turning into new enclaves for ex-villagers who had arrived by way of the West. In large part as a result of this, Poland was the one of the few places in Europe that escaped the worst of the global economic downturn, experiencing economic growth (albeit at reduced levels) and maintaining exports. At long last, and in spite of its best efforts to the contrary, Poland was getting its arrival cities.

THE FINAL VILLAGE
Shuilin, Sichuan, China

At bedtime, six-year-old Pu Ming Lin picks up his little sister, Dong Lin, four, and lays her on the mat between him and their 56-year-old grandmother, He Su Xiou. As the three of them curl up together beside the fading embers of the kitchen fire, they are lulled by the gentle snoring of the two fat pigs in the pen on the other side of the thin wall, the faint hum of the beehive on the wall, and the somewhat rougher snoring of their grandfather in the next room. These are the warm bodies in the village of Shuilin today. They are the only sorts of bodies to be found in most villages across China now: small children, livestock, grandparents. Anyone between about 14 and 55 years of age, including the parents of all the children, has vanished, leaving quiet evenings, empty rooms, and a palpable, constant ache.

They rise just before dawn, and Dong Lin and Ming Lin expertly build a kitchen fire to boil the morning's tea, their tiny hands pushing sticks into the grate to stoke the flames. At six-thirty, Dong Lin climbs on her grandmother's reed-thin back, Ming Lin grabs her callused hand, and they begin the careful half-hour walk, along narrow, muddy pathways across flooded paddies, to the village school. At 11, the old woman will return to bring the children home for lunch, during which they will sit on the porch and watch their grandmother work the fields; at two, she will return them, and then pick them up again at five, for a total of eight walks of two kilometers each.

"I never thought I'd have to raise a set of children at this age," says Su Xiou as she retrieves eggs from the ground to make soup for me. "It's because my son is not doing so well in Chongqing, he can't afford to move us all to the city and put the children to school there. But I don't mind. They have become very close to me—they are very obedient. Both of them say to me at night, 'Wherever you go, Grandma, I will follow.' " The children seem to worship their grandmother, clinging to her in the fields, though they relish the daily phone call from their father.

These are the children of Pu Jun, the 32-year-old Chongqing transformer builder we met in chapter 1. He has not seen them on a regular basis since Dong Lin was a few months old, almost four years before. But Jun is a devoted father, so he sends a large part of his pay to the village, 300 kilometers away in neighboring Sichuan Province, to support them. Lately, he has been sending about $150 a year. In his wealthier years, he sent back enough to replace the old mud-and-reed shack with a new cinder-block house with a strong concrete foundation, sturdy enough to have withstood the earthquake of 2008. The front room, an unpainted concrete cube, sports a color TV connected to a rooftop aerial, and the children speak almost every day with Mr. Pu on the mobile phone he provided them. In 2005, he tried to improve the fortunes of his parents' farm by investing his entire savings in a grove of mandarin trees, which would give them a cash crop and improve their lives considerably. But a terrible drought that summer killed the trees, so the family has returned to growing oil seeds, rice, and grain for their own consumption and selling one pig each year. "He is such a devoted and innocent man," his mother says as she shoos his children from a large pile of seeds, "and all he wants is to find some way to live in the same place as his children."

An entire generation of Chinese children has grown up without seeing their parents more than once a year, usually for a few weeks during the spring festival in February. Socially, this has created a generation who have identified with their grandparents and often formed close emotional bonds with these elders; this has led to the commonplace tragedy of teenagers having to endure the senility and death of surrogate parents who seem to be their only protectors and sources of love. The stress on the children, isolated from their parents and expected to use their educations to support their family's escape, is often overwhelming.[6] The strain placed on the village is equally profound.

Villages in China often serve not so much as centers of agricultural production but as "social buffers." It is a system popularly known as Li Tu Bu Li Xiang—"leave the soil but not the village"—turning the peasant homestead into a surrogate for the absent state. For most of the 140 million arrival-city workers who lack urban *hukou* or stable residency, the village is the only place to send children to school, to obtain medical help, or to get child-care services. These are overwhelmingly fee-charging services for migrants, unaffordable to most workers. Urban apartments big enough for a three-generation family are beyond the reach of all but the most successful workers. Even for those who are able to get schooling, sufficient housing, and support in the city, there are powerful reasons to keep one foot in the village. State pensions in China are negligibly small, and private pensions don't exist for most of the working class—Mr. Pu's father, who is a Korean War veteran and a former Communist Party village official, receives only $14 a month, and his is larger than most. Unemployment insurance and welfare are effectively non-existent for the floating population; the urban program known as the Minimum Living Standard Guarantee Scheme is unavailable to the village-born. Some estimate that 500 million people may be without any form of social assistance.[7] The village, and its subsistence crops, provide the closest thing to a social safety net for most arrival-city residents.

There is another, distinctly Chinese reason why families like the Pu clan are remaining on the farm. Agriculture is still officially communal. This has been only symbolically true since the reforms of the 1980s introduced the Household Production Responsibility System, in which farm families lease their land from the collectives and act as autonomous agricultural producers, able to consume, sell, or trade their produce as they wish. Nevertheless, the collective has the power to reallocate the land for best use. If the village committee decides that a family is no longer active on its farm, it can seize the land and deploy it more productively; if the collective decides to boost rural non-agricultural business—a good idea in principle—it will take land away from families who have moved to the city. In other words, families do not really own their farmland and cannot sell it to finance a full-scale move to the city. (Reforms in 2002 made this legally possible, but it remains very difficult in most villages.) And, conversely, the fear of having social-buffer land seized forces families to maintain a hold on the farm long after they have fully urbanized themselves.

At some point after 2004, the largest source of rural revenue in China ceased to be farm earnings and was replaced by remittances from the city;[8] much of this pays for the maintenance of the village home, as the village is functioning as a de facto child-care facility and retirement home. This remittance cost is one of the main factors that prevents arrival-city residents from saving enough to buy a property. The economic crisis that began in 2008 demonstrated how dependent China's arrival cities are on the village. In the early months of 2009, an estimated 20 million of China's arrival-city workers (from a total population of perhaps 150 million) returned to the village, abandoning their city quarters. But by September of 2009, after the economy had improved, Beijing reported that 95 percent of these migrants had returned to the city.[9] The village had functioned as an unemployment-insurance system, one whose price is the fracturing of families.

These millions of divided families have rendered the countryside incomprehensible. Although China's commercial farms are now able to produce enough food for the entire country and for the government to stockpile enough grain and pork for all of China to survive a nationwide famine of several months' duration, agriculture is nowhere close to the powerful export industry it could be, in large part because the land remains a fractured mess of non-commercial farms that serve social rather than nutritional or commercial needs. China now has about 200 million farm households with an average farm size of just over half a hectare.[10] Remittances from urban areas, combined with increases in farm income, have lifted more than 400 million Chinese, almost all of them rural, out of absolute poverty. Nevertheless, about 99 percent of those families that are still in absolute poverty live in rural areas.

Thus, the Chinese ex-villager is caught in an endless paradox, in which the farm village and the arrival-city neighborhood support each other's worst qualities, causing migrants, families, and entire communities to be trapped without a permanent and secure home. The reason why China has hundreds of millions of people floating rootlessly and inefficiently between arrival city and village, scholars at Oxford and the Chinese Academy of Sciences concluded in a major study, "is because no social assistance, public housing and schooling arrangements have been established for migrants to enable them to settle down on a permanent basis in cities." For those peasants who have found solid roots, home ownership, and thriving businesses in the arrival city, "the lack of such arrangements makes them unwilling or unable to give up their rural land, which, in turn, makes it difficult for those left in rural areas to expand their scale of agricultural production and secure their land tenure because too little extra land can be released to accommodate rural demographic changes."[11]

The "hollow village," as these rural enclaves of children and grandparents are known in China, has become a global phenomenon, as subsistence farming is forced to serve as a substitute for a proper social safety net. In Romania, hollow villages have become a national issue for related reasons. The millions of working-age peasants who have moved to the arrival cities of Italy and Spain to work have discovered school systems and social-service agencies that are closed to new arrivals (even from within the European Union) settling down or, in the case of Italy, a police and legal system that is actively hostile to arrival-city families. So Romanian villages consist of grandparents raising children with support from distant parents.

Nevertheless, it is becoming increasingly clear, especially after the dramatic migration followed by return in the 2008 crisis, that China's floating population creates true arrival cities, employing every strategy they can to become a permanent part of the city. As recently as 2002, only 7 percent of China's rural–urban migrants were able to bring their families with them. This number is gradually increasing, as the more successful arrival cities allow villages to die out. Shuilin, the home of Dong Lin and Ming Lin and their grandparents, is moving quickly in this direction. "We've passed the stage of just sending migrant workers," Pu Ze Shi, the retired village party official, tells me. "Now people are finding ways to leave completely." In 2000, the population was 2,500; now it is barely 1,000, almost all of them over 50 or under 15. Of this, village elders tell me that perhaps 10 percent are genuine permanent residents; the rest are searching for ways to leave. He Su Xiou, the grandmother, tells me that she is ready to give up the home that her family has possessed for hundreds of years.

"If Jun can do well in the future, if he can get over his financial troubles, we would love to move to Chongqing permanently," she says. "We're very old, we can't farm much longer, and I do not want my children to have to experience farming. If we could all move there, Jun will get to live with his children for the first time, and we very much want that. I know it will be bad for the village, but the village was never such a good place. We lived very badly there for a long time, and we owe it nothing. When we're gone, I won't ever come here again."

THE VILLAGE WITHOUT A CITY
Dorli, Maharashtra, India

The power of urban arrival may have a disfiguring effect on the shape of peasant life, but that should not be taken to mean that the lack of an urban connection is a peaceful alternative. I witnessed this vividly in the sun-blasted center of India, where a village of dung-and-mud huts distinguishes itself from its identical neighbors with a sign painted boldly on the outer wall, visible to passing vehicles: "This village is up for sale, including houses, animals and farms."

Like many visitors to Dorli, population 270, at first I took this Marathi lettering to be a gesture of protest or a rhetorical cry for attention, the sort of political statement that might not be out of place here on the outskirts of Wardha, formerly the seat of Gandhi's Indian Independence Movement. I was led into a dung-floored hut whitewashed the cheery local light-blue color; inside its single room, a dozen village men, young and old, squatted on the floor with me, leaning between the beds and the TV. They explained that their offer was genuine, based on what they saw as fateful logic, reached after months of heartbreaking calculations and debates. They really did want someone to buy their entire village and hoped some industrialist might be forthcoming, because all 40 families here had quite reasonably concluded that subsistence farming had become a deadly pursuit. Rather than riding the downward spiral of rural poverty to its agonizing end, they felt it was worth taking a long shot in order to make their escape to the comparative comfort of urban poverty.

"Why kill myself when I can get a new life with my land? We have all decided this—we realized that selling it all is the best way to get off the land forever," Chandrashekhar Dorlikar, 41, told me as he opened the village's handwritten account books. His moustache and beard were neatly trimmed, his clothes frayed; he was one of the few literate people in the village. He believed the fields and buildings could be bought by India's largest company, Tata Group, the Mumbai-based industrial conglomerate, for perhaps 20 million rupees ($400,000) or $10,000 per family—a vast amount of money for these families and almost certainly a completely unrealistic expectation. In earlier years, up to the end of the 1990s, each family here might have earned $2 a day, but, in the decade that followed, their household balances turned negative. Like peasant villagers in poor districts around the world, people here are choking on debt. Families typically owe banks and private lenders $500 each, close to a year's income. And the debt keeps mounting.

"We had in mind that if somebody buys it, we'd go into some urban area and take up trades," Chandrashekhar told me. "Even a rickshaw driver in an urban area makes enough that his kid can go to a convent school and he can cook on a gas burner. Here, we have to go to the village school and our wives cook on an open fire. So we'd use the money to move to urban areas where at least it would be better. On farming, we can't educate our children. The most education any of our children have is primary school. To go further we'd have to rent a room in town, pay for transportation and books—too expensive. We have spent the past 20 years living on hope, every year praying that we will get a good crop. We don't want to be dead— we'd rather be living in a slum."

That dichotomy is no mere metaphor, for aside from selling the entire village, or some major body part (as people in other villages have attempted), the only other popular way out of the rural trap in this region is a strategic death. At the very end of the twentieth century, farmers across the Vidarbha region (Dorli is near its center), deranged by crop failure and rising debt, weary of watching their families wither from malnourishment, discovered a strategy that could stave off the ruination of their families. There are few instruments of death on a poor Indian cotton farm: Sowing and plowing and harvesting are done, exhaustingly, by hand, and even sharp blades are scarce. The men here choose to wait until the early evening and head out into their fields, where they sit on the ground, survey the parched and lifeless soil around them, and drink a liter of agricultural pesticide.

This practice soon became epidemic. Between 1995 and 2004, according to a study conducted by the Mumbai economist Srijit Mishra, the suicide rate for poor male farmers in Maharashtra state nearly quadrupled, from 15 per 100,000 to more than 57, while for equally poor non-farm-owning laborers it rose only from 17 to 20 (for women it fell from 14 to 11). In some of the districts that surround Dorli, that rate has risen as high as 116, more than eight times the national rate for males. There is no indication that these numbers have since decreased. In 87 percent of cases, according to Mishra, the suicide victims were indebted, and the average debts are similar to a good year's income for a small farm. And, tellingly, in 79 percent of cases, the suicides were committed by drinking insecticide.[12] Hundreds of farmers in this region continue to take their lives every year. One need only visit a random village in Vidarbha, and any local will point out the many houses of recent suicides.

I visited two dozen such families, all housed in low-ceilinged mud buildings in various villages, most with electricity and quite a few with TV. There was a distressing similarity to their stories: The tiny, increasingly small plots of farmland, the fast-declining crop yields, the dependence on seed and fertilizer dealers for expensive inputs, the money borrowed, over and over, from state banks and black-market moneylenders to cover those farming costs, as well as mounting bills for the new fruits of modernization—electricity, TV, the ever-escalating dowry and ceremony costs associated with marrying a daughter, sometimes over-ambitious purchases like motorcycles. And, most significantly, the complete lack of any non-farm sources of income: Unlike peasant farmers in so many other places, the small-hold cotton growers of central India have no source of remittance from the city. In an age when family farms have become a mere buffer for urban economies, farmers in disconnected districts like this, with no direct relationship to the urban remittance economy, are struggling under an agricultural system that essentially assumes the existence of a parallel urban life, a support network in the slums of India's cities.*

Unfortunately, the slums are inaccessible to most of the farmers of this region. The nearest major city, Nagpur, is a difficult day's trip away, and it would require savings to make a start there. And, because of this region's cotton-based economy, its communication links are all directed toward Mumbai, an impossible 20-hour train ride away. The generation-long tendrils of seasonal and chain migration have not begun here. An informal survey of Dorli and its surrounding villages could not find a single villager who had even heard of someone who had moved to the city; without this sort of knowledge, migration is not even an option. Every village has access to at least one television and mobile phone and visits from urban-affiliated nongovernmental organizations and political parties, yet none of this has brought the city closer. The small holdings and strangling economics have made it impossible for farmers to migrate anywhere, even to the nearby towns of Wardha or Chandrapur.

In the Indian media, the farmer suicides have been attributed to numerous causes. It has become popular to blame globalization and U.S. policy: After all, the worldwide market price of cotton has plummeted since its twentieth-century peak, in part because of the U.S. practice of subsidizing its own cotton farmers, but also because there

---

* Such districts remain the norm in many parts of sub-Saharan Africa, especially away from coasts and major cities (north, east, and west Africans increasingly have ties to cities in Africa or Europe), in south India, northern Bangladesh, numerous districts of southeast Asia, and only a few very remote areas in South America. And they can be seen, to a far less deadly extent, in places like southeastern Poland, where farming remains at the subsistence level but, compared to the west and north, there has been comparatively little migration to western Europe.

is simply too much cotton on the worldwide market. While declining returns have certainly hurt, a simple examination of any cotton farmer's books will dispel this theory. Even if they were receiving prices equivalent to the historic peak price, I found that most of the farmers who took their lives would still have been unable to meet their costs and avoid spiraling debt with the money they earned. Their fields were simply too small and their yields too poor to make any economic sense with this crop.

Other reports have blamed the financial cost and declining productivity of genetically engineered crops and the commercial fertilizers they require. But the problem predates these technologies and is rooted in more basic costs of modern agriculture. Soil exhaustion has become almost universal: The over-fertilization and lack of crop rotation caused by the application of Green Revolution techniques to unsustainably small crops, without proper knowledge, has turned the huge yields of a decade before into a permanent famine. The farmers here have watched their crop yields plummet over the past decade and their expenses rise. Desperation, indebtedness, and suicide are the result. In other regions, closer to major cities, farmers in similar straits avoid this fate. Though the economics are equally impossible, they are bailed out, like the Polish peasants in Tatary, by relatives in the arrival-city slums of Nagpur and Mumbai. Without urban capital, this type of peasant farming makes no sense.

The most saddening sight in this region, beyond the devastated families of suicidal farmers, are the few farms that are operating at an appropriate size and capitalization level for commercial agriculture, with a few dozen hectares of fields, modern crop-management techniques, and water-preservation strategies. These fertile, profitable, high-employment farms are green oases amid the parched dun of ruined peasant lives, a constantly visible reminder to those families of just how easy it is, with some investment and savings from outside, to turn farming into a successful livelihood. "It is not hard to make a good and stable living farming around here—you just have to get enough land and manage it properly," says Subhash Sharma, 55, whose

10 hectares, with 45 employees paid $1 a day each, net him profits of almost $10,000 a year. Significantly, he and his father used their earnings from a move to Mumbai to finance the reinvigorated farm.

A generation ago, almost all the farmers in this region were positioned to become successes like Mr. Sharma. Their holdings were large enough, averaging more than eight hectares; a reserve army of agricultural laborers was available; and the Green Revolution of the early 1970s had delivered high-yield seeds, crop-management practices, and farming know-how that put a permanent end to major famines in India and made market farming a real commercial possibility. What should have happened here was what happened in most of western Europe in the eighteenth and nineteenth centuries: The more ambitious peasants expanded their holdings, took on workers, and multiplied their outputs, while the smaller ones sold their farms and either migrated to the city or became laborers on the successful commercial farms, and both the urban economy and the agricultural industry boomed, supporting each other.

But that sort of transition requires a functioning relationship with the urban economy, and India's impoverished rural districts have been deprived of this in several ways, notably by government policies that promote and even romanticize the small family farm. The most dramatic effect—the one most directly responsible for the suicide crisis—has been on land holdings. At some point after Partition in 1947, the farm families in this region abandoned primogeniture, in which the eldest son inherits the entire farm and younger sons became farm laborers or move to the city. Instead, after the death of the patriarch, the holdings are divided among interested sons. Across this region, farms quickly became smaller, with devastating consequences. Small farms lead to higher unemployment and declining yields, making a breakthrough into commercial success impossible.[13]

I visited the Chaple family, who live in the busy, crowded village of Rehaki and walk a kilometer to their fields. As late as 1970, their family farm was 35 hectares. The grandfather divided it among four sons, with 12.5 hectares going to one brother and 7.5 to each of the others. This was then divided again, leaving the next generation with no more than 3.5 hectares each. Today, some of them have only 1.2 hectares to farm. Such plots are so tiny that even poor farm laborers can save enough of their earnings to abandon a steady wage for the high risk of small-hold farming (and seed vendors have persuaded many to do so). Ramaji Chaple, one of the grandsons who inherited a 1.2-hectare slice of the original 35-hectare farm, spent $300 in 2007 on cotton seed and fertilizer and, in the autumn, sold his cotton for only $400, a typical yield that year. The remaining $100 was not enough to feed the family, to say nothing of paying the $500 in outstanding loans, and while he had wealthier siblings in town who offered small sums, there was no pressure-relief valve of urban migration either to help him escape or to provide financial support. In July that year, his wife, Mukta, found him lying stiff in the field, the pesticide bottle clutched in his hand.

"What India needs is more farm laborers and fewer farmers," says Anand Subhedar, a Vidarbha-based agriculturist. "We have created a situation where the farmers are gambling their lives with debt on the chance of getting a good crop, which hasn't happened in recent years. It would be far better if they were simply collecting a wage." But it is hard to make that break, because Indians are passionate about owning the land. They consider the land a goddess and pray to her. "The farmer doesn't know how to invest the money and make a better future for himself," says Mr. Subhedar, "so he will wait around until the last straw breaks."

THE ARRIVAL VILLAGE
Biswanath, Sylhet, Bangladesh

Given Biswanath's even more remote location, its isolation from any major cities, its tiny plots of land, and its dense population, this village in the Bangladeshi district of Sylhet might well have shared the same fate as Dorli, India. But Sylhet, an almost completely rural rice-farming district in the far northeast corner of Bangladesh, has one major difference: Since the 1960s, it has sent a continuous stream of permanent migrants to the arrival cities of London and other British centers. An estimated 95 percent of Britain's Bangladeshis hail from this small district, and the links have brought a surprising metamorphosis to the muddy villages here, as the back-and-forth flows of arrival-city migration and village-bound remittances have transformed the economy. In Sylhet, the relationship between the arrival city and the village has reached its dramatic, penultimate stage.

To drive into Biswanath is, at first, to enter any large Bangladeshi farming village. There are the tottering wood-and-corrugated-tin huts housing dozens of people who live on less than a dollar a day; there are children gathering fish in the rice paddies and adults reaping with scythes, pulling rickshaws, and selling anything they can lay their hands on. The poverty of rural life strikes first. Then, toward its teeming center, the village itself reveals the precise opposite: There are dozens of multi-story shops and even a full-scale shopping mall, Al Hera, which sports an escalator, smoked-glass windows, and air-conditioning, selling shoes and electronics and cosmetics and Western-style toilets, things never before seen in rice-farming villages. There are restaurants, fast-food joints, and kebab shops, many with English signs and names like London Fried Chicken, and an astonishing number of real-estate agencies. This is a highly urbanized village. Most of the villages of Sylhet district, unlike any of the other 64 districts of Bangladesh, have been similarly transformed.

The next shock comes just beyond the village limits, as you drive along the narrow lanes between the rice paddies, where the horizon is interrupted every dozen hectares by the looming spectre of an absolutely enormous modern house, three or four storys tall, usually with an ornamental roof terrace, an elaborate walled garden, and a circular driveway befitting the seat of a grandee of the Raj, all of it built in the grandiose architectural styles of the Persian Gulf or the wealthiest districts of Dhaka. Approaching these gleaming castles, it is quickly apparent that many of them are uninhabited and barely furnished, even though they are surrounded by rickety slum-housing developments full of people and rice fields swarming with farm workers.

These are the "Londoni" houses, owned and built in absentia by the families known as Londonis—the Sylheti term for anyone who has migrated permanently to any place in Britain. These palatial abodes typically cost tens of thousands of dollars to build, though they would be worth millions if they were built on such a scale in the West, and are often inhabited only a few weeks of the year, when the Londoni relatives come to visit. Somewhere near the big Londoni house is typically an impressive one-story residence, also built with British funds, occupied by the non-migrant relatives of the Londonis. And spreading out from these buildings are the far more humble residences of the many workers and servants, some locally born and some seasonal migrants from faraway districts, who have flocked to the fields around the big house because their livelihoods depend on the flow of Londoni money.

Even though the British-based Sylhetis often live in public-housing apartments and sometimes earn little more than the British minimum wage, those earnings are enough to have made them something akin to feudal lords in Sylhet. The villagers treat them as wealthy benefactors, and on their visits they often behave with the hauteur of nobles. Their wealth has created employment and construction booms, turning the region's villages into hubs, with their own migration waves and even small arrival cities of their own. A typical Londoni household will have a dozen or more hectares of cultivated fields, several large-scale construction projects, a few shops in the village and perhaps a share in a road-building or mosque-building project; it will provide direct incomes for between 12 and 100 Sylhetis at any time and will attract dozens of people from poorer regions of Bangladesh to the village, usually to live in "colonies," slum rental-housing developments built and owned by the Londonis.

In one large rice field in Biswanath, I met a gang of harvesters bent over the paddies, using their scythes to cut the rice, then bundling and tying it in an exhausting 10-hour day. Tariq Mia, 23, had come with most of the other team's members from Jamalpur, an extremely poor northern district more than 200 kilometers away, to spend half the year working the paddies in order to support his wife and children. Jamalpur is subject to the *monga*, a seasonal famine; death from malnutrition remains a tangible possibility there. During the harvest months, Tariq is able to make 3,000 taka ($60), a third of which pays for rent and food in the colony of slum shacks. The remaining 2,000 taka, multiplied by the four harvesting months, is more than double the annual earnings of a Jamalpur farm, enough to stave off starvation. Tariq and his team work under the watch of Cherag Ali, 30, a poor Biswanath resident from a non-Londoni family; he lives in a better-appointed shack in the village and earns about twice as much from the harvest.

These men work for Mominul Islam, a young man they consider the *malik* (landowner), who lives in the "blue house," a tidy, modern bungalow at the foot of the big Londoni house, surrounded by a fence and a well-kept decorative garden. Four decades ago, these fields were only three-quarters of a hectare and were harvested by the family who lived here; the land was subdivided from one generation to the next and approaching the sort of crisis we witnessed in central India. Then, in the 1960s, the family patriarch went to London, worked for a few years in a factory, then opened a north London takeout restaurant that did well off the booming economy; he used the proceeds to build the blue bungalow and to consolidate and expand the family's land holdings into more than 25 hectares. His London-born son, known to the family as Sufe Miah, went into small-scale property development during the British housing boom of the 1990s and used that money to build the Londoni house, to launch several housing developments in the area, and to open a string of shops and rental storefronts in Biswanath village, all during his twice-yearly visits from London.

Overseeing this small empire from the blue house, and employing and housing the rice harvesters, is Sufe Miah's nephew, the 21-year-old *malik* Mominul Islam, a laconic, soft-spoken man whose family, owing to the death of his father, has been unable to join the rest in migrating. Mominul has struggled with English classes and not yet managed to find any marriage opportunities in London, despite his attachment to Western-style motorcycle jackets, shoes, and football teams. Instead, he has become something of an overseer and a putative entrepreneur: He used some of his uncle's remittance money and one of the rental storefronts to open his own shop in the center of Biswanath, selling the sort of running shoes that are popular on the streets of London. He lives in the blue house with his mother and his three younger sisters and a brother who is enrolled in secondary school; he spends a good part of his time ensuring that the Londoni house is cared for, cleaned, and ready for one of his uncle's increasingly rare visits. The property costs 15,000 taka ($600) a month to maintain, 9,000 ($180) of which goes to the monthly salaries of two full-time, live-in servants, Masuk Ahmed, 56, and Moinul Ahmed, 25, peasant farmers who moved here from neighboring Habiganj district to take advantage of the Londoni money. They each send at least 80 percent of their salary back to their family, and they manage to visit their wives and children two or three times a year.

After the Western economics dipped into their credit-driven downturn and Britain faced a property-market slump in 2008, the remittances from Mominul's uncle turned into periodic gifts, then disappeared altogether. The construction stopped, and the whole enterprise had to be run from the revenues earned in Biswanath, mainly from the storefront rentals. This cutoff, repeated in thousands of households across the district, rapidly transformed the local economy from feudalism into capitalism, forcing non-productive enterprises to shut down. In Mominul's case, it was his shoe shop that had to go: He laid off his six employees and shuttered it. Altogether, at least two dozen people either directly or indirectly employed by the family have lost their jobs. The farm, previously operated out of a sense of charity and agrarian pride, suddenly became a financial consideration, and Mominul plans to turn out three crops a year and possibly switch to market crops.

What has happened in Biswanath? On one hand, it changed from a peasant economy into a highly dependent economy of tribute and monumentalism: The money from the arrival cities of Britain supports an economy that is sometimes driven more by pride than by economic reason. As the anthropologist Katy Gardner has documented in her exhaustive studies of the Sylheti economy and social system, some of the Londoni money goes to building roads and schools, consolidating farmlands and other productive investment uses, but just as much is spent on large houses, flashy storefronts, and other projects designed to raise the status of the family, improve the marriage prospects of the family members remaining in Sylhet, and produce the visible symbols of modernity and worldliness.[14]

But something more sustainable is occurring beneath this flash. As the Bangladeshi scholar Tasneem Siddiqui has shown in detailed studies of the economies of these villages, the money and knowledge from the arrival cities of London and Dhaka are creating consumer markets within the rural region (where consumerism, and the possibility of earning money, had not previously existed) and investments in high-productivity agriculture in Sylhet. It is a female-led form of progress, with women in the villages often being the leading figures investing in irrigation, craft industries, and agricultural marketing with the help of circular migrants.[15] Some Londoni investments take the place of an absent government: Aside from scores of English-language schools built by migrants and staffed by villagers, there are four full-scale colleges in Biswanath, all of them built and maintained with Londoni money, and all appear to be doing well, with full enrollments as local families have eagerly invested in postsecondary educations to give their children a better chance of winning immigration status or attracting a foreign spouse. The tighter Britain's immigration regime becomes, the more profit these schools make, and they appear to be improving the cultural resources of new

Bangladeshi migrants to Britain. But other Londoni investments, those with less value to the locals, have been killed off in the downturn. Mominul Islam's running-shoe store was far more devoted to expressing his tastes and Londoni aspirations than it was to creating viable markets and employment sources in Biswanath; it existed as a business only as long as it could be sustained by his family's remittance payments.

As a result of this bizarrely distorted economy, the Londonis have expanded their holdings, to the point that they own almost 80 percent of the land, even though they represent only a third of families here. But they themselves have ceased to be farmers: More than 84 percent of their relatives are no longer directly involved in cultivation. Instead, they earn their income from shops, construction projects, transportation, and other sources and sharecrop out their land in return for a sum that seems negligible compared to their new wealth. Most families now harvest only one rice crop a year, employing between five and 10 people, and a small but significant number, perhaps 10 percent, have left their land uncultivated—an extraordinary spectacle in a country that suffers from severe food shortages and is a net importer of food.[16]

But agriculture is no longer always the most sensible way for villagers to make a living. It makes more sense for a small core of people to operate small or medium-sized commercial farms, a larger group to work as farm laborers, and even more to work in non-agricultural rural jobs—a transformation that the Banglatown arrival city is at least beginning to accomplish. The same "deagrarianization" of the village is being seen in the better-off parts of sub-Saharan Africa and the Middle East: The arrival city is urbanizing the village, both culturally and in its forms of economic organization.[17]

All the ingredients are present in Biswanath for a shift to more sustainable village life, with high-yield, high-employment commercial farms. The land has been consolidated, the infrastructure has been improved, and the sources of investment are present. But outward migration remains the central and overwhelming function of this village, and the largest investments are devoted exclusively to huge and sometimes preposterous monuments to migration itself. This sort of village, and the insensibly large houses and disused agricultural land that characterize it, are increasingly common in the parts of the developing world that are linked to Western arrival cities, notably in Mexico, in northern Africa, and in the Pearl and Yangtze river deltas of China.[18]

Yet this economy, and its characteristic forms of architecture and employment, are strictly products of the arrival city's first generation. The second generation, the children born in the arrival city, have far less inclination either to send money back to the village or to build their status there; later generations are highly unlikely to continue such links. The question, then, is whether the flood of money and the shocking structural changes to the village can have a lasting effect once these direct physical ties are gone. Sylhet provides a useful test case, as it has experienced five decades of large-scale permanent migration to Britain. The steady streams of remittance cash have dwindled into occasional payments or strategic investments. The visits to the Londoni houses are increasingly infrequent. As the remittance money dries up, there is a sense that the displays of middle-class prosperity will fade. One scholar, after a detailed examination of a similar British-driven economy in Mirpur, Pakistan, described such villages as "a case of capital-rich underdevelopment" in which the prosperity is "only as stable as the continued inflow of remittances."[19]

Yet villages like Biswanath seem far more likely to become functioning centers of commercial agriculture. For the moment, the incentive to do so is limited because of Londoni money. Beginning around 2000, dozens of elderly Bangladeshis began moving back from "London" to spend their retirement in Biswanath, bringing with them British state and private-sector pensions that are major sources of wealth by Biswanath standards. They will be the final generation to deliver this kind of money, and some people here, realizing this, are beginning to plan for a self-sufficient future.

But this does not mean that the small peasant farms of the developing world will, or should, consolidate into large commercial enterprises of the sort that formed in the urbanization of Europe and North America. Clearly, some peasant farms are too small to support any kind of viable agriculture, but, for the most part, economists have found that smaller farms in poor countries have higher efficiency, greater profitability, and higher employment levels than larger farms, all other things being equal (this is the opposite of the case in places like Poland).[20] What they need is not size but investment: A fairly basic injection of money and basic knowledge will turn a subsistence peasant farm into a job-generating commercial farm. In fact, under-investment in agriculture is currently one of the most serious problems in the world, as the food shortages of 2008 illustrated. Change is beginning to occur—the large-scale Chinese investment in the farms of sub-Saharan Africa, for example, is slowly turning that region into the breadbasket it should always have been. In most places, though, it is the ties between the village and a distant city that will provide the investments for a second Green Revolution.

For some, the Londoni remittances have served as seed money for a permanent move into more remunerative businesses. In the village of Rajnagar, I met Montaj Begum, 47, who has three siblings and two children working in London, mainly in curry restaurants. At first, their remittances allowed her 11-hectare rice farm to be fully productive for the first time in decades. Then, she realized that her lifestyle had become reliant on the remittances, and the vicissitudes of farming were not going to sustain her. She saved two years' remittances, and she and her remaining relatives opened two shops in the village, a cell phone vendor and a window-shutter installer, and handed the farmland to a neighbor who was interested in modern farm-management techniques. "Before, our main source of income was the money from London, and we'd rely on it every month," she says. "Now the money is coming like a gift, only on holidays, because there are six children to support in London, it's much harder for them. But that's okay now, because we have our own sources of income here—the businesses pay their own money, so we don't rely on London money."

That may be the ideal end of the village: As a place where a few people run profitable farms, many more make their living working on farms, and others prosper in the local service industry. It is how the European migration put a decidedly unromantic end to the peasant village, and we can hope it happens the same way in the world's other two-thirds. The fate of the village rests largely in the way countries manage their major cities and in the rights and resources provided to the migrants living there. Conversely, the fate of cities and nations very often depends on the handling of villages and the people moving out of them. The badly run arrival city can turn the village into a prison; the badly run village can make the arrival city explode.

5

THE FIRST GREAT MIGRATION: HOW THE WEST ARRIVED

VILE PORTALS TO THE MODERN WORLD
Paris

When a skinny girl named Jeanne Bouvier made her first trip through the newly built outer walls of Paris in 1879, at age 14, she brought with her only two changes of clothing, which she wore on top of one another, a few toiletries she kept in a kerchief with its four corners tied together, and the timeless set of expectations that rural migrants bring to cities. She was alone, having made the long journey from the Rhone valley by coach and foot a few months before with her mother, who, after a depressing time trying her luck as a brush-dyer in the Paris outskirts, had given up and returned to their famine-blighted village. Jeanne continued on alone, plunging into the city's migrant-packed center. She joined the greatest surge of rural-to-urban migration the world had ever seen, arriving in Paris at the very apex of a 125-year transformation of the Western world. Like the hundreds of thousands of other peasant arrivals who formed a majority of the French capital's population in the nineteenth century, she was seeking nothing more than a source of cash income to send back home to the village and a place, any place, to sleep.

What she found was the first great arrival city of the modern world: not the largest one, since London and Manchester had by then far exceeded Paris in size, scope, density, activity, and horror, but certainly the most explosive. It was in Paris that governments made the first grave mistakes of managing the great migration, mistakes that are being repeated today. And it was in Paris that the arrival city became a political force capable of changing nations.

Jeanne descended into a maze of streets that native-born Parisians dared not enter, streets that the works of Victor Hugo, Honoré de Balzac, and Eugène Sue had transformed into popular bywords for filth, depravity, murder, disease, and ruination, streets that had already been the main stages of violent and history-altering uprisings and revolutions in 1789, 1830, 1832, 1848, and 1871. In the popular imagination, these neighborhoods were the repositories of the fallen, the hideouts of failed urbanites, the dwelling grounds for the animalistic ruins of humanity. Jeanne saw them for what they really were: a transitory home to millions who, having found something marginally better than the despair of the village, were seeking a permanent foothold in a better urban world.

Her first quarters, a tiny room whose only outstanding features were a bare plank bed and a rivulet of human waste running beneath its small window, did indeed confirm the worst images of the arrival city, as did her cruel employers. Within a year, after a series of unrewarding jobs as a domestic servant, she found distant relatives from her village working in the needle trades of Paris's ninth arrondissement, and they helped her find work sewing seams in the burgeoning ready-to-wear clothing industry. There, in workshops that would seem familiar, in both appearance and function, to those in the very similar arrival cities of Shenzhen and Dhaka today, she worked long hours for wages averaging two and a half francs a day.

And Jeanne Bouvier did what arrival-city residents were doing all over Europe: She calculated, and saved, and sent money home, with a constant eye to improvements. Her budget was rigid. From her earnings of between 12 and 40 francs per week (she was paid by the piece, so earnings varied widely), she spent 8.4 francs on food, 3 on rent, 3.75 on clothes; the rest was sent to the village or saved. "I would suffer any sacrifice to be able to buy what I needed to set myself up in a place all my own," she wrote.

> But to buy a bed and everything necessary to outfit it constitutes a considerable expense for a working woman who does not have a cent to spare and who is, moreover, without clothes or underwear . . . My ambition was to put together a life annuity and save enough to buy myself a little house in the country . . . I wanted to end my days there. To realize this dream, I had to sew my heart out, so I sewed with fervor.
>
> I rented a small room. I paid thirty francs rent in advance, including the tip for the concierge. This room was a horrible little hovel, but it had one virtue that I appreciated enormously: it was clean. The walls were whitewashed. It was not comfortable, but it was home. I also had bought a few kitchen utensils and some dishes, which allowed me to eat at home and to realize some savings on my food.[1]

Jeanne joined the great many workers, mostly female, who occupied the sixth, seventh, and eighth floors of buildings along Parisian streets—*sixièmes*, largely windowless rooms (because buildings were taxed according to the number of windows and doors) that often held a dozen people each, their hallways sometimes extending through the walls of adjoining buildings, creating a parallel "street in the sky" occupied entirely by village arrivals. In some districts, the Parisian arrival city was defined by this "vertical stratification," the established urban classes on the lower floors and the rural-arrival poor in the top two or three (an ordering that was later reversed by the elevator, introduced after the 1880s).

By Jeanne Bouvier's time, Paris had developed discrete, identifiable, segregated arrival cities. The city-born upper and middle classes increasingly lived in neighborhoods to the west, and village-born workers, would-be workers and the perpetually jobless occupied the districts in the center and the new, sprawling arrival cities to the northeast, east, and south, just outside the old city walls. As the central Paris of Haussmann and his successors became an increasingly beautiful web of boulevards and squares, its arrival-city majority were pushed farther and farther to the periphery.

Jeanne Bouvier's own life was both horizontally and vertically stratified, as she lived on the top floors in back-street neighborhoods jammed into the interstices of central Paris, mainly in the ninth arrondissement, in clusters of residential hotels and *garnis* (weekly-rental dormitory rooming houses, usually organized by trade). Many of these stayed in place until the 1960s, when the village arrivals of Paris were finally and forcefully moved into new, concrete high-rise blocks in the outer suburbs.

Jeanne, like the majority of Europe's arrival-city residents, would never return to her village, except for one or two brief visits—during which she was shocked to find that she no longer understood the regional dialect.* None of her Paris neighbors were planning on returning, either. Centuries of circular, seasonal migration had built links between village and city, and those circular migrations, involving hundreds of thousands of people across Europe from the Middle Ages onward, did not fully dwindle into permanent settlement until the First World War. Savoyard farmers came to Paris to work as chimney sweeps and carriage drivers in the winter; stonemasons and builders visited from the farms of Limousin; a constant supply of maids and prostitutes arrived for the season from Brittany. Then, as the city became less lethal and the countryside increasingly overcrowded, more and more of these farmers began staying in the city during the planting season. By the last quarter of the nineteenth century, in

---

* Another effect of the Parisian arrival city was to turn French into a universal language of France. In Jeanne Bouvier's time, only perhaps 40 percent of the population spoke French, and far fewer, mainly those who had worked extensively in Paris, felt confident speaking it; most spoke only regional tongues and dialects, such as Occitan, Burgundian, Breton, and Walloon. It was only at the beginning of the twentieth century that a majority of French citizens were able to speak the country's official language.

Jeanne Bouvier's lifetime, the majority of Europe's rural migrants were staying in the city for life, despite their almost universal initial expectation of a return.

Although she wouldn't return, Jeanne Bouvier would be able to buy herself a bed, on the installment plan, and eventually save enough money, through obsessive budgeting and rigid self-discipline, to live in a place all her own, away from the arrival city, within touching distance of the middle class. This would take her decades.*

Jeanne's migration had been one of hope but not one of happiness. Her parents, farmers and barrel-makers in the southeast of France, had been ruined by the great *phylloxera* infestation of the 1870s, which wiped out France's vineyards. Facing starvation, her father had sent his wife and children away to work. He ran the farm, increasingly with the help of Jeanne's remittances.

By relying on networks of fellow villagers in Paris to win her a stable place in the city, Jeanne Bouvier was typical of the citizens who made up the great European migration of the nineteenth century. Also typical was her sex. While the popular image has young men coming to work in factories and later bringing their families from the village, in reality it was more often the women who arrived first. The historian Charles Tilly found that domestic service, particularly among women, was most frequently the gateway into full rural–urban migration in the nineteenth century (as it often is today): "For the most part, the farmers who moved to cities found low-level employment in services and commerce . . . Indeed, over the last two centuries the most important single category of urban employment for rural-to-urban migrants within Europe has likely been domestic service. Only an undue concentration on males and manufacturing has obscured that fact."[2]

---

* Jeanne Bouvier would become, in the twentieth century, a labor organizer, feminist, amateur historian, and the author of one of the very few memoirs written by European rural-to-urban migrants.

THE FIRST EXPLOSION

By the late eighteenth century, when the modern arrival city had its beginnings, rural-to-urban migration had been part of human life for millennia. People had been moving from the country to the city since about 3000 B.C., when the first urban formations took shape in the Persian Gulf and soon spread across Asia and Europe. For the next 5,000 years, countless millions of peasants, and hundreds of thousands of regional elites, made the move to the city, most making seasonal or career-driven migrations but increasing numbers staying on. But it was not until the final half of the eighteenth century that village-arrival enclaves became a notable and influential feature of the urban landscape. Until then, cities had been tied directly to the agrarian population; from that point on, such arrival cities were the driving force in Western political change.

Much of this shift had to do with disease. For most of those 5,000 years, big cities functioned as "population sumps," to borrow the phrase of the historian William H. McNeill: They soaked up large numbers of rural people, held them for a few years, and promptly killed them, usually before they could reproduce or settle in any meaningful way. Cities, in the long centuries before most humans had developed immunity, sanitation, or medicine, were great pools of untreatable, lethal "diseases of civilization," such as smallpox, measles, and the mumps, infections that can be spread only by human-to-human contact in densely populated communities. These were joined, every few decades, by catastrophic outbreaks of epidemic diseases like bubonic plague. In every major city, deaths outnumbered births, and childhood mortality was especially high: The odds of surviving to adulthood in early modern cities were rarely better than even.

As a result, European cities as of the middle of the eighteenth century were growing by only 0.2 percent each year. The total population of western Europe in 1750 was only slightly more than it had been in 1345, before the plague first struck, and many Italian cities had not seen any population increase since Roman times. London in the eighteenth century was so lethal that it required an average of 6,000 rural migrants a year just to maintain its population of 600,000.[3] Cities, like armies, destroyed people almost as fast as they could take them in.

In the last half of the eighteenth century, and especially after 1780 or so, the dynamics began to change. In London, baptisms outnumbered burials for the first time in 1790, a trend that began accelerating dramatically after 1801.[4] Other European cities soon followed. In large part, this change came about because the tightening web of global commerce and communication had created a homogenous human pool of immunity across Europe and much of Asia, rendering many formerly lethal epidemic diseases endemic (that is, turning them into mere childhood diseases). This new immunity unleashed an unprecedented population boom—aided by, among other factors, younger marriages and more nourishing crops. In Europe and China, the rate of population increase grew between fivefold and sevenfold after 1750. Europe's population grew from 118 million in 1700 to 187 million in 1801 and would double again in the next century.

Most of those tens of millions of extra Europeans were peasants, as more than 90 percent of Europeans remained rural well into the nineteenth century. But the land couldn't support this expanded population. In places where inherited peasant land was divided among sons, as was the case in western and southwestern German states, the plots soon became unsustainably small, unable to supply even a single family's nutritional needs (as is the case in central India today); the ruined farmers were driven into the city. Elsewhere, younger offspring were simply forced to hit the road. "The surge of population growth that set in after 1750 thus put enormous and all but insupportable strain on village communities," McNeill observes. "Too many extra hands as they came of age had nowhere to go. Towns soon became desperately overcrowded by immigrants seeking a livelihood on the margins of urban society, and in the villages all suitable land was already taken up. It was against this background that the French Revolution broke out."[5]

The Revolution—or, at least, the specific events that propelled it forward—took place within a new sort of urban space, one that had not existed as such in previous generations. Populated with recent rural arrivals, it was a low-rent district offering a complex web of mutual-help circles, often organized around place of origin and profession. The historian Olwen Hufton provides an eloquent description of this new European site of rural arrival:

> Each town and city had its streets or entire *quartiers* gradually taken
> over and ultimately swamped by [rural] immigrants and their
> families and contacts. They were invariably the most derelict, dank,
> ill-lit and ill-provided for in the way of water supplies, areas about
> which public authorities demonstrated the least concern, but where
> lodgings could be cheaply found . . . These centers usually included
> important churches, cathedrals, and convents, for they were the
> oldest sections, mediaeval slums which were infested with rats and
> lice . . . yet their location meant that the immigrant was strategi-
> cally placed near the ports, docks, warehouses and near important
> arteries to public buildings. If he had to beg his living, what better
> place to command than the approach to the cathedral or the doors
> to convents? Many of the keepers of the *garnis* were his compatriots
> who had made out in the city; perhaps he could even expect a little
> credit . . . he had sisters and cousins who were urban *servantes*,
> brothers, uncles, cousins, friends who were *valets* and *domestiques*,
> and these lived in the prosperous sectors. If he sought a casual job
> on the streets or docks as *portefaix*, water-carrier, or errand goer, he
> needed to know where to go for jobs.[6]

France, by far the most populated and advanced country in Europe in the eighteenth century, was the first to experience a full-fledged arrival city. Paris in 1789 had an official population of 524,000, but a grave famine that year in the countryside had expanded that number to as many as 700,000, as tens of thousands of peasant women and men flooded into the city in search of cash incomes. Jacques Necker, the revolutionary finance minister, described a central city that today sounds strikingly like the Chinese cities of the early twenty-first century. Its occupants, he wrote at the time, were "the great 'floating' population of the hotels and furnished lodgings . . . many thousands of villagers from the surrounding countryside, driven by economic necessity, sought refuge within the walls of the capital."[7]

On the morning of 14 July 1789, most of these people awoke in alarmingly crowded quarters in the historic center of Paris, many of them having slept 15 or 20 to a room, only to vacate their *garni* beds for the day-shift sleepers; many had eaten nothing the previous day, because of spiraling bread prices, and had picked their way through two days of riots and looting. They were packed into slum dwellings in the Île de la Cité and the area around the Hôtel de Ville and Les Halles, and in a fast-growing arrival city in the Faubourgs, the dense and smoky neighborhoods just beyond the old walls. The Faubourg Saint-Antoine, home to tanneries and workshops, was the most volatile and densely populated; it also happened to sit directly behind the Bastille prison. Most of the men and women living here would have made daily excursions to the Place de Grève, a public square at the center of the Parisian arrival city, which, as well as being the site of executions, served as an open-air job fair for all manner of trades and domestic occupations.* Most, that day, would have found no work, the building boom that had expanded the arrival city in the previous decade having come crashing to a halt. In previous years, they would have returned to their villages at such news, but famine had made them desperate, and they lingered in Paris, listless and angry.

The Paris crowds who formed on the fourteenth and stormed the Bastille and sacked the Hôtel de Ville were almost entirely these people of the arrival city. A detailed examination of the arrest records

---

* The expression *faire la grève* emerged from this square; at first, it meant "to be unemployed," while today it means "to be on strike."

by the historian George Rudé led him to conclude that "the men and women who burned down the *barrières* were mainly drawn from the *menu peuple* living in the *faubourgs* on the outskirts of the capital"—in other words, the core residents of the largest arrival city in Paris, people with one foot still in the village. Of the 635 people captured by police during the storming of the Bastille, at least 400 "were of provincial extraction" and a significant portion were listed as being unemployed. These rural migrants were the original *sans-culottes*; the Revolution, first and above all, was an uprising of the arrival city.[8] And in the months that followed, the French Revolution continued to be an event of the arrival city. "The Paris crowds that propelled the revolution in its early days," one observer noted, "drew much of their fighting manpower from a floating population of recent migrants from the countryside."[9] It was these *sans-culottes* of the arrival city who, in 1793, propelled the Jacobins into power and further amplified the Revolution.

Yet, while the village arrivals were the reagents of the Revolution, they were never permitted to become its beneficiaries. During the next decade and a half of history-altering foment, absolutely nothing would be done to improve the conditions or standing of these urban arrivals (except counterproductive moves, such as fixing bread prices), or the nature and design of their neighborhoods. Instead, the French Revolution focused its attentions on keeping peasants in the village and making sure they stayed peasants. On the night of 4 August 1789, the Estates-General became the first European government to abolish feudalism formally in a set of decrees that limited the power of the nobility and clergy to control access to rural land, broke up the great landholdings, and, through a process of parcelization, gave peasants ownership of their plots, in theory at least. But there were few sources of rural investment. In many regions, intergenerational land division led to tiny plots unsuited to commercial farming. This was good for the idyllic image of the French peasant, but its humanitarian consequences were terrible. Thatched roofs may be picturesque, but life beneath them is short, hard, disease-ridden, and prone to bouts of starvation. This, in turn, led the peasants to accumulate debt or become dependent on systems very similar to feudalism. In practice, this singular focus on the countryside virtually guaranteed that the next century would be marked by a messy urbanization dominated by a febrile and neglected arrival city and an impoverished countryside.

Worst of all, the French farm economy was incapable of providing enough food to supply the city all the time. Even at the best of times, bread remained much more expensive in Paris than in London— workers in Paris spent 50 to 60 percent of their earnings on bread; in London, 35 to 40 percent. In Paris, food riots were frequent throughout the period, while in countries with more commercialized systems of agriculture they were largely unknown.[10] This is at least a partial explanation of France's famous lack of stability: Mass starvations and bread-price shocks preceded the 1848 revolution (which was almost entirely an arrival-city event), the July revolution of 1830, and the rise of the Commune in 1871 (which was launched in the arrival city of Montmartre). France's use of peasant parcelization, rather than urban reform, won a certain sort of rural stability, but its cost was a perilous loss of economic and political stability.

THE URBANIZING SHOCK OF ENCLOSURE

Elsewhere in Europe, an equally profound transformation was having an effect as dramatic as the French Revolution. In the Low Countries, in Scandinavia, in the German states, and, especially, in England and Wales, farmers were learning to intensify their yields and turn agriculture into a high-employment business through a set of innovations known as high farming. Beginning as early as the sixteenth century, but transformed into an almost universal practice in England and northwestern Europe between 1750 and 1870, farming became a high-productivity business by means of several innovations: large-scale drainage, irrigation, and use of fertilizers; new technology, such

as steel tills, seed drills, and threshers; better animal feed and selective breeding; crop rotation, buoyed by new fallow and fodder crops;
and high-yield food crops, like potatoes, turnips, and sugar beets.

In many ways the perfect complement to Europe's population
boom, high farming required far more labor per hectare, sometimes
by a factor of three, and therefore increased rural employment; it
also produced many times more food, ending the Malthusian trap
in which the land had seemed insufficient to support a growing
population and making its host countries far less vulnerable to food
shortages and famines. The extremely fast growth of urban populations created large and lucrative markets for cash crops and provided
a powerful incentive for landowners to shift to intensive commercial
farming.

High farming required common grazing and field lands to be
cleared, unified into sufficiently large holdings, and enclosed. The
lives of its inhabitants—the peasants, rural laborers, and landless
casual workers and vagrants—were disrupted dramatically and
sometimes tragically. Economic studies have shown that many
improved their lot, especially the better-off peasants who were able
to gain title to their land and become high-intensity farmers and
employers.[11] Viewed from the distance of the present, the sudden
shift to commercial agriculture across much of Europe looks like a
net gain. "Enclosure meant more food for the growing population,
more land under cultivation and, on balance, more employment in
the countryside; and enclosed farms provided the framework for
the new advances of the nineteenth century," one important historical study concluded.[12]

But this instant end to subsistence-level peasant farming, combined with the era's fertility boom, created a surplus population of
tens of millions who abandoned the countryside—by choice or by
decree—and sought work in cities, either in their own country or
across the Atlantic. In some cases, this was a flight of desperation. It
caused a massive shift from rural poverty to urban poverty, with
varied results.

Nothing anywhere in the West quite approached the horror or inhumanity of Ireland's transition from peasant agriculture, enacted by colonial laws that were often savage. Peasants who had been expelled from land of more than a quarter acre, for instance, were banned from receiving any assistance, even the workhouse. This rural restructuring by force, which never managed to produce a viable system of commercial agriculture (Ireland remained a net importer of food), compounded the potato famine of 1845–49, during which at least a million people died of starvation or disease and another million fled, without any prospects for work, into the arrival cities of England and North America, a loss of a quarter of the population. The Irish soon made up a significant part of the arrival-city populations of Manchester, Liverpool, Bradford, London, New York City, Chicago, and Toronto.

So sudden and dramatic was this migration that it briefly turned the arrival city into the hopeless slum of its popular image. During several periods in the first half of the nineteenth century, the influx of displaced rural families was large enough to force urban wages down to inhumane levels. Worse, in the century's earliest decades, the employees of the mills of northern England were largely children and women, who could be paid even less. The open sewers beneath floors and in uncovered gutters running behind the back-to-back houses were a great source of infection, so that western European arrival cities experienced three or four major cholera epidemics between 1830 and 1860, killing millions of people. Only the sanitary, housing, and humanitarian reforms of the second half of the nineteenth century ended this urban suffering.

Would Europe have been better off if other countries had followed the lead of France and ensured the right of peasants to stay on their subsistence farms? Or would the British approach of a sudden, sharp transition to commercial agriculture and urbanization have produced a higher standard of living in the peasant-dominated countries of western and southern Europe? This is more than a matter of speculative history, since it is precisely the question being asked by regional and national governments today in Asia, Africa, and South America.

One thing that did sharply distinguish the British and French approaches was the divergence between rural and urban life. In France, peasants and urbanites grew further and further apart in cultural and economic terms, whereas in Britain they tended to converge. In the 1860s, the French economist Léonce Guilhaud de Lavergne noted that in Britain rural and urban salaries were almost exactly the same, with no discernible difference "between the Londoner's way of life and that of the Cumberland man."[13]

On the eve of the First World War, agriculture employed 41 percent of French workers and generated 35 percent of France's national income; in Britain, 8 percent of the workforce was employed on the land, accounting for only 5 percent of gross domestic product. Virtually the entire rural population of England and Wales was absorbed into the arrival cities of London, Manchester, Liverpool, Bradford, Birmingham, Sheffield, and other industrial centers during this century. By the end of the great European migration in 1914, average British incomes—extending to workers in arrival-city slums— were between 15 and 25 percent higher than those in France, measured by purchasing power, although France had comparable levels of health, literacy, and education.[14] It is extraordinary that throughout this period Britain's population was growing at two to three times that of France, and yet somehow this demographic assault did not produce any social strains profound enough to threaten the integrity of the state. Certainly, there was considerable political upheaval in Britain throughout the first half of this period, resulting in confrontations, such as the Peterloo Massacre, and governments whose treatment of the arrival-city populations was, at best, indifferent and, at worst, savage and inhumane. Yet the new urbanites did not starve, and they did not, in general, feel stuck forever. Arrival was a viable possibility, so violence was rarely a consideration.

The nature of rural life had a direct and dramatic effect on the political character of the arrival city. If its residents arrived only when thrust out of their villages by rural food emergencies, then immediately suffered from the food-price shocks and urban unemployment resulting from those emergencies, then they tended to take action. To the revolutionaries of the time, this action was often mistaken for something else. This is vividly evident in Karl Marx's self-exculpatory masterpiece *The Eighteenth Brumaire of Louis Bonaparte*, in which he attempts to explain why the 1848 uprisings in Paris had failed to turn into the permanent socialist transformation he had predicted. He places the blame squarely on the peasants and the rural-born residents of the Parisian arrival city. The latter he dismisses as a consciousness-lacking lumpenproletariat, unable to understand their political place the way a city-born worker could. Much like the novelists of the time, he had failed to notice that the village arrival, not the urban worker, had become the driving force in society.[15]

THE GREAT AGE OF THE EUROPEAN ARRIVAL CITY

By the middle of the nineteenth century, Europe's cities had become unrecognizable to those monarchs and planners who had attempted to give them shape, order, walls, and boulevards. All of that grandeur had been swamped and rendered minuscule amid the great arrival cities that choked their inner quarters and engorged their outskirts, turning the official districts and their monumental buildings into mere asterisks.

The elegant plan of Berlin, laid out in the eighteenth century in neat grids of boulevards by the planners of the Hohenzollern court, was quickly overwhelmed by the rural tides, its planners humiliated by an unmanageable pace of population growth—a leap from 197,000 people in 1816 to 431,000 in 1841, and then twice as many again in 1871, and almost two million at the dawn of the First World War. The German countryside was cleared of peasants in the nineteenth century, following England's enclosures by almost a century at an even more rapid pace. With the exception of a few monumental quarters in the very center, it seemed as if Berlin was all arrival city: In 1885, 81 percent of men employed in food supply, 83.5 percent of builders, and over 85 percent of those in transport had been born in villages. They had all moved, by choice or force, into a city that found itself unable to broaden its physical expanse, forcing a huge number of people into a limited area. By the last quarter of the century, Berlin was the most densely populated city in the world.

The arrival city in Berlin was based on a grim form of tenement housing erected at great speed to fill accommodation needs around the edges of Vienna, Warsaw, Prague, and St. Petersburg. Such buildings were, and still are, known as *Mietskasernen*, described by the architectural historian Joseph Rykwert as grim human warehouses: "block-size buildings, often five to seven stories high, with several interior courtyards to act as light-wells, though they were usually too narrow to admit much light . . . As their name implied, they were built to maximize rents, even if their exteriors were often stuccoed and moulded to maintain the more or less civilized patination of city streets."[16]

If the arrival cities of central Europe were packing impossible numbers of people into airless, inhumane vertical stacks within a dense, depressing grid, those of western Europe and England, far larger in scale, often seemed to evade order and reason altogether, throwing people into endless, seemingly arbitrary rows of shacks that barely qualified as housing, stretching across fields on the edge of town, filling derelict and unused properties near the mills and factories just outside the center.

Although the squalor of the arrival cities of London and Paris attracted literary fame, the most startling of all might have been the vast expanse of shantytown housing that overtook Barcelona. This was an urban emergency on an impossible scale, for Catalonia, unlike any other place on the Iberian peninsula in the nineteenth century, had industrialized on a large scale; the wages paid in its factories were double those in Madrid, and the displaced peasants of Spain and southern France, their land overwhelmed by population growth and frequent famine, headed there in great numbers. Between the mid-eighteenth century and 1854, Barcelona's population grew from 35,000 to 175,000, inside a very limited area defined by the old city walls. A majority of its residents wound up living in the most dire sort of unplanned slums, prone to disease outbreaks and cholera epidemics in what was considered the most unsanitary city in Europe. Even more so than Paris, the arrival city of Barcelona, neglected by all levels of government, became the site of violent unrest, with a century-long sequence of uprisings, revolutions, and riots that were perhaps the worst in Europe. Because of this crisis, and because of the particular genius of the urban planner Ildefons Cerdà, Barcelona became one of the first cities to embrace the arrival city in its urban plans. Cerdà's famous extension of the city, the Eixample, provided not only sanitation but the possibility of a toehold of ownership in the city for a generation of rural arrivals. It was certainly not sufficient to accommodate the masses who kept arriving through the early twentieth century, which was rife with arrival-city explosions, but it did set an example for cities in the future.

HOW THE NINETEENTH CENTURY WAS BUILT
London

Five years before Jeanne Bouvier made her trip from the Rhone valley to Paris, a similar journey, under equally urgent and traumatic circumstances, was made by two peasant tenant farmers from a thatched-roof village in southeastern England. In 1874, amid the final sweep of enclosure acts, a young married couple felicitously named Will and Lucy Luck, found themselves evicted from their cottage. They packed their few possessions onto their backs and walked the 50 kilometers from Luton to the fast-expanding outskirts of London.

They ended up in the arrival city that had spread outward from the edge of the Regent's Canal near Paddington Station during the previous decade; its long rows of houses had mainly been built by speculative developers hoping for buyers among the lower middle classes moving outward from the City of London along the new tramlines. Such people simply didn't exist in great enough numbers to fill the suburbs, especially in the long economic depression that had begun a year before the Lucks came to London. As developers would learn throughout the century, the larger human flood is not outward from the city but inward from the fields. Their neighborhood, like much of London's ballooning periphery, became an arrival-city slum.

The Lucks found themselves surrounded by former tradesmen, farmers, and rural workers from villages near theirs in Bedfordshire, drawing them into the tight social networks that led to employment. Lucy soon found work as a straw plaiter in one of the many hat shops in their district; Will's equine skills led to solid work as a horse-keeper for the railway companies. They both made many times more money than they would have been able to earn in the village and eventually established a comfortable life in the secure reaches of the middle classes.[17]

Millions of people from across Britain were following the Lucks's path to London, in what, until the late twentieth century, was history's largest rural-to-urban migration. London was by far the largest city in the world, and at almost any time in the nineteenth century at least 40 percent of its citizens were born outside the city. By 1901, the metropolis contained a startling 1.3 million rural arrivals, up from 750,000 only 50 years earlier, with another 50,000 or so arriving from the country each year throughout the last half of the nineteenth century. The largest group were women: In 1881, London had 1,312 women for every thousand men, mainly because so many more women came from the country to enter domestic service.

Nineteenth-century London was infamous for its eastern and southern slums—densely packed rookeries of dark, stinking houses with open sewage beneath the floors and no source of fresh air, rented by absentee landlords at per-foot rates that were higher than those in Mayfair, with dismal sanitary conditions that led to frequent cholera outbreaks and rates of violent crime and child labor, which transformed them into emblems of Dickensian fiction and radical social reform.

But these were not London's arrival cities. The historian Jerry White's careful study of population statistics has revealed that the desperate poor of London were not the same people as the rural arrivals of London. "It was not in central London that newcomers took root," he writes. "Provincial-born Londoners seemed most comfortable at the edge of London, that great new belt of the Victorian metropolis emerging from 1840 to 1880. The old troubled central area, inherited from the eighteenth century, was left to the cockney. Increasingly so as the century wore on."[18] The dispossessed were not migrants. Bethnal Green, widely considered the worst slum area in East End London, had the highest proportion of London-born residents in the entire city: 83.5 percent in 1881. "Poverty and distress is home-made," the great demographer Charles Booth wrote at the time, "and not imported from outside." Of course, given the huge influx, it is statistically likely that virtually every native-born working-class Londoner in the nineteenth century, including the destitute, had at least one parent who had arrived from the village. It is probably best to describe these terrible East End and South London neighborhoods as a sort of economic flypaper, trapping those who had fallen afoul of the tough upward scramble of the arrival city proper.

London's great arrival cities took shape instead on the periphery, around the places where rural migrants disembarked. In the first half of the century, these enclaves were built by seasonal laborers on the semi-rural edges. The roads to London, when seasons changed, would be packed with rural tradesmen: brickboys from Devon, shipbuilders from the east coast, and women, domestic servants, from virtually everywhere. There was also a constant back-and-forth flow of labor to the cattle-sales settlements in Islington and Holloway and the market-farming enclaves in Chelsea and Fulham. Typically, farm women from Shropshire would walk to Fulham, find work on farms there, carry their produce to Covent Garden every day, and then walk back to Shropshire at the end of the season. This circular path continued up to the end of the 1860s, when better conditions and transportation links allowed many of them to settle and form families in Fulham. Hackney and Bethnal Green served a similar function for villagers from the east. The Irish made similar migrations, in which single men worked on the potato and wheat farms of London's outskirts, remitting money back to Ireland in large sums and slowly drifting into the city, forming the great Irish arrival-city enclaves of St. Giles and Whitechapel. The famine sent tens of thousands of Irish flooding into London in the 1840s and 1850s, into overcrowded rooming houses in failed arrival cities around the metropolis, giving them a reputation for destitution and insalubrious living. But the economy bailed them out: By the 1880s, the Irish were, by and large, a well-integrated part of London life.

In the second half of the century, the London arrival city formed, at a scale never seen before, around the end-of-line railway stations. Migrants from Wales and Cornwall settled around Paddington, joined by rural laborers who walked in from closer villages. The very poorest of them, those driven out of the countryside by desperation, tended to settle in the rough enclaves of North Kensington and Notting Dale, a former pig-farming area, which became an infamous slum. They were joined by navvies from the railway and destitute inner-city slum-dwellers who had been forced out by redevelopment. Those from the north and Scotland, as well as a considerable population of Irish, made the flight into Camden, settling in rooming houses expanding outward from Euston, St. Pancras, and King's Cross, in some cases joining the huge crews that built those stations. Essex villagers arrived in the city and expanded outward, the poor laborers settling around the docks, the more prosperous artisans and craftsmen finding homes in the aspirational rural-migrant enclaves of Leyton, West Ham, and Walthamstow, where they were joined by the clerks and office workers of the lower middle class moving outward from the city. Those from Kent wound up around Deptford and Greenwich. A similar stratum of arrival formed in the south, creating poorer and less poor arrival cities around Lambeth and Southwark.

Many of the arrival-city slums of London were built by property-development corporations and were intended to be neat suburbs for the emerging lower-middle classes, but a speculative real-estate bubble and a gross overestimation of the numbers of clerks able to buy homes meant that many became village-migrant enclaves as soon as they were built. Places like Lisson Grove, in Marylebone, or Portland Town, northwest of Regent's Park, or North Kensington all turned straightaway into rooming-house slums. Some streets in those suburbs fell to the point of being counted among the most disreputable places in London. Campbell Road, Holloway, or Sultan Street, Camberwell, or Litcham Street, Kentish Town, all became synonyms for crime and violence, despite having been built by developers and promoted in lavish advertising campaigns.

But London also had its self-built shantytowns in the outskirts. At various points in the nineteenth century, places like Camberwell, Deptford, and Holloway were home to large squatter enclaves of very poor rural arrivals (mixed with inner city castoffs). And, while social mobility remained a visible and concrete goal for most migrants, rural–urban migration was by no means always an ascent to better living standards. A significant number of the thousands of abandoned children who roamed the streets of London, according to the Victorian reformer Thomas Barnardo, were "victims of the family dislocation involved in mass migration to London."[19] At least half of all prostitutes at any time were born outside London. As everywhere, the move to a city almost always meant an improvement in livelihood—but one that was not without risk.

London in the latter half of the nineteenth century became famous for the wide range of public-housing schemes developed by philanthropic and government bodies. These were often admirable. But they also had little relationship to the actual needs of the people flooding into London, and they often made matters worse. First of all, there never was very much of it. By 1905, after half a century of building, London's nine public-housing companies and trusts had managed to house only 123,000 people "or little more than the population increase of Greater London for a year and a half."[20] And the philanthropic housing tended to be located where the arrival cities weren't: Whereas more than 8 percent of Westminster residents were housed in public-housing blocks, only about 2 percent of those in the East End were. As the geographer Richard Dennis has noted, social housing actually amplified the spatial segregation of London by class—a pattern that seemed to be repeated across Europe.[21] Urban planning, in London as in Paris, had little effect on the success of the arrival city.

ARRIVAL WHERE?

The first great wave of rural-to-urban migration was not anticipated, comprehended, or managed by any government; in fact, by the time its 125-year course had run, it had overwhelmed and destroyed a great many governments and created a number of new ones, just as the final wave of migration is doing today.

The European arrival city remains a source of great controversy. Was it a perfect engine of advancement, a "land of boundless opportunity," as the Victorian booster Samuel Smiles wrote, where men of "no particular class nor rank" can "come alike from colleges, workshops and farmhouses—from the huts of the poor and the mansions of the rich," and turn themselves into "great men of science, literature and art?"[22] Or was it a place where millions of people, cruelly and unjustly expelled from the peaceful certainties of peasant life, were thrust into generations of filth, disease, proletarian servitude, and consumerism? The latter view is forcefully argued not just in

Dickens and in Friedrich Engels but in that masterpiece of historical narrative, E. P. Thompson's *The Making of the English Working Class*, which forcefully casts the entire era as tragedy.

The first view is cruelly deaf to the terrible struggles and punishments of the poor. But the second is equally deaf to their motives, for any detailed study of the nineteenth-century city reveals that most of its newly arrived inhabitants were not at all passive victims and that the social mechanisms of the arrival city most often functioned as a great collective instrument for raising living standards above the levels of perpetual rural poverty, if not higher.

It is now possible to address this question with facts, for the past two decades have seen a revolution in the techniques of analyzing social mobility—both intergenerational mobility (did you end up better or worse off than your parents?) and intragenerational mobility (did you end up better or worse off than you were born?). The most comprehensive and well-documented study of the mobility question to date, conducted by the British social historian Andrew Miles, found that the arrival city changed its nature as the century went on. After mid-century, there was a change: Social barriers became more and more permeable, and both sorts of mobility increased throughout the century's final decades.

A man's chances of escaping the income category of his birth rose from one in three at the beginning of the nineteenth century to one in two at the end. By that time, between a quarter and a third of the British middle class and an eighth of the higher professional and managerial classes comprised people who had been born in the lower classes, most of whom had presumably used the arrival cities of London and Manchester as their gateways to advancement—a higher level of mobility, by Miles's measurement, than existed at the end of the twentieth century.

There were limits to this mobility. While a majority of poor people entering the city were able to rise within a generation from unskilled working-poor status to the far more comfortable and stable skilled-worker or tradesman status, only 5 percent of working-class men at the beginning of the twentieth century were able to obtain middle-class status.* Much of this has to do with property owner-ship. In nineteenth-century Europe, it was almost unthinkable for even the most elevated members of the working class to purchase the land beneath their feet. Thus, comfortable-artisan living was often the highest attainable level for a rural arrival.[23]

It was the chaotic, mercantile arrival city, not the well-ordered rural village or regional town, that made this upward mobility pos-sible. At some point in mid-century, the arrival city turned from a trap door into an escape hatch. The economic historian Jason Long has found that between 1851 and 1901, in England and Wales, half of all sons ended up in different classes than their fathers and that the rate of upward mobility was 40 percent greater than that of downward mobility.[24]

But, contrary to Smiles, this was no simple matter of self-help and individual guile. The years of increasing social mobility, in fact, also happen to be the years during which public education, child-labor laws, hygiene and housing reforms, and rudimentary social welfare were introduced, and numerous studies have found that the two trends tracked one another. Indeed, during that first great human migration, you could describe two eras of the arrival city: the one before 1848, when urban life was tempting but the odds of failure were no better than even, and the one after 1848, when a better life, for your children, if not yourself, was more likely than not.

The year 1848 marks a significant fulcrum point. After the Europe-wide wave of revolutions and uprisings that year, which seriously threatened the viability of the state and the economic order, the arrival city became a focus of official attention for the first time in history. The reforms didn't happen quickly, and they were often ineffective, but they did begin to change the hopes of the poor. It was in 1848 that the first English Public Health Act was enacted,

---

* Those 5 percent of escapees from the working class were able to make up 33 to 50 percent of the middle class because the middle class was so much smaller in number.

that child labor was banned, and that the first real public-housing development was proposed. None of these reforms would really be comprehensive or properly funded for decades, but they began having a gradual and noticeable effect on social mobility. A number of recent studies, drawing on large sets of records, have found that such reforms served to block the transmission of poverty and the creation of permanent pauperism and that social mobility increased as public education and social-welfare policies were introduced.[25] It was this shift to state involvement, more than anything else, that transformed the nineteenth-century arrival city. Before 1848, it was a destitute place; in the second half of the century, with government investment and outside attention, it became a great engine for progress and growth.

THE TRANSATLANTIC ARRIVAL

If you wanted guaranteed social mobility, you had to cross the Atlantic. The difference was great. If the *fin-de-siècle* European arrival city gave the poor villager a passing chance of securing a better life, in the New World it was almost certain. Throughout the nineteenth century, North America offered stunning levels of upward mobility. One study found that, in the United States, 81 percent of sons of unskilled laborers moved up into higher occupations, compared with only 53 percent of British sons, and downward mobility was also lower.[26]

This was well known to people in even the most remote rural villages of Europe, and the resulting response created the largest international migration in human history. Between 1800 and the First World War, about 50 million Europeans left the continent permanently for a new home, and as many as 65 million emigrated for part of their lives. By the end of the nineteenth century, fully 20 percent of Europeans had moved to the Americas, Australia, or South Africa. More than half of those migrants wound up in the United States.

And, during the key period between 1846 and 1890, almost half of them came from Britain and Ireland.

It was overwhelmingly a rural-to-urban migration. The Europeans who came to the United States, Canada, Australia, and New Zealand did not generally move first to a metropolis within their own country; they moved straight from the village to the New World, usually following paths laid by neighbors and friends. By the end of the century, 80 percent of migrants had a relative waiting for them. And, as the historian Leslie Page Moch has chronicled, it wasn't just villages that moved across the ocean but the most remote and deprived villages: "In Italy, they were the provinces around the Alps to the north and east of Milan and around the southern Apennines. The people most likely to leave Spain and Portugal were from their Atlantic islands (Canaries and Azores) and from the mountainous northwest corner of the Iberian peninsula . . . Scandinavian emigrants most likely came from the mountains of south-central Norway and south-central Sweden, Oland Island, and the Danish Islands of Bornholm and Lolland-Falster. The Scottish highlands sent dis-proportionate numbers abroad early in the century." People from such remote locations were isolated from information about urban jobs in their own countries; it made just as much sense to migrate overseas.[27]

Records show that the steep rise in emigration rates in most European countries was driven largely by the demographic and economic changes in the countryside, which also drove people to the cities of their own countries. Indeed, when labor shortages began to appear in the cities of Europe, emigration rates to the New World tended to decline, as peasants decided it was more economical to move to their own nation's arrival cities. These were not ignorant and desperate peasants blindly seeking opportunity; overwhelmingly, they were well-informed people making a calculated move from a rural to an urban life.[28]

And, almost always, it was an urban life they were seeking. While a small minority migrated from European farms to the larger and more fertile plots in the New World (where mechanical cultivation made farming a much more profitable endeavor), most wanted to give up farming altogether. In 1880, only 10 percent of foreign immigrants to the United States were living in rural areas.

HIDDEN ARRIVALS
Toronto and Chicago

In 1905, Joseph Thorne decided he'd had enough of the cockney slums of Bermondsey, South London, where he and his wife seem to have wound up after falling afoul of London's arrival cities, and arranged passage to Canada under a contract that indentured him to a year's farm labor. He sent most of his income home. He then worked in downtown Toronto for a year, saving a small pocketful of money, which he used to buy a sliver of land in the wastelands beyond the city limits—in an ungoverned and unmapped area known as Silverthorn, which was unknown to Toronto officials but teeming with clandestine settlement. He got himself a shovel, dug a hole in the ground, covered it with tin sheeting, and called it home. A few months later, his wife and five children arrived from London, and he scrounged enough wood and cardboard to build a two-room dirt-floor shack.

All around him, spanning the horizon, were similar shacks, lean-tos, and hovels, all built by their owners, all recent arrivals from Europe. This thick ring of shantytown development, resembling in many ways the peripheral slums of Asia today, surrounded and overwhelmed Toronto. When we think of the North American arrival city, we tend to imagine the tenement blocks of New York's Lower East Side. In reality, European villagers were just as likely to enter the city by building their own unregulated settlements on the outskirts.

The Royles, neighbors of the Thornes, arrived just before the First World War from a rural village with almost nothing to their name, bought a load of second-hand lumber from a job lot on a demolition site, hauled it out by horse and wagon, and used it to build a two-room shack. Wilf Royle, who spent his childhood in this fast-expanding settlement, described the scene around him: "It was quite a while before there were sewers of any kind and floods were notorious. The traditional outhouse was the only sanitation and everybody had one. There was no garbage collection in those days . . . people got rid of their garbage the best way they could. Some burned it, some buried it and some just left it hanging around."[29]

This shack-town slum, making up much of what is today a central-Toronto district known as York, was not an exception. Most of the eastern, northern, and western outskirts of the city were thickly encrusted with these self-built centers on mud roads without piped water or sewage; they covered the neighborhoods known today as Etobicoke, York, the Junction, North York, East York, Davenport, Broadview, and Coxwell. Such shack towns propelled the growth of Toronto in the decades before the Great Depression. And in many other North American cities, arrival cities materialized without permission in this Mumbai-style accretion of owner-built shack housing.

We owe this new understanding of the informality of the North American arrival city to the Canadian geographer Richard Harris, whose study *Unplanned Suburbs* scrutinizes property records to reveal that self-built peripheral housing of this sort represented at least a third of all housing in Toronto at the time of the First World War—a figure that later scholars have estimated at as much as half of Toronto's pre-Depression housing.[30] Such settlements remained a prominent but rarely mentioned feature of urban life until the late 1920s, when the city annexed these communities, paved them, installed services, and rebuilt most of them in standard styles.

In many places across North America, millions of formerly rural Europeans (and a large number of formerly rural black Americans making their own great migration) were repeating this classic approach to settlement. While Toronto had the most dramatic number of such shantytowns, they were also major features in the blue-collar outskirts of Chicago, Milwaukee, Detroit, and, later, Los Angeles, with unapproved, owner-built shack housing constituting as much as a third of new construction in those cities. They were a major part of Chicago's periphery in the decades before the Depression, defining then-unincorporated neighborhoods, such as Stone Park, Oak Forest, Burnside, Robbins, large parts of Gary, Hegewisch, Garfield Ridge, and Blue Island, and pockets throughout the west and southwest.[31]

The outstanding feature of these settlements, aside from their spontaneous form and their haphazard appearance, was that virtually all of their residents owned the land their shacks stood on. Though the land had often been subdivided without approval by speculators who had bought plots of farmland or uncleared forest and sold slivers for perhaps $200 apiece, governments and banks usually recognized the title deeds. As we've seen throughout the developing world, land ownership offers a clear path to social stability and often to middle-class vitality, as long as governments are willing to help.

What made North America in the late nineteenth and early twentieth century so different from Europe—and so different from North America today—was the scale of home ownership among the newly arrived poor. Blue-collar workers, in both Canada and the United States (and very likely in Australia), had rates of home ownership that were far higher than those of any other social class. As the historian Elaine Lewinnek has shown, one-quarter of all Chicagoans owned their own homes between 1870 and 1920, a rate that rose to nearly 50 percent in the city's poorer neighborhoods. The drive to save and scrounge earnings, however small, to buy a plot of land or put a down payment on a small home was almost a religion among the rural-immigrant working classes of the time. Similar rates of lower-income home ownership have been chronicled in Boston, Detroit, New Haven, and Toronto. And the numbers were also surprisingly high among blacks and women.[32]

The result was an extremely high rate of upward social mobility—a trend that ended only in the second half of the twentieth century, when cities became more zoned and regulated, barriers to home ownership and property financing became more difficult, and the pathways from lower- to middle-class status came to be defined by much-harder-to-obtain forms of higher education and loan capital.

FAREWELL TO ALL THAT

Back in Europe, the industrialization of farming continued to throw millions of people off the land, in numbers that reached their peak in the early twentieth century, and while the vast majority were absorbed more or less comfortably into the arrival cities of Europe and North America, there continued to be frequent arrival-city failures, especially in the more peripheral parts of the continent. The results were increasingly explosive.

Toward the end of this period, a young man was born in a Balkan farming village; as the second son of nine children, he did not inherit any land, and work near his home could not be found, so he made various failed attempts to enter urban life through the region's disjointed arrival cities, eventually joining a floating population of casual laborers who lived on the edge of urban poverty. The humiliation of this experience, amid the riches of the Austro-Hungarian Empire, radicalized this young man and his milieu. When Gavrilo Princip pulled the trigger that began three decades of war, he was giving violent expression not only to the tortured politics of central Europe but also to the dismal failure of many European governments to comprehend or manage the expansive new communities of former villagers forming within their cities. Like the revolution that began this 125-year transformation, the gunshot that ended it was a product of the arrival city.

By the time the smoke cleared, the world had changed. War, even more conclusively than peace, had served to urbanize the West, and those temporary innovations of the First World War, the passport and immigration control, became permanent features of the nation-state. Those would become the principal elements of migration when, in the decades after the Second World War, the world's newly awakened south and east would begin sending their villagers out to their own arrival cities and those of the West. Though the numbers and distances would give this final migration a scale never seen before, they would follow patterns that ought to seem terribly familiar.

6

THE DEATH AND LIFE OF A GREAT ARRIVAL CITY

Istanbul

After you have awoken at sunrise in your motionless hillside village, walked down the rock-strewn lane into the valley, waited at the side of the lone paved road, and then bumped for long hours along an asphalt path that follows the Silk Road's route to the very westernmost tip of the Asian continent, you find yourself in a place called Harem. It does not offer, as its name might suggest, any kind of alluring sanctuary or fragrant Oriental specter; in fact, Harem is a place of anonymous, unadorned reinforced-concrete modernism and constant noise and bustle, of hasty lunches sold over smoldering wood fires and hucksters shouting their offerings; it is the place, more than any other, where the great transformation of Istanbul, and then of the Turkish nation, has had its origin.

Harem is a bus station. It is here, decades ahead of the rest of the Eastern world, that the great migration has taken place in its most dramatic fashion. And it was here, while most of the world wasn't watching, that the migration built, for the first time, an arrival city that was large and powerful enough to take over a nation. What began at Harem, and exploded over an amazingly short period across Istanbul, offers a foretaste of the transformations, both exciting and threatening, that are about to sweep across half of the world.

If you begin at Harem, you will find the future of the world's cities.

The Harem bus station was erected in the 1950s, when the modern Turkish road system first made it possible for people to move efficiently across the country's expanse. Since then, it has been the main landing point for a constant flood of people arriving, usually with their few possessions in plastic bags, from villages in central and eastern Anatolia. In four decades, these arrivals have increased the city's metropolitan population from under a million in the late 1950s to about 14 million today. Until 1973, when the first bridge was built across the Bosporus, Harem was the last stop on a path that had been the central trunk of the Silk Road; it remains the final destination for many. During the 1980s and early 1990s, half a million villagers a year were settling here, and, even though Istanbul is routinely said to be "full," Harem is still a key point of arrival for the 250,000 or more new residents who add themselves to Istanbul's population every year.

It is here that Istanbul's periphery begins, symbolically and functionally, although Harem itself is physically near the center: if you pause in the middle of its asphalt expanses, as few people do, you have a clear view across the ship-clogged Bosporus to the domes and spires of the Blue Mosque on the city's storied European side. The well-established residents of that older Istanbul are often unaware of this dusty bus terminal's existence, which may help explain why the explosion of the outskirts has given them such an unnerving shock. The Istanbul of literature and legend, the entirety of Byzantium and Constantinople, is today little more than a flash of greenery and historic domes along the banks of the Bosporus, a tiny museum trapped within a dense, uninterrupted crystalline growth of human settlement many times its size.

Given the importance of Harem in modern Turkish history, the station offers little to commend itself—a few low-slung concrete buildings, brash ticket booths run by competing bus companies, vendors selling hot, sesame seed–covered *simit* rolls, piles of duffle bags and cardboard boxes, and bus drivers standing on the concrete, hawking their destinations: "Bilecik, Bozüyük, Eskişehir! Leaving in five minutes, hurry hurry hurry—beautiful Bilecik!" The arrivals stream off the buses day and night, after journeys of up to 20 hours, and depart quickly for parts of Istanbul that do not appear on tourist maps, places that didn't exist 20 years ago, pasture fields transformed overnight into dense thickets of megalopolis.

THE ARRIVALS FIND THEIR PLACE

One evening in the early winter of 1976, a shy, moustached young man named Sabri Koçyigit arrived in Harem. It was not his first visit to Istanbul, as the vicissitudes of his family's tiny, unproductive grain farm in the hilly Sivas region of central Turkey had often forced his father to come to the big city as a seasonal laborer, sometimes with his young son in tow. But this time, at age 31, Sabri was here to stay. He was determined to change things in a lasting way, to make a new home for his young family, and he had vague aspirations of larger, more dramatic changes. He also had no money at all.

In his father's time, an arrival in Harem would lead inevitably to a ferry ride across the Bosporus to Istanbul's European side, a makeshift home in an industrial district, and a tentative place among Turkey's growing army of industrial laborers, some seasonal but most becoming permanent residents. The 1950s were a potent time for Turkey. Half a century before most other poor nations opened their economies, Turkey was feeling the pains and stresses of a fast change from an agricultural to an urban, industrial economy. Prime Minister Adnan Menderes put an aggressive and largely admirable emphasis on ending his country's subsistence, peasant-driven agriculture system, shipping 40,000 tractors into the countryside between 1951 and 1953, subsidizing a national industrial economy, and building a modern highway system to replace the ancient dirt tracks of the Silk Road. It was an impressive success, creating industrial agriculture well ahead of most countries. But Menderes did little to prepare for the flood of peasants abandoning the land for the better prospects of the city. His economy was ready: Turkey's industrial boom needed all the Anatolian laborers it could get. But they had nowhere to live, salaries that were generous by village standards but desperately inadequate in the city, and nothing resembling a welfare state to support them.

So, encouraged by Prime Minister Menderes to develop their own solutions, the new urbanites found their own way of creating shelter. One observer described what they did: "Those working in the factories thought nothing about building houses in the immediate vicinity: one-story, often with a garden for personal use . . . this led to the emergence of settlements which were not produced for a market value, but built by users with their own hands for personal use. This land-taking was by no means legal under applicable law. Nevertheless, it was considered legitimate, and not only by the occupiers."[1]

By 1976, this ad hoc system had become a potent institution. When Sabri arrived, he knew what to do: He spent a few weeks gathering downtown with fellow villagers, like-minded peasants mostly from the Alevi minority that dominates the Sivas region; some, like him, also had Kurdish roots.* They were giddy, hopeful gatherings, full of men and women willing to work hard. Then Sabri turned his back on the European side, got on the road toward Ankara, traveled until the buildings disappeared beyond the horizon, and stopped at a nearly empty, rock-strewn valley. "There was nothing here, and it looked terrible—just trees, rocks, dust, garbage, not even a good path," he recalls. This, Sabri and his fellow rural émigrés decided, would be home.

In the early months of 1977, Sabri did what tens of millions of rural Turks have done. In an unnoticed place on the edge of town, he built a rugged but rudimentary house that was not supposed to

* Alevis, who make up between a fifth and a quarter of the Turkish population, are historically Shiite Muslims (the majority of Turks have Sunni backgrounds). Persecuted by the Ottoman Empire, they moved to the most remote and agriculturally marginal Anatolian villages and thus were among the first to migrate.

exist. Sabri knew what he had become. In the 1950s and '60s, when they started to appear amid Turkey's industrial boom, these build-ings, and the communities they formed, were given a name that was uttered with distaste by the better-off residents of central Istanbul. It combined the word for "night" (*gece*) with the word for "arrived" or "settled" (*kondu*). The *gecekondu* (pronounced "getchy-kondoo") became, for many years, the menace on the frontier, a word that perfectly captured the sense of shock and alarm these "night-arrivals" provoked within the city they had already long since encircled and overwhelmed. As the 1960s wore on, that initial shock evolved into a begrudging, if fearful, acceptance. *Gecekondu* residents happened to be much-needed laborers. They also happened to be voters and potential taxpayers—which would prove important.

"It was just an empty place—bushes, rocks, that was it," Sabri remembers today, sitting at his friend's double-glazed-window shop downstairs from his office, in a place that has become a dense and central part of the urban expanse. In 1977, it was a rubble-strewn, tree-lined deep valley far from the outermost reaches of Istanbul, its twisting dirt roads leading to a meat-processing plant, some stone quarries, and a dump that held all the garbage of Istanbul's Asian side. Most of it looked barren and uninhabitable. Its steep valley walls seemed ill-suited to any kind of housing, there were no water or sewage lines, and the roads were often so rough that you couldn't reach Istanbul itself without riding a tractor. But it possessed a qual-ity that Anatolian peasants had learned, over the previous two de-cades, to value dearly: ambiguous ownership.

Sabri's friends, most of them fellow Alevis from Sivas who'd come to Istanbul months earlier, had found this forlorn valley through the courts. In earlier times, it had been known as the Hekimbaşi Estate, a large plot of idle agricultural land, which, since 1874, had belonged to an Ottoman prince. In 1923, after the Ottoman Empire had col-lapsed and the secularist, modernizing regime of Mustafa Kemal Ataturk turned Turkey into a republic, it became illegal for royalty to own land, and the estate became the property of Turkey's Ministry of the Treasury. Starting in the 1940s, the prince's descendants launched a series of lawsuits that were not to be settled until the 1990s, and the descendants tried to sell plots of the land to various private owners to pay for those lawsuits, leading to even more court conflicts over their right to do so. Nominally government land, it was, like much of the emptiness surrounding Istanbul at the time, legally beyond any official use.[2]

"This place was the very edge of Istanbul. There was nothing here. It was the outskirts. It wasn't even the edge: there were fields between here and the edge of the city," Şükrü Aslan, the author of a history of this neighbourhood[3] told me as we stared from an impossibly steep road across the dense, five-story-high urban expanse that covers most of the valley today. "Nowadays you could even consider this central Istanbul!"

In theory, the land was there for the taking. In practice, settling it would be a difficult and deadly operation, one that would combine military tactics with criminal affiliations and violent revolutionary confrontations. By the time the 1970s had ended, this nocturnal home-building mission had turned Sabri into a very different sort of man and Turkey into a very different sort of country.

THE ARRIVAL CITY AS A MARGINAL MENACE

Just before dusk one evening in February of 1977, a team of men arrived on the edge of the valley in tractors, carrying basic hand tools. As darkness fell, they sunk their spades into the dry, tough soil and began to dig trenches for the foundations of houses. Just before dawn, dirt was raked over the surface, so that daytime passersby and police might not notice what had occurred. The next night, the team arrived with large red bricks that had been made from mud in a nearby facility. Overnight, they assembled walls, building without mortar, plastered the outer walls with mud, inserted basic doors and windows and covered the roof with corrugated metal sheets. The team would leave, sleep through the day, and prepare to help others build their houses, as families moved into the new structures. Literally overnight, as the name *gecekondu* suggests, a community was born.

The mass seizure of unused urban land became an international phenomenon in the 1970s, as poor countries wrestled with a stagnating global economy and unsustainable levels of debt, abandoning notions of state-funded housing reform and leaving their rural migrants to fend for themselves. In Ecuador and Colombia, these acts became known as *invasiones*, were organized with military efficiency, and developed into a politically potent movement.

Sabri and his friends, having heard about some of these tactics, decided that the helter-skelter Istanbul land grabs of previous years wouldn't give them lasting homes. The old *gecekondu* methods had become risky: The government and the police, fearing that millions more citizens every year would be demanding water and sewage lines, had become far more vigilant, demolishing settlements as soon as they began. At the same time, the building of squatter housing had become an underground business. "By the time we arrived, there was a *gecekondu* mob-mafia," Sabri told me. "The communities would have to make regular payments, and in return the mob claimed they would negotiate with officials and stop the *gecekondus* from being demolished. They'd spend the money having nice dinners with guys from the ministry. These guys were violent—they had ripped off other *gecekondu* communities and gambled the money they had collected."

To counter the mob and the government, Sabri and his colleagues began organizing regular meetings to plan the construction of their neighborhood. There was an election, and "people's committees" were formed. Sabri was elected to head one committee. They were determined to build their neighborhood in a more deliberate and organized way than their *gecekondu* predecessors. They planned street layouts and even space for small parks, unheard-of features in the chaotic world of Turkish squatter towns. The meetings attracted students and political activists from the far left, who volunteered their planning skills and lent this community a revolutionary air. Sabri found both his ideology and his voice at these meetings, losing his peasant's reticence and making heated speeches, eased with the glimmers of self-effacing wit that temper his speech, and people began to listen to him.[4] It was a dangerous pursuit. By 1977, the *gecekondu* had become less peaceful places, as a second generation grew up without their parents' job prospects and with few ties to the culture of the central city. In response, the government had become hostile toward *gecekondu* communities, which struck them as hotbeds of anti-government activity and which were often populated with Alevis, Kurds, and other restive minorities.

In the fight for space in the city, the main weapon of the rural émigré is physical presence. The undeniable reality of thousands of families living on the peripheral land in sturdy, self-built houses had often been enough for Turkish governments to allow communities to stay and sometimes even to receive utilities. In the 1960s and '70s, amnesty laws had turned thousands of self-built squatter communities into legitimate, tax-paying, and vote-delivering neighborhoods and their tens of millions of citizens into full participants in the economy (but not resolving the question of who owned the land).* Sabri and his neighbors, like millions of others who poured into Istanbul in the late 1970s, hoped that they would turn into recognized citizens.

Over several nights of sweaty work that month, 300 houses were built in their corner of the valley. By the end of 1977, another 3,000 houses had been added, populated with poverty-fleeing and fortune-seeking émigrés from across central and eastern Turkey. The meetings became crowded and complicated. The poorest and most deprived villagers from their region, the committee decided, would be the first to get houses. They would conduct research to

---

* In 1966, the Turkish government passed Law No. 775, which legalized all existing squatter settlements (but did not give title deed to the land) and required the owners of squatted land to transfer ownership to the municipalities. This law was updated periodically to regularize new settlements and remains in force today.

make sure the families were really in need and not just searching for housing bargains.

The neighborhood had grown to the point that it needed a name. On May Day in 1977, an annual labor gathering in Istanbul's Taksim Square, attended by 150,000 people and infiltrated by feuding parties of the far left, turned violent. The police opened fire, panic erupted, and, by the end of the day, an estimated 39 people had been shot or trampled to death. The deaths galvanized Turkish society, especially among Alevis and Kurds, who felt increasingly targeted by a government that was promoting a rigid Turkish identity. At a meeting days later, the villagers voted, with Sabri's support, to call their community 1 Mayis Mahallesi, or "May 1 Neighborhood." With this name, their community became a provocation.

THE ARRIVAL CITY IN DIRECT CONFRONTATION WITH THE OLD CITY

By this point, the *gecekondu* had become a source of panic among government officials and secular urbanites. Urban planners in central Istanbul were watching their carefully made housing plans, their greenbelts and infrastructure strategies, collapse under the weight of hundreds of thousands of villagers a year flooding into the fields on the edge of town. The character of Istanbul's population was changing: Formerly a largely secular and uni-ethnic place, its majority in the outskirts now contained millions of Alevis, Kurds, and observant Sunnis whose women covered their heads; their politics, on the far left or right, were equally alien. Worst of all were their communities, chaotic ad hoc messes piled onto Istanbul's elegant if threadbare boulevards. One planner wrote of Istanbul: "As the political control of cities with an urban squatter problem passes from the presently established urban society into the hands of the emergent urban squatter society, who have little or no heritage of city-dwelling, and who at present have no training in or administrative knowledge of city maintenance, it can be expected that essential services will diminish until they finally break down and collapse."⁵

Yet if someone had visited this valley from one of the arrival cities of China, India, or South America, it would have seemed luxurious. Neat, brick-walled structures that eventually had stone floors, *gecekondu* houses averaged between 600 and 1,000 square feet. They usually had courtyards and small gardens. Though considered ugly and unsanitary by mainstream Turkish architects and urban planners at the time (and the hygiene levels certainly were lacking), these rugged, haphazard houses later came to be praised for their tight-knit beauty and their intrinsically earthquake-proof design: "Typical *gecekondu* settlements are composed of one- or two-story houses with gardens or courtyards," one admirer wrote 30 years later. "There is an irregular settlement pattern with narrow paths and passages between the plots. This kind of space is a result of a long-term consolidation process and provides a special kind of environmental quality for the inhabitants. The built environment offers variety, flexibility in the uses of immediate environment of the houses, fluid spaces between indoors and outdoors and an opportunity for socialization." Established city-dwellers looked at the outskirts and saw a million rural villages popping up. In reality, though there were certainly aspects of village life in the *gecekondu*, the houses and their surroundings bore little resemblance to the villages their occupants had fled. "*Gecekondu* houses are not pure replicas of original village houses; they are not products of traditional ways of construction," a Turkish historian notes. "They are rather new inventions."⁶

The new residents of May 1 enjoyed a life that offered many more economic opportunities than their parched and oppressive Anatolian villages had. They were making enough money to send significant sums back to those who remained in the villages. But it was, in many ways, a more difficult life. "They had to get water from a 15-minute walk away, and carry it home," the historian Şükrü Aslan remembers. "It wasn't until 1979 that the Greater Istanbul municipality built a water pipe going overland . . . Electricity was illegal—engineers, left-wing guys, helped bring the wires here—it was guerrilla electricity. There weren't proper roads for cars—there was only a mountain road that tractors could cross—all bread, food, was brought on a tractor, sold off the back of it."

The children, who outnumbered the adults, were a bigger problem. By this point, Sabri had moved his wife and his two young children to May 1, and for weeks the children roved the streets. Finally, the residents built their own school, and the government actually provided teachers. "It was a strange situation—an illegal neighborhood, but a legal school, with a government-appointed head teacher," Sabri recalls. Slowly, entrepreneurs provided transportation by bus and *dolmus* (a collective taxi that is a key form of travel for the Turkish poor), linking them to Istanbul itself. Physically, it was becoming something like a real neighborhood.

Politically, though, it was far from calm or comfortable. In the 1970s, the political identity of Turkey, which for half a century had been governed by a paternalist state secularism, was suddenly up for grabs. Much of the pressure came from the arrival cities, which were now recruiting their villagers along ideological lines. Some *gecekondu* neighborhoods were populated with right-wing nationalists, associated with the Grey Wolves, the fascist front organization of the right-wing National Action Party. Some were Islamist, giving their support to the Muslim fundamentalist National Wellbeing Party. And others, notably May 1, were left-wing. It was these Marxist groupings that were seen as the greatest threat to the Turkish state. This was the height of the Cold War, and it seemed as if Turkey might topple into a communist revolution.

Sabri's remote valley began appearing in the headlines during the summer of 1977. In a neighborhood just up the hill, where the women generally wore headscarves, a group of Islamist party supporters had built a mosque on privately owned property. The owner, who lived in Germany, sued them, and the Islamists occupied the mosque in protest. The police watched but didn't intervene. They were worried about the politics of the outskirts, but the Islamists weren't their concern. The May 1 residents, who were Alevi, Kurdish and left-wing, were what worried them. "We were both ethnic and political minorities, and we were living on the edge of town," Sabri explains. "We were the ultimate outsiders, even though we wanted to be part of Turkey, and they treated us like invaders."

Over that long, hot summer, the May 1 neighborhood became the site of violent clashes with right-wing and Islamist gangs, with the police and with the Turkish military. There were murders, pegged to both residents and outsiders, and newspapers reported that the neighborhood had become a dangerous no-go zone. The city's social-democratic government, facing what seemed to be a mounting insurgency in its outskirts, announced that it would have to act. The residents of May 1 prepared for a confrontation.

Early on the morning of 2 September 1977, Sabri walked along the potholed mud road to the edge of the neighborhood with his wife and sons, aged 5 and 10. He told the boys to gather stones, sticks, anything that could be thrown. The police arrived in squadrons, wearing white helmets and bulletproof vests, with their pistols drawn. They were joined by armored vehicles, behind which came the bulldozers. The battle lasted all day. By the end, 12 residents of May 1 had died, dozens had been hospitalized, and their neighborhood had been demolished.

The houses would be rebuilt, but Sabri's life did not get easier. Although his politics, like those of most Alevis at the time, were on the left, he was alarmed by the deadly terrorist extremism that had been taken up by the second-generation youths of the arrival city. Militant groups from the right and left and various religious factions seized control of *gecekondu* neighborhoods, declaring them "liberated zones," whether their residents were sympathetic to their cause or otherwise. The walls of May 1 became covered with slogans of feuding leftist and Maoist militant groups: Revolutionary Way, Liberation, the Progressive Youth Association. "They built a kind of military base here, in the middle of the neighborhood, and after that the soldiers were here all the time," says Mehmet Yeniyol, who came here as an idealistic 35-year-old teacher and helped build the first school, in 1977. "Before they built it, even the municipal police couldn't get into this neighborhood. It was guerrilla war."

In the media, in Parliament, and in academic discussions, Sabri and his neighbors had become symbols of the looming showdown between villagers and urbanites. *Gecekondu* people were no longer described as rural migrants but as a potentially threatening population who were destroying the values, institutions and social order of the city."[7]

But those who were watching closely at the time realized that these weren't backward village cultures reproducing themselves on the edge of town: This was an entirely new politics, born in the outskirts by the children of rural immigrants, shocking to their largely apolitical peasant parents. "These young people have no meaningful role in our society, few opportunities for work and have dissociated themselves from the values of their traditionalist families," an Istanbul psychiatry professor concluded in 1978. "They feel isolated and powerless and are easy prey for the extremists."[8]

The social order on the outskirts broke down further. Sabri found that his people's committee was dividing its energies between the utopian task of rebuilding a neighborhood for poor villagers and the rather dirtier work of staving off threats of further demolitions and increasingly violent incursions from conservative and Islamic groups from neighboring migrant settlements. Gangs patrolled the streets, beating up young men who had the wrong political affiliations or, perhaps worse, no affiliations at all.

THE OLD CITY TAKES CONTROL OF THE ARRIVAL CITY

One afternoon in 1978, the committee, and the neighborhood's utopian ambitions, were blotted out of existence. Sabri describes the event as a dark mystery: "Five right-wing guys came into a coffeehouse here, claiming that the whole neighborhood was originally their property. They were swearing, and they were armed. I wasn't there, this is what I heard. There was a fight, and these guys' dead bodies were discovered in the stone mines." A police investigation— what Sabri calls a conspiracy—blamed the people's committee, and Sabri in particular, for the five murders. With help from his network of villagers, he fled, leaving his wife and children alone in their *gece-kondu* house in the center of the neighborhood. For the next three years, he lived in hiding in the lawless villages of southeastern Turkey, not far from the Iraqi border.

In the weeks after he went into hiding, the violence rose to an extreme pitch. Dozens of similar incidents inflamed the *gecekondus* and sometimes spilled into central Istanbul and Ankara. One day in December 1978, a confrontation in the southern Anatolian town of Kahramanmaraş (which had been home to many of the settlers in the May 1 neighborhood) between left-leaning Alevis and militants from the fascist Grey Wolves turned violent, killing over 100 people. Days later, tanks rumbled into the streets of Istanbul's outskirts, strict curfews were applied, and soldiers roamed the cities with rifles ready. The government had declared martial law across Turkey's most populous provinces.

Yet even this did little to curb the violence. In the period after martial law was imposed, it was reported that an average of 16 people a day were being killed by guns and bombs in Turkey's cities.[9] In the view of a Turkish military that had increasingly lost faith in the country's elected leaders, the chaos was entirely the fault of the arrivals living in the *gecekondu*: "It is these neighborhoods," *The New York Times* reported from Istanbul, "that have become recruiting centers and battlegrounds for the terrorist bands that have brought Turkey to the edge of anarchy." According to army claims, by 1980 the *gecekondu* had become home to 20,000 active extremists on the right and the left.[10]

On 12 September 1980, that violence abruptly ended. The Turkish military, declaring the country's secular state gravely threatened, seized control in a long-threatened coup d'état, the third since 1960.

About 100 MPs and political leaders were imprisoned or placed under house arrest, including both the prime minister and the opposition leader. Generals took over ministries, and officers took direct control of neighborhoods. Opposition politics, radical or otherwise, were illegal, and enforcement was strict and summary. As many as 250,000 people would be imprisoned, and many of them tortured.[11] Migration from villages to cities was abruptly halted. All citizens would now have to carry documents stating where they lived, similar to the *hukou* certificates used in China. The slogans on the *gecekondu* walls were ordered painted over, and the neighborhoods, residents say, became eerily quiet.

The problem of the lawless frontier of the *gecekondu* was solved in a quick and expeditious manner, which would end up having a surprising and ironic effect on Turkey's future power structure. It was simply declared, shortly after the coup, that all neighborhoods would now have to be legal. Officers were ordered to call up three representatives from each neighborhood. Those representatives were ordered to gather in a crowded meeting room in central Istanbul one day, each neighborhood assigned to a desk bearing its name. A senior officer strode across the room, surveying this new and unfamiliar cartography, when he spotted the offensive words "May 1." He stopped at the desk, turned to the three representatives—Sabri's former comrades—and ordered them to take down their neighborhood's sign immediately and change the offending name to "Mustafa Kemal," after the father of Turkey's secular revolution.[12]

Sabri was running out of places to hide. The army, in a drive to "Turkify" the population, was driving Kurds and Alevis out of their villages throughout eastern and southern Turkey. After he'd been at large for three years, the military caught up with Sabri in southeastern Turkey in 1981. The trial was swift. He was found guilty of three offences, including "being a member of a political group." He would spend the next five years in prison, facing beatings and complete isolation from his family and the suburb he had launched.

THE ARRIVAL CITY TRANSFORMED

When he stepped out of his cell in 1986 and hitched a ride back to
his house, Sabri at first felt certain that he had taken a wrong turn
or perhaps entered the inner city rather than the rural-migrant outskirts. "It didn't look anything like it had when I'd left—it had become
a completely different place," he remembers. The streets were nar-
rower, the buildings much bigger and painted in bright colors, a mad
bustle of commerce on the sidewalks. Cars were everywhere. The
soothing regularity of *gecekondu* rooftops was gone, with many of
them replaced by taller buildings.

Over the next several days, as he reacquainted himself with his
wife and his sons and received a warm welcome from his old neighbors, he realized that far more than the neighborhood's name and
appearance had changed. Its people, its politics, its attitude, its standing in Istanbul, its role in Turkey, all had been turned upside down.
While he'd been in prison, Turkey's arrival cities had undergone a
transformation unlike any in the world.

The military dictatorship had ended on an unpromising note in
1983, when the head of the military had called elections after introducing a highly restrictive constitution. Most well-known leaders had been
banned from politics, and many parties had been outlawed. The election was won by Turgut Özal, an economic manager who had partici-
pated in the military government, and his newly formed Motherland
Party. There was no reason to believe that Özal would be anything
other than a military-loyal bureaucrat. Throughout the 1980s, though,
he remade Turkey in dramatic ways, opening its economy to international trade and investment, modernizing its monetary system,
replacing the disastrous import-substitution economic plan with a
system based on export-driven growth, and building modern infrastructure and government institutions. But nothing was quite as revolutionary, or quite as subtle and inconspicuous, as his solution to the problem
of angry, rootless squatter communities on the urban outskirts.

Soon after taking office, Özal introduced Law 2805, an amnesty law for *gecekondu* squatters. This one was different from the amnesties of the 1960s and '70s, though. Rather than just turning the squatters into accepted taxpayers, it granted them formal ownership of their makeshift houses and title deeds to the land under them. Millions of precarious and uneasy "overnight arrivals" who had been at war with the city were transformed, almost literally overnight, into property owners with a stake in the economy.

Changing the self-built houses into parcels of real estate had a rapid effect. The constant flow of arrivals from the Anatolian villages—which was to become a deluge in the 1980s—guaranteed that land values would increase. With this simple act, the *gecekondu* houses were turned from a threat to the state into an instrument of state welfare, and in fact into a rudimentary substitute for a welfare state. As one Turkish writer noted, "*Gecekondu* houses became the most important social security object for at least two generations of families who have no access to state social security instruments."[13]

Özal recognized that this property would be used as seed capital, allowing poor peasants to start small businesses, build up savings, earn rental incomes, and use Turkey's precarious banking system to withdraw equity from their homes. He had created the beginnings of a new middle class in the outskirts, though he probably didn't realize the full political repercussions of this. He did recognize, however, that this was a potent way to defuse the political threat of the arrival cities. In 1988, he boasted to a reporter that he had won over the outskirts by replacing the passions of revolutionary activism with the more pedestrian delights of home ownership: "We have given land certificates to those people, they own land and now their buildings, their streets are clean, they now have playgrounds for children, sports installations for the young, and therefore they vote for us, not for the left."[14]

As Özal hinted in that boast, it was not a simple matter of granting ownership. The administration of Istanbul was spending heavily on bringing infrastructure to these newly legitimate and tax-producing communities. Their property wealth did not turn into entrepreneurial wealth automatically; that required schools, transportation networks, links to the city's economy, and the rudiments of life. By 1987, 74 percent of established *gecekondu* houses in Istanbul had tap water (though most had lengthy cuts in the summer), 90 percent had indoor toilets, and 91 percent had electricity.[15]

The end of the military junta, and the possibility of their becoming actual urban homeowners, motivated millions of peasants to consider leaving their villages. Istanbul saw at least half a million new citizens arrive every year between 1984 and the end of the 1990s. Turkey's governments, eager to win the confidence of new voters in the outskirts, acted quickly to turn these new arrivals into homeowners, extending the amnesty law in 1984 and 1986 to include the latest *gecekondu* arrivals.

By end of the 1980s, almost 80 percent of *gecekondu*-dwellers in Turkey had either title deeds on their properties or government certificates that would eventually entitle them to formal legal ownership of their houses.[16] And this was a huge number of people. By 1989, the *gecekondu* neighborhoods made up two-thirds of Istanbul's urban space. Sabri's neighborhood, which had been the remotest edge of town when he fled the police, was now virtually part of the center. To see it on a map today, Mustafa Kemal seems to be about three-quarters of the way into the center of Istanbul, with a dense spray of rooftops extending far in every direction, from the Marmara Sea to the Black Sea.

Turkey had become a nation of arrival cities. In its three biggest cities alone, the *gecekondu* stock was estimated at two million units, housing a population of at least 10.2 million people. By 1986, half of all Turks lived in cities, up from 20 percent in 1950, making Turkey probably the first major developing country to cross this boundary.

This shift took Istanbul's established residents entirely by shock, and they didn't know quite what to make of it. "The unexpected New Istanbul, which emerged within the space of one generation, caught the locals by surprise," one more sympathetic member of that group wrote. "In an attempt to overcome one's own speechlessness, the term 'uniqueness' came to explain it all: A catastrophe of such a scale has happened only to us."[17] This wasn't quite historically correct, of course: The "catastrophe" of Istanbul's sudden explosion was strikingly similar to the transformations that overtook the cities of Europe and North America in the nineteenth century. But it would become a political catastrophe for the Istanbul elite, who were suddenly outnumbered by a new, arriviste middle class whose women often wore headscarves and who were already adopting their own, seemingly alien forms of political power.

For Sabri, it was a catastrophe of a different sort. The years of military control, and the sudden inclusion in urban society, had succeeded in depoliticizing much of his neighborhood. In the words of one observer, "the Alevi identity replaced the leftist one."[18] Land ownership had allowed many squatters to sell their houses, for good profits, to outsiders. The Mustafa Kemal neighborhood now had 50,000 citizens, many of whom had no memory of its years as a center of rebel activity. Persecuted minorities were joined by thousands of poor members of Turkey's Sunni majority. Sabri realized, with some bitterness, that Özal had been right—that his comrades (not to mention his own family) had become comfortably middle-class citizens carefully guarding their property values. "The reforms," Sabri tells me, "turned us all into property owners, and it changed the way we think—we all started to think the way that owners think. In the end, we created a petit-bourgeois culture."

But then he breaks into a smile. "I don't regret it—we have no regrets," he says, with good reason. In 1989, when the neighborhood's borough was able to vote in municipal elections for the first time, those neighbors elected him leader of Mustafa Kemal, under the banner of a left-wing party, with 75 percent of the vote. During his terms in office, he was to oversee another overnight change, one that would again completely transform the appearance and character of the neighborhood. It was a change that would effectively eliminate the *gecekondu* as a form of dwelling.

Prime Minister Özal's 1983 land-ownership law had quietly intro-duced a potent innovation known as the Improvement Plan. In order to integrate these districts into the city and rid them of the most unsanitary or ill-constructed houses, the law allowed neighborhoods to improve their chaotic slums in three ways. First, they could choose conservation, in which existing *gecekondu* houses were legalized, physically improved, and provided with public services. The second choice was redevelopment: replacement of the existing stock with apartment blocks. And the third was clearance: selling off and bull-dozing the *gecekondu* and selling the land to developers for profit.

What Özal could not have foreseen was that almost none of the *gecekondu*-dwellers would choose to keep their homes. For a great many residents, it was hard to resist the possibility of turning their self-built house into a multi-story building that would be worth much more and generate a constant stream of rental income. Others were tempted to sell their homes, for a sum they'd never seen before, to a group of developers, in exchange for which they'd receive ownership of one of the condominiums and a share of the rental income of the rest (a popular Turkish arrangement). Even those who would have preferred to stay in their little house with its neat courtyard soon found themselves feeling otherwise. "I would not like to tear my *gecekondu* house down and build again an apart-ment house," one well-established resident said at the time, "but if the neighbors do it, I also have to. Otherwise, we would not get any sunshine in the house."[19]

The Improvement Plan in Mustafa Kemal changed the place over-night. In 1989, an Istanbul mayor friendly to left-wing causes granted Sabri's constituents the right to build apartments up to five stories. Almost everyone took him up on the offer. "If you were to have visited here at the end of the '80s," the historian Şükrü Aslan says, "you would still see entirely *gecekondu* houses with gardens around them—but as soon as it was permitted, people tore them down and built larger buildings. This happened all at once, just like the *gece-kondus* themselves. People saw that their land was worth more, so they said, 'Let's start using every square millimeter.' It switched almost immediately from an idealistic mentality to a much more profit-driven one."

Today, Mustafa Kemal looks nothing at all like a squatter settlement, unless you know where to look. In a back street, you will occasionally spot a lone example of the old self-built houses, which now sport attractive paint jobs, red-tiled roofs, smoking chimneys, and satellite dishes; they represent perhaps one building out of every 20. For the most part, the busy streets are lined with modern stuccoed and painted buildings, almost all exactly five stories tall, with shops on the bottom floor and apartment balconies (also studded with satellite dishes) above. A slash of multi-lane highway, built in the 1990s, cuts through the bottom of the valley, its noisy shoulder lined with the old *gecekondu* houses, some of them cut in half by the land appropriation. This time around, the residents didn't mount a violent protest against the government. They were paid good money for their land, so they moved on without complaint, usually to more desirable *gecekondus*.

Sabri Koçyigit tells me this story on an outrageously hot July day, just before a national election. He is running, not for the first time, as a parliamentary candidate for the far-left Freedom and Solidarity Party; the stretch of the busy street around his office is strung with the party's banners. After I drop in on his campaign office, decorated with images of protesters and triumphant workers, he takes me downstairs to drink tea in the shop of his friend, who sits behind a lavish hardwood desk facing a display of sophisticated double-glazed windows—a commodity whose increasing popularity among the former peasants is a good indication of the neighborhood's rise.

Today, beneath his balding pate and his salt-and-pepper mustache, Sabri's easygoing demeanor still occasionally rises to heights of principled anger, especially when we come to the treatment of Turkey's Kurds and Alevis at the hands of the army. When we discuss the changes that have overtaken Turkey, and especially the settlements outside Istanbul, his bitterness seems a well-worn posture, one he delivers with a smile. "Look, the voters here are not revolutionaries any more, I will admit that—the money is keeping people away from their old principles, and their votes are easier to buy."

Indeed, while the former May 1 neighborhood still votes more heavily for the far left than most neighborhoods, it no longer gives victories to Sabri or his comrades, who haven't won an election since the 1990s. The majority of its votes in 2007 went to those old enemies, the Kemalists of the Republican People's Party. Sabri's party attracted 0.15 percent of the national vote and came a distant second here. It is, he says, a sign of the bourgeois culture that's overtaken his neighborhood.

It then strikes me to ask him what has become of his hand-built *gecekondu* house. Does it still look the same? Has he added double-glazed windows? Could I possibly visit? With a sheepish smile, he looks to the floor and points across the busy road. There, perched on a prime corner lot, is a large five-story building whose street level sports a chicken restaurant, a delicatessen, two cell-phone shops, a clothing store, and a travel agent, with a couple of dozen large rental apartments upstairs, a formidable rent-generating enterprise. "That," he says quietly, "is what I have done with my house."

I tease him: "So it seems that the outcome of your years of Marxist struggle has been your own transformation into a petit-bourgeois member of the dreaded *rentier* class." He frowns, then looks up and laughs brightly, raising his finger to the sky: "Absolutely not! No matter what has happened, I will not accept the name petit bourgeois! That name cannot possibly apply to me. I have always been a communist."

Like so many of his squatter neighbors, though perhaps more entertainingly so, Sabri is still coming to terms with the strange twist of fate that has turned them from the midnight diggers on the outskirts into the menace on the outskirts and then, finally, into members of Turkey's dominant economic and political class.

THE NEW ARRIVALS CONFRONT THE ARRIVAL CITY

To see what has happened to the Turkish arrival city in the years since its success, you should leave Sabri Koçyigit's office and walk several blocks uphill, to a slightly more chaotic street, and take a seat in a café called Hope. Behind its faux-rustic façade, the hand-hewn wood benches are covered in carpets, and the walls display deliberately corny pastoral scenes. This is what Turks call a "folklore bar," an increasingly popular institution in the arrival cities of Istanbul and Ankara, a hangout for the generation who arrived here in the 1990s and after.

The handsome, stocky man with the neatly trimmed beard who brings you your tea is named Kemal Doğan. This place is his—that is, he rents it, as he does his apartment. If Sabri's generation became lavish homeowners, Kemal's generation are, for a number of reasons, perpetual tenants. He called the place Hope (*Umut*) shortly after he took it over in 2000, after his newborn son. His interests, like those of most of his generation, were in working hard to make enough money to support his family, not in building any kind of ideological utopia. He, too, got off the bus at Harem. It was 1993, he was 23, and life had become unbearable in his family's home of Erzincan, in Turkey's far east. There had been a serious earthquake, the military-ethnic conflicts were endless, and his family didn't have the money to go into farming in a serious way. He knew that there were plenty of Erzincan residents, including several of his uncles, living in a certain neighborhood in Istanbul, so he rode a bus across the country to check it out.

The millions of people who arrived in Istanbul's outskirts in the 1990s had quite a different experience from those of the previous four decades. They, too, came from villages whose agriculture had stopped needing labor and were seeking better jobs in the city. But they were arriving in a different world. The spectacular balance of economic growth and social improvement that had marked the 1980s had come crashing to a halt in the '90s as unsustainable levels of government debt led to a rapid currency devaluation, throwing the economy into turmoil. And the old economy of secure, long-term industrial jobs in state-supported enterprises had disappeared, replaced with a diverse trade-driven economy, which offered more opportunities but less job security.

The arrivals were a different group, too. If the previous generation was drawn by promises of employment, this enormous group was largely pushed out by rural deprivation, especially in the war-torn east, where the Turkish military was shutting down hundreds of villages and expelling their residents. These victims were forced to move as entire families, and they had little opportunity to adjust to the contours and rhythms of urban life. "Poverty among newcomers was so high that they could not even afford to build a *gecekondu* house," one observer wrote. "There was a lack of unoccupied land. People could only find accommodation in old and consolidated *gecekondu* areas as tenants." By the end of the 1990s, the proportion of tenants in the former *gecekondu* neighborhoods had reached 80 percent.[20]

Kemal followed the hopscotch pattern of the second-generation migrant: First he got a job in a furniture shop, and he rented an old *gecekondu* house. It belonged to his uncle, who had been one of the revolutionaries who built this place in the '70s. Actually, it was only half a house: his uncle had built at the bottom of the valley, and when the highway came along, he'd happily taken the money to have his house bisected. Kemal spent some money renovating the place, making it habitable, installing a satellite dish. He brought his mother and his little sister over to live with him. The noisy half-house became impossible, so he rented a flat on the third floor of one of those innumerable five-story buildings.

He worked in the furniture store for two years, then in an insurance company's branch office. Then he took a job managing a school cafeteria. His wife worked as a secretary, then as an accountant. No matter how traditional their background, Turks of Kemal's generation have learned that husband and wife both must work. Across the road from the high school was an abandoned café, so he rented it, bought the contents of a village's old bar from a friend, and, when his son was born, he painted a sign reading "Hope." The two jobs complement each other nicely but don't earn him enough money to buy a place.

Home ownership is an unobtainable goal for many members of this generation. The signs in the real-estate agent's shop attest to the astonishing rise in the price of self-built homes: "*Gecekondu*, 3 rooms, 60,000 new lira, 170 square meters . . . *Gecekondu*, with deed, 85,000 new lira." In other words, those rudimentary abodes, built with stones, hard labor, and hope, are selling for $40,000 to $55,000 each, and in adjoining districts they cost considerably more. A well-paid factory worker might earn $18,000 a year. Something has changed, and it isn't just the land prices.

Kemal and a good number of his customers seem to have done well in the optimistic years of the early twenty-first century, making the slow march into the lower ranks of the middle class in Turkey's fast-reviving economy. And they weren't hurt by the recession that began in 2008, whose effects on credit and employment largely bypassed Turkey. These are upwardly mobile arrivals. Nevertheless, they have little sympathy for the idealists who built this place—in fact, most of what they express is scorn.

And no wonder: what is visibly, painfully missing here is the assistance of the state, the good schools, transit networks, and social services that allow villagers to turn their children into full-fledged urbanites. Without a significant government role, this laissez-faire development has made the neighborhood a distinctly uncomfortable place for those on the lower rungs. Kemal and his tea-drinking customers say it's abundantly clear that home ownership alone isn't creating decent public facilities and that the failure of government to produce these things has led to an uneasy political situation. Kemal, who, like most people here, knows Sabri Koçyigit and his legendary reputation, explained to me why he has turned his back on such heroes. "Their radical political groups should get a grip on and think twice," he says. "It is the ordinary people who get stuck in the middle."

When he first came here in 1993, Kemal says, those rebels had got ownership of their houses, and the wide streets were becoming narrow streets. Private land had created prosperity but also selfishness: People expanded their properties to the maximum extent of their title deeds, building over sidewalks, parks, semi-public squares. There was a reluctance to sacrifice land, or raise funds, for parks or better schools. There is no municipal tax system, so the presence of the state is a matter of political largesse, which hasn't been forthcoming here. One scholar observed how the combination of private ownership with an absent government changed the appearance of the Istanbul arrival city: "[T]he spatial characteristics of the *gecekondu* settlements, with low-rise houses and surrounding gardens, is lost. The newly emerged environment is poor in its open, public and semi-public spaces."[21]

For Kemal, this was a betrayal of the neighborhood's values. "All the ideals of building cultural centers, public libraries, parks, they all were destroyed. Now it's all a heap of concrete. Those days rent was cheap. But people acquired the taste of money and became degenerate. They have forgotten the fact that they were poor once."

THE ARRIVAL CITY FINDS ITS OWN POLITICS

Contrary to the fears of the military authorities, the founding politics of the May 1 neighborhood never became the politics of Turkey, or even a plausible opposition. The pinnacle of left-wing success was achieved in 1989—the election that brought Sabri his moment of power—when a social-democratic party swept Istanbul. But that was the left of an old, disappearing Istanbul: Its policies were aimed at those voters who had real jobs with real companies, not the *gecekondu* residents, whose lives tended to take place almost entirely off the books. It was not until the crisis years of the 1990s that a political party arrived that was born and nurtured in the arrival cities, which promised the sort of aid and support that mere property ownership hadn't delivered. It was even called the Welfare Party.

The party's mayoral candidate, Recep Tayyip Erdoğan, was in many respects the quintessential *gecekondu* citizen. He was not technically from the fringes, having been born and raised in Kasimpaşa, a poor quarter near the Bosporus (poorer, in fact, than most *gecekondu* neighborhoods are today). But his life was that of the arrival. His family had migrated to Istanbul from Rize, in the far northeast of Turkey; they had developed the culture of arrival, religious and veiled; he spent his youth selling *simit* bread on the streets, scrambling to make an urban living.

His electoral victory in 1994 was decisive and, to almost everyone in central Istanbul, deeply alarming. Support for his Welfare Party had come from mysterious places far outside the city's old borders. And he was not what urban Turks considered an acceptable politician: He was openly religious; his wife wore a scarf over her head. It was conventional then, as it is among some today, to call him an Islamist.

By 1994, the established population of Istanbul had ceased to have any electoral influence: they had been swamped. In that election, the *gecekondu* neighborhoods contributed 60.4 percent of votes cast—the first time they'd outnumbered the urbanites. By then, almost 75 percent of Istanbul's population was estimated "to have a relation with *gecekondu*"—that is, rural roots and a background in the city's outskirts. The outsiders had become the sole source of power. As one Turkish analysis of vote results concluded: "That population of Istanbul, whose majority now has rural roots and is still experiencing the transition process from rural to urban life with dominant informalities in their living situations, has found its representatives."[22]

Erdoğan strolled into the void of Turkish politics in the 1990s, becoming mayor of Istanbul when the secular Turkish republic seemed to have failed most of its citizens. The economy was a catastrophe, reaching a complete collapse in 1994, and the city appeared to many to have become a garbage-strewn mess. He was a powerful enough force that even the residents of Mustafa Kemal gave him their vote.

The Welfare Party did bring something to the arrival city. In a thousand concrete ways, its campaign offices took the role that might have been occupied by the state, filling the gaps in a laissez-faire urban economy that left former villagers without support. One observer remembered its "army of covered women," who "were there to help the sick land a hospital bed, to distribute food on freezing winter days, to provide a small present to newlyweds, to help with the cost of a funeral."[23] The party's message also happened to appeal to the basic conservatism, driven by fear of urban perils and the collapse of old family certainties, that animates almost all immigrant communities, especially those living in the dangerous and precarious precincts of the arrival city. It tried (unsuccessfully) to outlaw adultery, and some female candidates covered their heads, a taboo in Kemalist Turkey. To villagers who were used to seeing women coddled and covered—not out of especially strong religious convictions but out of comforting custom—the city seemed full of family-destroying menace, and the party offered an alternative.

In 1997, the Welfare Party was banned from national politics by the Constitutional Court, at the insistence of the military. Erdoğan spent 10 months in prison for giving inflammatory speeches. In 2001, as Turkey experienced another financial meltdown, the Welfare Party split in two: Its Islamists formed the Felicity Party. Erdoğan and his allies, who were always more interested in social and economic policy, formed the Justice and Development Party (AK Party), which quickly became known as the ultimate outsiders' party, the national voice of the *gecekondu*. It seemed inevitable from the beginning that it would end up leading Turkey.

One neighborhood uphill from Mustafa Kemal is a hub of the new politics, a place called Bitterwater. It got that name in the late 1970s, when the villagers arriving here stayed up all night digging trenches and wells, which yielded water that was almost undrinkable. Today, it is one of the fastest-growing places in Istanbul. Life here is effectively controlled by the land registrar, a man with enormous political power, as he is able to declare people legal residents, enabling them to receive health care, schooling, and, possibly, ownership of their properties. He tells me that five or six new families come to his office every day, newly arrived from the villages. Some 18,000 people arrived here last year.

When people started coming here in the 1980s, residents say, this was a largely apolitical place. True, women in the neighborhood were more likely to cover their heads—a rarity then in Istanbul and still illegal in public places—but it was not because they were especially religious. Several women here explained to me that the custom is as much for practical reasons (the women tended to be agricultural laborers, working in the hot sun of Anatolia) as for any deep tie to Islam. Still, you're far more likely to see headscarves here, and there are certainly more minarets poking above the storefronts.

As the economy collapsed and families in Bitterwater became desperate for assistance, it was not the Turkish government but the AK Party's "small army of covered women" who provided it. Today, you can see the impact of the new politics everywhere in this neighborhood. The land registrar is a Felicity Party man, and his office contains the extraordinary juxtaposition of the mandatory Kemal Ataturk portrait hung immediately below an Islamic text. From the same desk, he delivers welfare certificates and collects donations for a new mosque.

Erdoğan's AK Party exists here as the neighborhood's capillary system, delivering fresh blood into the area's isolated, depleted households. I spent a day here, just before Erdoğan's second prime ministerial victory, with a young woman named Kadriye Kadabal, a university graduate who strolled the back streets in a white dress and a chic white headscarf. It was apparent that she knew every family by name, every house and its precise history, and could stroll with impunity through any door. She dropped in on one family, living in a collapsing rented *gecekondu* house, and quietly helped them obtain a government card that would provide free drugs to their sick child. Another family received a box of food; a third got a discreet payment for expenses while the father was tending to a family disaster. She described herself as having no complaint with Turkey's secularism but was motivated by her personal faith. "According to our religion, the one who can sleep when a neighbor is hungry, he is not one of us. That is our motto."

This is how the AK Party works in the streets. Kadabal oversees two dozen households and reports to Ali Tunel, the 36-year-old owner of a successful small furniture factory around the corner. He supervises 30 volunteers, who provide financial, medical, and bureaucratic aid to 700 families here. There are hundreds of men like Tunel in Istanbul. The party receives donations from supporters who have become wealthy, directed at its aid organization. "It is the AKP that fixes things around here between the rich people and the poor people," says Tunel. "You should think of us as a conduit."

AK Party officials bristle at comparisons to Hamas and Hezbollah, Islamic movements that employed similar community-organizing techniques, and prefer to mention the U.S. Democratic Party in the Tammany Hall days. They usually argue that the party is Islamic in the way that Germany's Christian Democratic parties are Christian— that is, the faith is a symbolic touchstone, not a fundamental societal goal. When Erdoğan first became prime minister, in 2003, few urbanites believed this, and many saw him as a Trojan horse for Islamism. Those fears had a genuine basis among a moderate, educated Turkish minority who had somehow managed to maintain the Middle East's only secular democracy (save for periodic military coups) for eight decades. Yet their fear of the AK Party was also a direct reflection of their fear of the arrival city. Once again, we see the old narrative of the conservative, backward villager bringing a village culture of religion and repression into the cosmopolitan realm of the city.

Yet Erdoğan won successive elections without bringing any popular support for political Islam with him. In fact, he seemed to devote most of his energies to integrating his country with Europe and strengthening its economy, ending the impasse with the Kurds in the southeast, and trying to stop the courts from punishing political dissidents. In an apparent reversal of his erstwhile adultery law, he also passed a dramatic women's-rights bill that outlawed honor killing and made rape, even within marriage, the most serious sort of crime, the strongest law of its kind in the Islamic Middle East. Clearly, forces other than religious conservatism were emerging from the *gecekondus*.

In 2006, scholars at the well-regarded Turkish Economic and Social Studies Foundation, a non-partisan academic think tank in Istanbul, produced an extraordinary large-scale study, which revealed that Turks had become dramatically less interested in any form of religious politics, even as support for the AK Party rose. The scholars interviewed 1,492 people across Turkey in 1999 and again in 2006. Those who supported the idea of Islamic sharia law declined from 21 percent of Turks in 1999 to only 9 percent in 2006. Those who felt that there should be Islamic political parties dropped from 41 percent to 25 percent. And the number who said that they would never want to live in an Islamic state increased from 58 percent to 76 percent. The proportion of women who were wearing Islamic headscarves, contrary to expectation, had dropped from 16 percent of the population to 11 percent. (The number who wore the more concealing chador had dropped even more sharply, from 3 percent to 1 percent.) But in one area, tellingly, there was an increase in religious sentiment: those Turks who identified themselves as "Muslim first and Turkish second" had increased noticeably, from 36 percent of the population in 1999 to 45 percent in 2006.[24] What seemed to be happening could be described as a privatization of religious belief. As in much of Europe and North America, religion had become a matter of personal identity and pride, a self-affirming membership in an order that transcended the troubled realm of the nation, rather than a totalizing ideology of omnipotent social control.

It is abundantly clear that these changes were a direct product of the arrival cultures of the *gecekondu*. It was here, in these hybrid sites of village attachment and urban adjustment, that, after 80 years, the personal display of Islamic identity became part of Turkish life again, and the Islamic identity became part of Turkish politics. But it was also here that Turkey opened up to Europe, to trade, to an individualistic form of life that was not governed by any overarching ideology. It was, in a way, a victory of the arrival city not just over the politics and the demographics of the nation as a whole but over its mind. As one Turkish observer wrote, the acceptance of the arrivals had "turned the *gecekondu*, as an ersatz city erected in self-help, into the actual metropolis—initially in terms of urban development, then culturally, later politically, and since recently economically as well."[25]

THE ARRIVAL CITY ABSORBS THE OLD CITY

If you're standing in Bitterwater and you try to look toward the center of Istanbul, your view will be blocked by an anomalous sight: 10 apartment buildings, spaced close together in a tight circle. These are not the poured-concrete public-housing monoliths that are peppered across the outskirts but elegant, glass-curtain buildings with handsome glass balconies, condominium towers that would look familiar in Rotterdam or Santa Monica. They sit, like a strange glimmering mirage, in the center of a welter of ragged *gecekondu* neighborhoods and light-industrial back streets, as if a perfectly round crater has been blasted out of the poor housing and a residential rhinestone inserted in its center. A high wall separates this enclave from the surrounding houses; the only way in is by car, through a security gate where visitors must leave their ID cards before entering the underground parking facility. Above the gate is a sign identifying the complex, in English, as Sinpas Central Life.

Once inside this walled-off space, a very different sort of neighborhood reveals itself. The streets are cobblestoned and immaculately clean. Security guards, wearing sheriff-style badges, are visible everywhere. The central circle is filled with greenery and features a large fountain-spurting pond with a children's island at the center. There is a gym (its sign reads, in English, "Wellness Club"), a Turkish bath, a medical center and a large and well-staffed day-care facility, all for the exclusive use of the residents of the 386 condominium apartments. The people who live here, according to sales manager Habip Perk, are almost entirely young couples who grew up in central Istanbul, born to families who had lived in the city for generations. They move here because the old city has become crowded and expensive, its infrastructure crumbling. It has become home to Istanbul's real poor (far poorer than the *gecekondu* residents), who have brought with them crime and drugs. And these outskirts neighborhoods have a reputation for being more earthquake-proof.

Companies like Sinpas are here to cater to them. Sinpas has become a force in the old *gecekondu* settlements, stealthily buying up large blocks of self-built houses, negotiating development rights with local officials, and demolishing those blocks to build middle-class enclaves. The firm's glossy color catalogue, with the English title *Sinpas Love Story*, showcases these urban islands, whose names are all English: Aqua City, Istanbul Palace, London Palace, and the delightfully titled Avant Garden. Half a dozen major firms are building similar settlements.

They are appealing to a market of Turks who are members of a new, globalized middle class, whose lives have more in common with the middle classes of Europe or North America than with the old Turkish state-led middle class. The growth of the arrival city, and the increase in its real-estate values, has created an exodus of this class into the outskirts. "In the last two decades," one Turkish study concluded at the end of the 1990s, "middle and higher income groups have taken a growing interest in peripheral land. They no longer feel safe and comfortable in central urban areas. Increased private car ownership and the building of expressways have also helped to shift middle class housing preferences."[26]

On the fourth floor of one of these buildings lives Şeyda Gurer, 30, and her husband, Ahmet Uzun, 34. They are both mid-level employees of the Turkish branches of multinational pharmaceutical firms: Ahmet is with Novartis, in sales; Şeyda is with Pfizer, in marketing. When I visited, she was in the midst of a six-month leave to care for their three-month-old baby, Yigit. They bought their two-bedroom apartment in 2004 for $172,000, after saving for almost four years to make a $74,000 down payment. As an investment, it had been wise. By the end of 2006, similar-sized apartments in their building were selling for $262,000. As a life experience, it had been the shock of discovering the existence of the outskirts.

"Two years ago, I had never heard of this part of the city," says Şeyda. "I was born in Istanbul and had never heard of anything so far outside—I thought the city ended before you got this far out." Their apartment has the universal look of the deracinated second-generation upstart: new furniture, clean hardwood floors, a clumsy surround-sound TV system, a few tasteful photos on the wall, and a lot of blank white space. Şeyda says that their biggest reasons for moving out of the historic city, aside from their inability to afford an apartment that was up to their standards, were crime and parking. "This is the outskirts, and it takes us away from all that," she says. "It's very nice living here because you have 24-hour security. And ample car parking—plus you have your own social facilities. It takes one hour to get to the city center, so we can go there for shopping."

I ask them what they think of their new neighborhood, with its colorful history and its mysterious back streets. Have they tried any of the better-known eateries? Have the area's famous furniture shops attracted them? Şeyda and Ahmet tell me that they, like most of their neighbors, have never set foot in the *gecekondu* neighborhood. They leave the parking garage in their cars, drive through a few of its streets, and head downtown. In the year and a half they have lived here, they have never walked the streets that adjoin their own compound. "We actually don't know the neighborhood," says Şeyda. "We just know this place."

———

While the wall between the globalized middle class of multinational employees in places like Sinpas Central Life and the poorer, entrepreneurial middle class of the *gecekondu* settlements seems almost impermeable—both physically and culturally—the similarities between these two groups have become increasingly apparent. They share a disinterest in the old nationalist politics of Kemalism, whose endless disputes over the Kurds, over the right to express "un-Turkish" dissent, and over Cyprus have cost the Turkish economy dearly. They share an interest in European integration, even if the *gecekondu* middle class wants to enter Europe in Muslim headscarves and the Sinpas middle class would prefer to enter in Yves St. Laurent scarves.

In 2007, it first became apparent that these two middle classes, who still seemed barely aware of one another, had begun to unite their interests. For the first time, a significant proportion of Turkey's old middle class voted for Erdoğan's AK Party. A number of Turks recognized this result as a watershed, as a harmonization of the arrival-city values with the nation's values. The political writer Zafer Senocak saw it as a pivotal event in which "the social climbers from the provinces have taken their place at the table. Perhaps they don't even want to elbow the others aside."[27]

Meanwhile, the packed little buses keep arriving at Harem. The emigration from the Anatolian villages has slowed, but still perhaps 250,000 new people a year arrive in Istanbul, a growth rate that some consider unsustainable. At the very edges of Istanbul, you can still see the geometric, frostlike patterns of *gecekondu* rooftops spreading. The land is much harder to find, limited essentially to the forests and water reserves in the north and to the purchase of private farmlands (at a steep cost) on the European side. Some have declared this the end of the *gecekondu* era. "Unlike its precursor," the writer Orhan Esen believes, its neo-*gecekondu* variant "does not represent a collective settling at an industrial center offering employment, but impoverished families who have found their individual stopgap solution at a remote location without any urban context or foreseeable future benefits . . . A place of the losers."[28]

It is tempting to declare that the arrival-city adventure has reached its end, to decide that the destitution in this latest wave of squatter settlements does indeed make them "a place of the losers." The city of Istanbul seems to believe this and has launched a large-scale slum-clearance project intended, in theory, to replace all "crooked buildings" with high-rises. But it is useful to note that these "losers" on the far edge of town are not choosing to move back to the poverty and oppression of their villages and are not seeing their lives get any worse. It is equally useful to remember that this, "a place of the losers," was exactly what people were saying in 1976. Those losers ended up changing the Middle East.

7

WHEN THE MARGINS EXPLODE

Emamzadeh 'Isa, Tehran

The metropolis of Tehran cascades from the snowy heights of the Alborz mountains into the salt flats of the Dasht-e Kavir desert, its houses transforming along the way from steel and glass, to stone and wood, to sand and mud. If you follow the city to its southern limit, then past it, through several kilometers of crude-industrial hell and out into the desert's fringe, you'll find a perimeter buzzing with furtive activity, with home construction and arrival and return, with vehicles bearing the license plates of faraway provinces, with secretive new settlements emerging from the sand.

This is the place where the 1979 Islamic revolution found its body of support and its motivating cause. And now it is here, on the even more distant fringes, where the new Iranian generation is pulling itself up from the earth, attempting to make an urban start, experiencing profound frustration with the failures of the Islamic government, and, perhaps, planting the seeds of the next great change.

At the very end of Tehran, just beyond the city's municipal limits, where buildings and sand melt into one another, a cluster of perhaps 200 haphazardly built houses is carved into a seemingly arbitrary patch of desert, separated from anything else by patches of wasteland, around a small mud dome. It would be easy to mistake the dome for a natural formation, were it not for the flag and the muezzin's loudspeaker at the top, which reveal it to be a Persian shrine, this one built 800 years ago in honor of the prophet known elsewhere as Jesus Christ. The shrine, Emamzadeh 'Isa, has given this settlement its name.

Fifteen years earlier, the mud dome had been the only feature on the landscape. Then, in the 1990s, one or two houses appeared. At the beginning of the twenty-first century, streets and electricity arrived: The man who owned the land had persuaded a local official to allow, or at least to ignore, his subdivision of the land. These houses at first were crude constructions of handmade bricks, with water tanks on top, but some owners have slowly added wrought-iron gates and stucco or even marble cladding. Gas, electricity, and water lines are connected, though water is still delivered by truck. Satellite dishes proliferate.

"This is a good place to live, because it's one of the few places where someone from a village can buy a house today, if he has saved for many years," says Jafa Asadi, a 40-year-old resident of Emamzadeh 'Isa, who runs one of the three real-estate agencies whose improbable presence marks the most visible and successful form of commerce on the arrival city's dusty main street. "Most people here are small traders, craftsmen, or self-employed as construction workers, mechanics, technicians. The majority of people here came from rural areas; they are farmers' sons—they learned a skill or a trade and used it to urbanize themselves," he tells me over tea. The land was very cheap at first—for $1,500 you could buy land, and for another $1,500 you could buy a small house. Then you could bring your family. Around 2000, these houses were selling for $3,000 to $4,000; now they are perhaps $20,000. "It's good business for us," Jafa says. "And some of the farmers' sons who moved here are using the property to build a business, if they're lucky. Those who got in during the early years are doing well. Those who came later have a harder time."

For 28-year-old Soheila, who arrived here in 2005 from a mountain village in the far western district of Luristan, there is none of this mood of optimism.* We sit down on the top floor of a barren café, and she stares at the floor, speaking quietly but reddening with exasperation. "My parents gave up everything to come here, and they saved all their money to get me into university," she says. "But now they have nothing, no work, just this house in the sand. Me and my friends are all alone here, there's no places in school. We were promised so much and there's nothing." A petite woman who averts her gaze shyly, she nevertheless wears only the legal minimum head covering, a hair-revealing bright red "bad hijab" that ex-villagers wouldn't have worn a generation ago. They wouldn't have spoken out against the government, either, but almost everyone I met here expressed a deep and abiding fury with president Mahmoud Ahmadinejad, who was elected on promises to improve the lives of the urban poor. And, in private moments, some of the otherwise pious people here speak of their frustration with the revolution itself.

In the summer of 2009, this improvised fringe of Tehran became, improbably, a site of dissent. In those troubled months after Ahmadinejad's second, contested election victory, there were no protest marches here, no banners hung from windows or occupations of buildings. Those events were mainly in the middle-class districts of central and northern Tehran, carried out by students who had less to lose (though some lost their lives). Here, something far less visible took place. After the sun had set on summer nights, people across the southern outskirts took to rooftops near public streets and chanted, in slow chorus: "Allahu akbar, Allahu akbar"—God is great, God is great. To an outsider, this might seem a show of faith and support for the Islamic regime. In Iran, it is a forbidden act of dissent: It was the rooftop chant of the 1979 revolution; during the 1980s, here in south Tehran, it became a derisive message fired back at the regime. In 2009, it became almost habitual, infuriating officials, leading squads of Basij, the Revolutionary Guard volunteers, to raid rooftops and arrest, and sometimes kill, those doing the chanting.

* I have omitted Soheila's surname to protect her security.

Most people in Emamzadeh 'Isa come from the villages of Luristan or from the country's far northwest; some are ethnic Turks or members of other non-Persian minorities. The men came first and worked during the late 1980s and 1990s in Tehran, staying in rented rooms in the nearer outskirts, before saving the money—or using family farming revenues—to buy a plot and build a house in Emamzadeh 'Isa. People who have arrived more recently, from the countryside or from central Tehran, are forced to rent rooms in the houses out here, at rates that rise faster than incomes. Some of the original inhabitants, after less than a decade, have moved back to their villages in order to rent out all the rooms in their houses, since the landlord's income exceeds any kind of employment a migrant could get.

Property prices in these far-fringe settlements are rising steeply for a reason known to all poor Tehranis: there is nowhere else to go. The city has aggressively, and sometimes forcefully, prevented any new settlements from forming. Indeed, Iranian studies show that rising prices, and the lack of any new low-cost housing developments, are forcing workers out of the central city and even its more established arrival cities and into these settlements—thus making them unaffordable for the latest wave of rural émigrés.[1] The casual laborers occupying rooms out here in the far edge are realizing they won't have any way to bring their families over or get a place of their own.

The Tehran urban planner Esfandiar Zebardast warns that an explosion is waiting to happen here on the edges of Tehran. "The rigidity of the urban planning system in Iran to adapt to fast demographic shifts, due to land-use restrictions within the city and rigid municipal boundaries, and the investments in infrastructure that are not commensurate with needs, have resulted in the spill-over of low-income urban groups into the periphery, the un-serviced areas," he writes. As a result, about five million people, or 40 percent of the population increase that has expanded Tehran to 13 million people, now live in informal and mainly unrecognized settlements such as slums and shantytowns on the edges, a number that is growing.[2]

As this is occurring, the Iranian economy is caving in on these people. A state-run industrial sector and limited trade or investment provide jobs for the regime-connected elite workers, and a great vacuum for more recent arrivals. Forty percent of Tehran's population, according to the Iranian Chamber of Commerce, lives below the poverty line, and half are unemployed. And, in a sign of the regime's failure to provide for the arrival city, the usual escape route of education is virtually non-existent in Iran. In a typical year, 1.5 million graduates apply for only 130,000 university places.

The last time this convergence of circumstances took place—a rush into the city, a land-price increase, and a harsh government crackdown on the availability of non-planned land—Iran's arrival cities provided the fuel for an explosion that changed the world.

A SPARK IN THE DUST

If you look north toward central Tehran from the rooftops of Emamzadeh 'Isa, beyond a kilometer of wasteland, construction sites, and dirty roadside industry, you see rows and rows of identical, low-cost modern apartment blocks. This place, once the outer frontier of Tehran but now an official suburb of more than 400,000 people with a dozen of its own outskirt communities, is where you will find the beginnings, and the most powerful causes, of the Iranian revolution.

Eslamshahr was Tehran's first arrival city and remains its largest. It was built as a warren of narrow, mud-walled buildings, slowly supplanted with brick and serviced with electricity tapped illegally from the city's power grid and water diverted from the mains. Unusually, most of its plots of land were formally purchased by the settlers from generally private landholders (who had no legal permission to subdivide their land). From the beginning, as it rose from nothing in 1968 to 10,000 houses in the early 1970s to hundreds of thousands in the 1980s, Eslamshahr has offered a parallel, highly organized but legally clandestine society and government, a model for all future arrival cities, independent from Tehran's municipal authorities and Iran's ruling regime—and frequently at war with them.

In media accounts, the 1979 revolution's flashpoints are conventionally identified as the holy city of Qom, where the Ayatollah Khomeini and his circle of clerics delivered their rhetorical barrages against Shah Mohammad Reza Pahlavi after returning from exile in 1978; or in the bazaars of central Tehran, where the wealthy merchants merged their religious pieties with anti-modernist fury to back the Ayatollah's movement. Yet these explosions occurred long after the revolution was well under way, and they would not have been society-altering events if this had merely been a revolt of the mosque and the bazaar. The revolution was not, until its final moments, an Islamic movement, and its motives and causes were not religious. It was a revolution of the arrival city, and its main cause was urban property.

As recently as 1963, when the Shah began his "White Revolution" to industrialize Iran's economy, Tehran had been a small city without any major slum or shantytown developments, in a country that was largely rural. What happened over the next 16 years is an object lesson in the mismanagement of rural–urban migration. Rather than the Shah's goals of creating "a prosperous, healthy, literate, well-housed, and largely (90 percent) urban society . . . with industry emerging as the employer of perhaps 40 percent of the labor force,"[3] Tehran became, in less than a decade, the most migrant-packed city in the world, experiencing an urban growth rate higher than Calcutta, Bombay, Mexico City, or Manila. In 1956, only 31 percent of Iranians lived in cities; on the eve of the revolution, almost half did. And this enormous population shift occurred without any serious state investment in the migrants' futures, without any government effort to turn the millions of new arrivals into urban citizens, without any effort to acknowledge the existence of arrival cities. As we shall see, the Shah turned the noble motive of urbanization into a self-defeating catastrophe.

The White Revolution was the Shah's attempt to preempt the possibility of a full-fledged "red" revolution—for the forces of the left, and not of Islam, were seen as the sole threat to his regime. He attempted to do this, at a rapid pace, by bringing about the sort of change in Iran that had occurred in the West during the decades of the Enlightenment. "You are all going to have to run to keep up with me," the Shah boasted. "All the old economic and political feudalism is over and done with. Everybody should benefit directly from the product of his own labor."[4] There was nothing misplaced about the Shah's ambitions in themselves; in fact, he was seeking exactly what every developing-world leader should: an economy based on industry and services, a largely urbanized population, and a higher standard of rural living provided by an agriculture system that abandoned feudalism for intensified, high-employment food production.

The plan failed first in the countryside. Iranians were overwhelmingly villagers, and most of those villagers were peasant farmers, who grew by hand for their own consumption and paid feudal-style fees to owners who often lived elsewhere. The agricultural reform, which affected the majority of the population, seemed a simple matter: Redistribute the land, and let agriculture become an industry.

By 1971, when the land reforms were complete, it should have been apparent that the goal wasn't being realized. About half of the best land, much of it owned by government employees or military officers, was neither redistributed to peasants nor mechanized into productive farms; the owners bribed officials to have their estates classified as industrial farms, even if they weren't, or they simply stole the subsidies, or they "divided" out the most unfertile pieces of land and handed them to peasants. "Only a minority," one study concluded, "practiced capitalist agriculture, using wage laborers, machinery, and production inputs such as fertilizers. The government did not encourage modern production techniques."[5]

By the 1970s Iran was a net food importer, to an increasingly large degree. Imports were rising by 14 percent each year, so that by the time of the revolution almost half the country's food was imported. The newly liberated farmers couldn't compete with the imports, so the peasants became ever more indebted to the government, to the banks, and to private moneylenders. This led to a mass exodus, in which hundreds of thousands of peasants and workers left the villages every year. "Many abandoned the routine life of two bowls of rice and a jar of yoghurt in a cavelike adobe house of the village for the uncertainty of life in the city which promised, at the least, minimum wage for manual labor," the scholar Tahmoores Sarraf wrote in his memoir. "Thus, instead of increasing consumption in the rural areas, the strategy reduced the rural population and agricultural output."[6] By 1978, three million working people had moved from rural areas to Iran's major cities; counting their families, this meant that between nine and 12 million people had made a rural–urban migration in only 15 years.

When those villagers arrived in the city, there was nothing waiting for them. The Shah's spending on factories and urban redevelopment projects was legendary and widely self-promoted, so it was with genuine bewilderment that millions of people found that they were not wanted in Tehran and unable to live or educate their children in even the most rudimentary conditions. The Shah had created a Potemkin façade of industrial growth and urbanization—a national automobile industry, attractive downtown buildings, and universities—but had paid little attention to either the rural or the urban livelihoods of the actual citizens who would form the majority in this new society. As a consequence, the number of illiterate adults rose from 13 million in 1963 to 15 million in 1977.

By 1979, 35 percent of Tehran's population of five million lived in slums, squats, and makeshift settlements, with a million living in the new arrival cities on the edge of town. Those numbers kept growing. To keep the city appearing "modern," the Shah's regime aggressively pushed squatter-dwellers out of the center and into the unseen outskirts of Tehran, often using force to do so. Huge construction projects were taking place in central Tehran, but they involved universities, military barracks, automobile factories, government buildings, hotels, and airports. Little was spent on housing or the development of residential communities, except for the middle-class developments in the north.

"High rents effectively barred most people from the central zone of large cities," the Iranian sociologist Misagh Parsa concluded in a study of the revolution's causes. "As a consequence, shantytowns sprang up on the outskirts of urban areas. In Tehran, at least twenty-four large shantytowns containing thousands of families had arisen on the edge of the city . . . These shantytowns provided notoriously poor living conditions. Houses were generally erected by family members themselves, who were forced to pay exorbitant prices for black-market building materials. Drinking water was supplied by private companies at 72 times the rate within the city. Whereas 80 percent of the city budget was allocated to provide services for the wealthy inhabitants of northern Tehran, shantytowns lacked running water, electricity, public transportation, garbage collection, health care, education and other services."[7]

Despite having become one of the world's leading oil exporters during a decade of rising petroleum prices—or more likely because of this—Iran's economy became inflationary and failed to produce jobs. By early 1979, one Iranian cabinet minister estimated that in Tehran 700,000 people were employed in "dead work," such as the sale of chewing gum on the streets. Urban land prices increased daily. Between 1967 and 1977, Tehran property increased in value by over 2,000 percent. In 1975, in an attempt to control land speculation, the government forbade the selling of vacant land, a move that severely exacerbated the problem. By the end of 1977, every day 3,500 Tehran families were searching for somewhere to sleep. In southern Tehran, each single room was occupied by an average of six people. Between 1967 and 1977, the percentage of urban families living in a single room rose from 36 to 43; on the eve of the revolution, 42 percent of Tehran's inhabitants lived in "inadequate" housing, usually single rooms in slums.[8]

These numbers became an embarrassment to the regime. In the summer of 1977, the Shah began to respond with bulldozers. By the end of the summer, the slum-demolition plans met fierce resistance within Eslamshahr, where the community took up arms against the police and bulldozers. Entire families were buried in their houses, but the community was organized enough to keep rebuilding, rewiring, and replanning the new town, resisting the regime and becoming increasingly desperate for any new form of government. [9]

"I am inclined to believe," the scholar Leonard Binder wrote after spending the late 1970s in Iran, "that the extent of the opposition to the Shah was not primarily because of his repressive treatment of the opposition, but because of the outrageous simple-mindedness of his modernization programs which attacked the quiescent and made political activists of them. The Shah had gone out and created a mass opposition and therewith a responsive audience for the small groups of extremists on the right and the left who had taken up arms against the regime." [10]

AN IMPLOSION FROM THE EDGES

The 1979 revolution was an event deeply rooted in the arrival city. According to the Iranian political scientist Ali Farazmand, it was "rural migrants who participated in the massive anti-regime demonstrations in the streets during 1978 . . . These migrants whose living conditions were growing worse every day were among the early demonstrators in the streets of the major cities. They became targets of the revolutionary organizers, religious and secular as well as left and liberal, who focused their attention on the urban poor . . . Both religious leaders and liberal leftist political organizations targeted these migrants as well as the other lower- and lower-middle-class people who dropped to the poverty line during the 1970s." And no wonder. At that point, 94 percent of Tehran's working-class population had been born somewhere else, usually in a village. Even in major factories in Tehran, whose workers were the blue-collar elite, 80 percent of workers were peasants or sons of peasants who had migrated to the city. [11]

There was every reason to expect a mass revolt against the Shah, but no reason to expect it to be an Islamic revolution. "The vast majority of participants in the revolutionary uprising," the most comprehensive study of the revolution's social origins concludes, "did not indicate in any way that they wanted to establish a society based on fundamentalist principles."[12] According to the sociologist Asef Bayat, who observed the revolution closely, "most of the poor seem to be uninterested in any particular form of ideology and politics."[13] There was every reason to expect this to be a liberal-democratic revolution, a turn to Turkish-style Kemalism or European-style liberalism.

But it was the cleric Ruhollah Khomeini who most vocally, and most credibly, promised the rural migrants a place to live—in fact, in his speeches of early 1979, he promised all Tehranis, and all peasants, their own land. "This Islamic revolution is indebted to the efforts of this class, the class of shanty dwellers," he said that February. "These South Tehranis, these footbearers, as we call them, they are our masters . . . they were the ones who brought us to where we are. Everyone must have access to land, this divine endowment . . . no one must remain without a dwelling in this country." Furthermore, he said, electricity and water should be provided free of charge to the poor. His deputies, horrified by this promise, begged him to make rural reforms instead, warning that such promises would unleash even greater waves of urban migration. But he knew that his revolution would not succeed unless he won the unqualified support of the slum-dwellers.[14]

His message was efficiently spread through the mosques, a recruiting network of the sort that the liberal-democratic and Marxist parties did not possess and did not seem capable of replicating. Even as he promised free land and housing, Khomeini kept the Islamic nature of his revolution obscure, couching it in the language of nationalism and democracy, referring to it as an "Iranian revolution" or a "republic" when addressing less religious audiences and avoiding discussion of Islamic policies.[15] There is every indication that ordinary Iranians, when they voted over-whelmingly for Khomeini's government in the referendum of March 1979, believed they were voting for a nationalist, liberal-democratic party that happened to have a mullah for a leader.

As the revolution turned theocratic, rejected the republican con-stitution, expelled the liberal-minded president, executed many of his colleagues, and turned the Ayatollah into a perpetual, all-power-ful Supreme Leader, it was safe from the anger and disillusionment of the secular middle classes because it carefully maintained the loy-alty of the far larger mass of arrival-city residents. The squatters won their justice when former Tehran mayor Gholamreza Nikpey, who had ordered the bulldozers to Eslamshahr, was taken before a revo-lutionary tribunal, given a summary sentence, and promptly exe-cuted by firing squad.

A SOCIAL CATASTROPHE

The rhetoric of free land had been heard by the poor, not just in Tehran but throughout the country, and it had its effect. Within months, the flood of migrants from the years of the White Revolution had turned into a torrent the likes of which the world had never seen. It seemed, for a while, as if the entire city's perimeter was up for grabs. Tehran's population more than doubled in just a few years.

In Tehran, I spoke with Mitra Habibi, an urban planner who wit-nessed these events, and she explained the inevitable logic of this exodus: "The revolution had persuaded a large group of people who were living outside Tehran, in the countryside, to come to Tehran, because they were saying that those who were living in Tehran will be given land, and those who have occupied land in Tehran will be given a house. That was the reason why the population of Tehran so quickly grew from three million to seven million, because the people had been given the idea that the revolutionary government was there to support the oppressed poor people, so they started thinking, 'Whenever we go and we take the land, we confiscate or we occupy the land and start to build the house, it will be legitimated by the revolutionary government.' "

As a result of this pressure, the rising cost of the war with Iraq, and the rather evident fact that the outskirts-dwellers had never been terribly interested in Islamic ideology or Koranic law, the revolution soon turned on its village-arrival supporters. In 1983, after Tehran officials begged him to declare a state of emergency, Khomeini deemed migration a "major social problem" that must be stopped. It was a complete reversal of the rhetoric that had led the urban poor to support the revolution in the first place and a complete misunderstanding of the potential value of these migrants. As Asef Bayat wrote, "Whereas the poor viewed migration as a means to a better life, for the authorities it represented a 'social catastrophe,' 'the most important problem beside the war,' and 'a major threat to the revolution and the Islamic Republic.' "[16]

During the next twenty years, five comprehensive laws would be passed to regulate urban land, most of them restricting its use and exchange. This gave the government a de facto monopoly over the use of land, which raised prices. There were also large-scale public-housing construction projects, financed through petroleum revenues, almost all in the form of massive Soviet-style blocks of apartment towers. But this low-income housing was available only to workers employed full-time by corporations or governments, a condition that effectively excluded an estimated 60 percent of households.[17]

As a result, the arrival-city residents of Tehran were forced to plan for themselves. And, starting once again in Eslamshahr, that is what happened: They autonomously organized their own administration, an ad hoc, practical-minded municipal government that seemed oblivious to the ruling Islamic regime. Young architects and planners donated their efforts to replace the medieval-looking lanes with straight, wide streets; engineers tapped into the city's electrical and water systems. In 1986, Eslamshahr issued its first development plan.

In the early 1990s, in a bid to halt the expansion, the Tehran government turned Eslamshahr into a formal, incorporated city. With almost 400,000 residents, it immediately became one of the 10 largest cities in Iran. This had two effects. First, it created a land-price boom in Eslamshahr. Second, the prospect of taxes, utility bills, building standards, and other costs of legitimate urban living proved too daunting for many of the poor, casually employed residents. Within a short time, Eslamshahr had spawned its own arrival cities. Two new settlements, Akbar Abad and Sultan Abad, appeared just beyond its incorporated borders and started growing fast. Within a year, these two villages had expanded into a dense urban expanse of 110,000 people.*

A major bulldozing and slum-clearance campaign was launched. In the summer of 1992 alone, 2,000 homes were destroyed. Confrontation between squatters and police became increasingly violent, reminiscent of the worst years under the Shah. Eslamshahr exploded again in 1995, in some of the most serious riots Iran has seen since the revolution. The cause was anger at rising government bus fares between the periphery and the downtown core, where most arrival-city residents work. But the protests took on an increasingly anti-regime tenor.

The regime was unable to snuff out the new arrival cities on the edge of Eslamshahr, and, by now, Akbar Abad and Sultan Abad have been able to win themselves a begrudging legitimacy from the government, though without any parks or schools, these settlements remain dusty, primitive places. When I visited Akbar Abad, I found myself in the midst of a sizable neighborhood of low mud houses being transformed piecemeal into four-story apartments, its residents all from one district in the central province of Yazd. As these sub-settlements have become increasingly legitimate and inaccessible to rural migrants, they themselves have thrown off new arrival

---

* The names of these settlements were later changed by the government to Nasim Shahr and Golestan, though they are still widely known by their original names.

cities on their own peripheries—one of them being Emamzadeh 'Isa.

During the Ahmadinejad years, the Islamic regime, thrust into power by arrival-city residents on promises of property rights, did everything it could to deter migrants from settling in the margins, while trying to avoid the violent clashes that marred the 1990s, using quiet strategies such as the mass reforestation of vacant lands on the outskirts—using nature, rather than violence, to make it physically impossible to arrive. This tack has had limited success. A fifth of the Iranian population now lives in Tehran, eight million in the city proper and perhaps as many more in the outskirts. There is a real sense that those living on the southern fringes have no path toward inclusion in Iranian society: They are forced into permanent marginality.

In the streets of places like Emamzadeh 'Isa, this is breeding resentment. Village migrants are no longer the submissive, conservative, and religious people they were once thought to be. Detailed surveys by scholars Amir Nikpey and Farhad Khosrokhavar found that the citizens of Tehran's outskirts have become deeply opposed to religious politics.[18] "This young generation has a totally different point of view toward the revolution," Nikpey told me. "They are not the young people of 30 years ago who backed the revolutionary state—this generation has no connection to the revolutionary values. They are still mainly believers in Islam, but the majority are saying that we must separate the church from the state—and that the state cannot gain its legitimacy from religion." This is a new outskirts, as urbanized as anywhere in the center. Women here are marrying at 28 rather than at 13, as they did in 1979, and having 1.7 children per family, rather than 7, as they did in the 1980s—and women here have more education than men, just as they do downtown.

A succession of Iranian governments has repeated the mistakes of the Shah: treating the arrival cities as a threat rather than an opportunity; failing to give them the physical or financial resources to grow, instead focusing on the lower middle classes of the downtown core; and, in the process, creating a huge division of wealth. The Islamic regime, despite its oil money, has not been able to stem the accretion of blocked lives on the fringe. Out here on the edge, it feels as if history is repeating itself. These are patient, conservative people, unwilling to risk everything for a mere political statement. But if they find their path into sustainable urban life blocked by the state, then they will explode, once again, into the center of Iranian life.

Petare, Caracas

What happened to the arrival-city residents of Tehran has been repeated across the developing world. Revolutionary movements originating in the wealthy center, probably beginning with the Jacobins in 1789, have used the grievances and frustrations of the arrival city as their source of ideological and human support and then abandoned those communities as soon as they came to power.

A most extreme and fascinating variation on this theme is found in Venezuela, where the "Bolivarian revolution," which began with the election of Col. Hugo Chávez to the presidency in 1999, promised to produce a South American government focused exclusively on the arrival city. Turning the rural-migrant slums into the symbolic instrument of their legitimacy, the Chávez regime managed to stoke these marginal lives into a revolutionary conflagration and then to provoke a fresh crisis in the arrival city.

To understand what went wrong, it's worth speaking to the residents of Petare, an enormous shantytown community that covers a large upper slope of the Caracas valley, a dense warren of streets that overlooks the wealthier city below. The slums of Caracas are likely the most vertical in the world; rural arrivals have spent decades staking their claims on theoretically uninhabitable rock walls, the residents of Petare jerry-building steep cascades of squatter settlements, which are both physically and economically precarious.

Its people—they number between 400,000 and 900,000, depending how they're counted—have been described from the beginning as Chávez's most ardent supporters and most lavishly rewarded beneficiaries. The Mexican writer Alma Guillermoprieto described this slum as embodying the essence of the Chávez revolution. "Petare has . . . possibly more *chavistas* [followers of Chávez] per square foot, and more cohesively organized, than anywhere else in the country. It is in Petare that Hugo Chávez's ambitious social welfare programs are implemented most ambitiously, because he has turned the poor into his de facto party, and as a result, whether his presidency stands or falls can be determined by the residents of this *barrio*."[19]

These would prove to be prophetic words, as we shall see. It is no surprise that a new sort of arrival-city politics arose in Venezuela, for this oil state has had huge arrival cities longer than most countries. Venezuela was one of the first developing countries to make an urban transition, its population becoming 61 percent urban by 1961. From 1941 through 1961, the annual growth rate averaged more than 7 percent, greater than any other city in Latin America. As in Iran, ultra-rapid migration was encouraged without much consideration for either village or urban destination. During the 1970s, rising petroleum prices created an employment boom in Caracas, and governments encouraged tens of thousands of villagers to migrate to the city, tolerating their "land invasions" and occasionally granting them ownership of their squatter homes in exchange for electoral support.

The economy was virtually engineered to prevent a decent urban transition. Beginning in 1970, food prices were set by a Law of Agricultural Marketing, and then price controls were extended to 80 percent of wage goods in 1974. This was accompanied by the massive subsidizing of goods at the consumer level, notably food and gasoline—an expenditure that amounted to 7 percent of government revenues—and rigid currency-exchange controls. These policies continued in the 1980s, this time without the oil revenues to back them, leading to staggering government debt. Together, these rigid policies had several effects. They destroyed the agricultural industry, sending hundreds of thousand of people fleeing the villages for Caracas, and they provoked high levels of inflation, which destroyed the non-oil-productive economy. This, in turn, led to double-digit unemployment, which struck just as the slums on the outskirts were becoming most crowded.

In 1989, as the government was forced to abandon its gasoline subsidies in order to receive emergency bailout loans, the slums of Caracas exploded into days of violent rioting and repression known as the *Caracazo*. Bodies shot by government soldiers were dumped in Petare. This set the seeds for Chávez's unsuccessful coup attempt in 1992 and then his successful presidential election, built on the support of arrival-city residents, in 1998. By that point, Petare was badly in need of state support: The endless shantytown slums of Caracas were becoming unlivable, their canyons of sewage undermining the very hills that supported them, causing their roads to collapse and entire neighborhoods to plummet off the hills in rivers of mud and human waste. There were no jobs, and crime was rife.

The Bolivarian revolution seemed to be made for the arrival city, and Chávez was lucky enough to launch it just as petroleum prices were beginning their decade-long climb, providing him with the resources to support it. By 2003, Chávez had established the signature programs of his revolution, the "social missions" (*misiones*) aimed mainly at the urban poor. Key programs were Mission Robinson and Mission Ribas, which taught basic literacy and skills-training courses to Venezuelan adults; Mission Mercal, which provided subsidized, low-cost meat, grains, and dairy products in the barrios; Mission Barrio Adentro, which provided free health care in the slums; and Mission Hábitat, which was intended to replace slums with 100,000 new units of high-quality housing per year.

There is no question that large sums of money were poured into the arrival cities of Caracas during the first decade of the Bolivarian revolution or that the arrival-city residents appreciated any food, health care, and money that came their way. Yet it quickly became apparent that the social missions were doing nothing for the arrival city in terms of its most important needs: land ownership, business opportunities, an autonomous economy and a pathway into the middle class. The residents of Petare knew what was needed for this but were never asked.

They soon realized that the social missions directed at their barrio had not delivered. While the free food and money brought about a decrease in absolute poverty during the period in which the money was coming, the arrival-city residents complained that nothing lasting was being built. This was often literally true. Housing construction never really got going; 150,000 homes were meant to be built and fewer than 35,000 were, many of them social-housing apartment blocks that didn't suit the needs of arrival-city residents. There was never any effort to give the arrival cities a chance to determine what housing suited their needs. Such long-term investments never became a priority, and, in fact, declined: average per capita levels of public spending on housing dropped by a third between the 1990–98 period (against which Chávez had campaigned) and his own 1999–2004 period.[20]

As for the education programs, these have been shown in extensive studies to have produced no measurable decrease in illiteracy.[21] The writer Tina Rosenberg, on a visit to a slum near Petare, was surprised to find how Mission Ribas functioned: "Political and ideological training, Ribas officials told me, is the top qualification for a facilitator. I attended a session for new Ribas students in Las Torres, a La Vega barrio near the top of the mountain. After Ribas officials told students how to register for classes and what would be expected of them, María Teresa Curvelo, the district coordinator, began a 90-minute talk about a referendum of great importance to the government . . . Afterward we rode down the mountain in a truck. When she got out, I thanked her. 'Fatherland, Socialism or Death!' she replied."[22]

At the end of 2008, Petare rebelled. Along with many other poor urban neighborhoods, it turned against the revolution, defeating the Bolivarian candidates in regional elections and protesting against the failure of the social missions. Petare's member of Parliament, Jesse Chacón, one of Chávez's best-known allies, was defeated by

Carlos Ocariz, a social-democratic opposition candidate. "There were people who got tired of the same old thing—it was payback," said Arleth Argote, a 31-year-old voter, who had enthusiastically backed Chávez during the previous decade, then became frustrated as the arrival city failed to evolve into a thriving community. "People are tired of living poorly," Ocariz told reporters. "It was a struggle between ideology and daily life."[23]

What Chávez had done, in essence, was to replace existing state programs with his own "revolutionary" programs, staffed by volunteers and visiting Cuban professionals, and with an ideological, rather than an economic or social, mission. The largest sum of money was spent subsidizing consumption, which did not change the underlying conditions and often replaced programs that might have done so. As a result, rather than improving life, these programs actually caused a sharp decrease in the material conditions of the rural-migrant poor. Between 1999 and 2006, the proportion of Venezuelan families living on dirt floors almost tripled, from 2.5 percent to 6.8 percent; the percentage with no access to running water rose from 7.2 to 9.4 percent; the percentage of underweight babies rose from 8.4 percent to 9.1 percent.[24] Despite the rhetoric, Chávez decreased the proportion of public spending on health, education, and housing compared with the years leading up to his attempted coup. Most tellingly, social inequality actually increased during the years of the revolution, according to the regime's own estimates.* It has been described as a process of "hollow growth": Even though the oil-dominated economy grew by 9 percent each year in Chávez's first decade, it failed to create jobs, and half of Venezuela's factories closed their doors between 1998 and 2008, mainly because price and foreign-exchange controls made it impossible to do business.

That view was reinforced by Edmond Saade, a generally

---

* The Gini Coefficient, the standard measure of inequality, in which zero indicates perfect equality and a one indicates complete inequality, increased from 0.44 to 0.48, a significant jump, between 2000 and 2005, according to the Venezuelan Central Bank.

regime-supporting scholar who runs the Caracas-based Datos research firm. He realized, a few years into the regime, that the money spilling into the arrival cities of Caracas was leaving no lasting effect. "The poor of Venezuela are living much better lately and have increased their purchasing power . . . [but] without being able to improve their housing, education level, and social mobility," he told an interviewer. "Rather than help them become stakeholders in the economic system, what [the Chávez regime] has done is distribute as much oil wealth as possible in missions and social programs."[25] In the view of disgruntled regime supporters, Chávez had done exactly what previous governments had: poured oil money into the economy, thus causing inflation and destroying the possibility of slum-based entrepreneurship, and given vote-winning handouts to the people on the margins, ignoring their real needs. "Despite its revolutionary rhetoric and its curtailment of democratic institutions," the economist Norman Gall concluded in an impressive study, "the 'Bolivarian Revolution' seems merely to be continuing the history of colossal waste of oil revenues, disorganization and failed investments that have impoverished the Venezuelan people in recent decades."[26] By the end of its first decade, the first great South American revolution of the arrival cities had fizzled, failing to deliver the rural migrants anything it had promised. Chávez, his popularity fluctuating wildly, turned his attention toward dramatic seizures and nationalizations of foreign companies, all but forgetting the promises of housing, development, and more prosperous slums. In Petare, time froze.

This was, like its Iranian cousin, an explosion from the urban center that simply used the arrival city as fuel. There is another way arrival cities can explode: by developing their own potent political movements and sending them inward to seize the political center of the larger city, and possibly the nation. The arrival-city takeover of the city and the nation is a new phenomenon but is likely to become the defining political event of this century, as neglected ex-migrant communities, which, in many countries, will soon represent a majority of the population, demand their own representation.

Mulund, Mumbai

Sanjay Solkar, whose annual journey to his southern Maharashtra village we followed in chapter 2, returns to spend his nights in a tiny concrete room, perhaps two by three meters, in the back of a narrow tea shop on a crowded street outside the Mulund train station in northeast Mumbai, in a busy and thriving district where slums and lower-middle-class apartments are jammed together. At night, this slight, quietly determined 20-year-old shares its bare floor with four other young men. Sanjay's possessions—a blanket, three changes of clothing, and some papers—are piled in a corner of the room. His earnings, amounting to barely a dollar a day, are all sent back to his village; he gets his meals and spends most of his spare time in the shop. He sees his immediate family once or twice a year, at rice-harvest time and during major festivals. It would seem to be a fragile, precarious, lonely existence.

Next door to the tea shop, however, is another narrow building that offers Sanjay a surrogate family, a welfare system, and a source of physical security. It is an odd-looking place, fronted with a wood panel painted to resemble a comic-book entrance to a stone temple, adorned with flags and banners bearing a tiger logo. It functions as a social club, a meeting point, and a de facto employment center and welfare office. It is the place that guarantees Sanjay's job security; where he can get small loans for transportation to Mumbai and back and gain his place in the social network of the slums; where he can someday seek a better job or find someone to pay the bribes to obtain a license for a vending cart or a skills-training course; where he can go to seek better-quality slum housing when he and his family become permanent urbanites; where they will be able to seek sewage hookups and fight to keep their slum from being demolished for middle-class developments; and where they stand the best chance of someday gaining ownership of the land beneath their home. In exchange for this camaraderie and support, if he avails himself of its services,

Sanjay will be expected to give money, when he earns enough to contribute a share; to participate in political campaigning, when it's election time; to lend his bodily presence, when protests or occupations are called for; and, should the arrival city erupt again, to be willing to commit acts of violence against religious and linguistic minorities.

This is the local *shaka*, or branch office, of the Shiv Sena, or Army of Shivaji,* which counts Sanjay among its hundreds of thousands of members. It is an ethnic movement, political party, and organized-crime body that has ruled the city since the mid-1980s. In the process, the Shiv Sena has irrevocably transformed the city's character, its mood, and even its name. Across Mumbai, and especially in slum neighborhoods, 224 *shakas* and about 1,000 sub-*shakas* serve as organizing points for a startling range of activities, from social work and housing aid to extortion and protection rackets to election campaigns and violent battles against non-Hindu street vendors and shops that dare print their signs in English. These more aggressive activities, all in the name of defending the Marathi-speaking Hindus of Mumbai, have earned the Sena its reputation as a threatening and fascistic movement, one that has terrified India's secular establishment and launched waves of violence against Muslims on an unprecedented scale.

But to see the Shiv Sena strictly as an ethnic-chauvinist movement is to miss its crucial role in the process of rural–urban migration, in the settlement of slums, and in the building and maintenance of the arrival cities, which are the key feature of modern Mumbai and home to half of its 20 million people. This arrival-city role may seem surprising in a movement that was built on opposing the migration of outsiders into the city. But, in violently enforcing its ideas about who should be excluded from and invited to join the arrival cities of this megalopolis, the Shiv Sena has come to be the quintessential political movement of the great migration: a fascism-from-below that has

* Shivaji Bhosale was the seventeenth-century Maharashtrian Hindu who led an uprising against the Moghul rulers of the region and established a Marathi empire; he is a folk hero among Maharashtrians and low-caste Hindus across India.

taken the bitter struggles of rural–urban arrival, the competition for scarce housing resources, and transformed them into the defining politics of a city, a state, and, sometimes, an entire nation.

Bombay, as Mumbai was known historically, is located near the intersection of Gujarat and Maharashtra states, the former tradition-ally known for commerce and the latter more for farming; it has always been a polyglot city, its mixture of Muslims and Hindus speak-ing Gujarati and English in business, Marathi (the language of Maharashtra) and Urdu (the main Muslim tongue) in the workplace and the home, and, in the streets and shops, usually Bombiya Hindi, a variant of the national language peppered with words and expres-sions from those other tongues. In the decades after the Second World War, Bombay's rising cotton-industry fortunes drew millions of poor Maharashtrian farmers to migrate into the city, especially after India decided in 1960 to redivide its states along strictly linguistic lines, cre-ating a larger Maharashtra with Bombay as its capital. Many of the Marathi-speaking migrants expected this new status to turn them into a dominant class, and they were surprised to find themselves just the same as before, a plurality but not a majority, neither the wealthiest nor the poorest group, suffering the same unemployment as anyone else during the economic downturn of the mid-1960s.

When the editorial cartoonist Bal Thackeray launched the Shiv Sena movement with a protest rally in a park in 1966, the targets of his rage and resentment were fellow Hindus—those who, he claimed, had moved to Bombay from Gujarat and other northern states to take control of businesses and those who had migrated from Tamil Nadu and other southern states to take all the white-collar jobs. Sena vol-unteers began torching South Indian cafés in efforts to stop the "inva-sion" and launched campaigns to lobby for restricting white-collar positions to "sons of the soil" (as they referred to Maharashtrians). It was an anti-minority movement, with a distinctly middle-class tone, among the largest of the city's minorities, a group that was as much an immigrant or "invader" community as any other.

But this ethnic-rights movement soon encountered the problem, and the opportunity, of the arrival city. By 1965, the increasing pace of migration had created over 3,000 Bombay slums and more than a million slum- and pavement-dwellers. For the first time, they were seen as a major threat to the city's well-being and a potential key political constituency. For the arrival-city residents, the constant, burning issue was the scarcity of livable land (and, in Bombay, the concept of "livable" has always been stretched to human limits) and the struggle to hold on to it. This was really an issue of land tenure and housing policy, but it was easily recast by Shiv Sena leaders as one of inter-ethnic competition. In the early 1970s, the party made its first major moves into the slums. It organized its rural-migrant *dadas* (*shaka* leaders, or literally "big brothers") and sent them out to encroach on public land—both to create new arrival-city enclaves for the Maharashtrian villagers entering Bombay and also for the developers of middle-class housing blocks, who now had to pay the Shiv Sena to obtain it.

While they engaged in this lucrative franchise, the *dadas* became big brothers in a more personal sense. For the Marathi-speaking rural migrant, the Shiv Sena became the sole point of comfort and order amid the chaos of the fast-expanding city. The ruling Congress party, which had heretofore served Bombay well with its Nehruvian mission of inter-ethnic harmony, had become a threat to the slum-dweller. In the 1970s, it turned to economic and demographic authoritarianism, its signature policies being mandatory birth control and slum clearance, and its near-exclusive focus on India's rural development treated cities as an inconvenient afterthought. Those policies missed the point of rural–urban migration and failed to see that Indians did not, on the whole, want to be farmers with large families but were lacking effective pathways to urban life. The rural-focused policies of Congress left migrants trapped in a limbo that was neither rural nor urban. Shiv Sena was able to step into this space. The typical rural migrant, the sociologist Sujata Patel observed in her study of this period, has

broken the bonds of village community life but has not become
part of an urban-industrial culture. In these circumstances the need
for an equivalent "village community" becomes translated into an
affiliation with the other members of small slum communities, with
the slums being organized into clusters of regional, ethnic and
religious groups . . . The Sena's policy of organizing people at their
point of residence has helped to mobilize this deprived populace,
especially the young male migrants. For young male under-
employed slum dwellers the Shiv Sena represents the family, and its
local chief becomes the "father" or the elder brother, "*dada*." It
gives them a sense of identity, organizing them into various
cultural activities as they "hang around" in corner *paan* shops. It
taps their restlessness and articulates their anger at being part of
an unrecognized element in the city.[27]

By the end of the 1970s, Bal Thackeray's movement had become
a fixture in the slums, but it had produced no discernible political or
demographic gains. It had, however, turned Thackeray himself into
a major celebrity, the "Al Capone of Bombay," the subject of a cult
following. But his movement was losing its impetus. By this point,
most Marathi speakers were more successful and no longer saw
southerners and Gujarati businessmen as a threat. Thackeray realized
that he needed a larger target and a more sensational approach. He
found it in the politics of *Hinduvta*, the Hindu-supremacist movement that views India's Hindu communities as the original, authentic
Aryan race of India, drawing on the same confusion of linguistic and
racial categories that created Nazism in Germany (both movements
were inspired by the same European thinkers). This provided him
with a powerful ideology, with a built-in enemy in Bombay's large
Muslim community, and with a constituency in the Hindu slum-
dwellers, who could easily be persuaded that their Muslim neighbors
were competitive "invaders."

From the beginning of the movement, Thackeray had kept a

portrait of Hitler in his office, next to a snarling Bengal tiger. In 1984, as Shiv Sena was becoming a national political movement and the first major anti-Muslim riots were sweeping across Bombay, he explained in an interview exactly how his anti-Muslim campaign was modeled after the Third Reich: "Now I like some Jews, they have a warrior-like thing . . . But Hitler found that not only were they the corrupt people but they also didn't behave. He realized that 'if I don't drive them out, then my country won't come up.' You may condemn that kind of act—even I would condemn. It is not the only way, this gas chamber and all. I don't like. But you may drive them out—things like that. It is all right. But don't blame the man. He wanted to bring his country up and he knew what were the evils."[28]

So Thackeray invited Gujaratis and South Indian Hindus to join his movement, began publishing his newspapers in Hindi as well as Marathi, and fomented a Hindu–Muslim conflict where none had existed. Muslims were not obvious targets: It was impossible to claim that they were taking jobs or educational opportunities away from Marathi speakers or that they were migrating to Bombay to steal jobs. Muslims are at least as well established in the city as Hindus are and had lived as neighbors for centuries. But there was a new atmosphere in Bombay in the 1980s. The big textile mills were closing down forever, after the catastrophic strike of 1982 drove the industry to seek lower-wage locations around the world. Suddenly, people on the lower rungs of the working class were thrust into the informal service economy, out of the one-room concrete *chawls* and into the proper slums, out of permanent lifetime employment and into the chaos of selling, hustling, and finding a living. This created insecurity and discomfort and made nationalist, jingoistic politics seem more appealing.

This mood was particularly acute for rural-migrant women, who, during the fabric-industry boom, had often maintained ties to the villages, calling themselves "visiting wives." Now, they were finding themselves transformed into permanent urban residents, full-time workers in domestic service and retail, and often their family's primary breadwinners. Shiv Sena, heretofore a very masculine movement, suddenly held an appeal to Hindu working women, and the *shakas* eagerly incorporated them by organizing the *Aghadi*, a women's branch. The social anthropologist Atreyee Sen, who spent a year living undercover within the Shiv Sena women's organizations, found a movement that used rural–urban migration to build an ideology of hate.

> Poor slum women joined the violent Sena ethno-nationalist movement because the organization provided shade from what they described as "the scalding effects" (*man jalana*) of urbanization, industrialization and migration in Mumbai . . . Within the Sena they felt "connected"; the feeling of community that was lost through rural-urban and intra-urban migration was replaced by "Maharashtrianism" . . . Most women, who mourned the lost vitality of community life in villages, seemed to have regained their traditional group solidarities. Thus the *Aghadi* gave slum women a chance to assimilate into a new social and political network, within which they could resolve their urban insecurities and experiences of alienation.[29]

On the other hand, for the hundreds of thousands of men who flooded into the city from the villages, a migration that accelerated to record levels in the 1980s, there were two possibilities: You could join the Shiv Sena's cult of violence, benefiting from the Sena's many forms of assistance in exchange for participating in acts of gangsterism, expulsion, or destruction, or you could live in fear of the Shiv Sena and very likely become its victim. "Youth in general, and particularly the growing minority devoid of strong ethno-regionalist affiliations, esteem the urbanite and tough image of the Shiv Sena," one scholar who spent time within the movement observed. "The organization is as *tej* (tough) as Bombay is. Joining it is considered as a way for learning the city codes and becoming integrated . . . the organization thus puts before the in-migrants a choice: *The first term is a proposal for complete integration . . . The second term is complete exclusion.*"[30]

By the end of the 1980s, it became possible for the Shiv Sena to turn that dichotomy into a city-wide ideology. Starting with its municipal election victory in 1985, the Shiv Sena controlled the Bombay mayor's office and other municipal bodies continually for the next two and a half decades. By 1992, it had an active membership of 300,000, exceeding the size of the Bombay police force (of course, many police were also Shiv Sena members). That strength of force, and the rising pitch of intolerance emanating from Bal Thackeray and the *dadas*, combined to form a highly combustible mixture.

In December of 1992, it ignited. The cause was unlikely. In a remote corner of Uttar Pradesh state, in northeastern India, a crowd of 150,000 Hindu nationalists destroyed the historic Babri Mosque. In faraway Bombay, there were rumors of Muslim reprisal killings; these were inflamed when the Shiv Sena decided to hold a march in support of the activists implicated in the destruction of the mosque, and to hold it in the narrow laneways of the Dharavi slum, whose 800,000 residents include sizable Muslim communities. Some Muslims reacted angrily, and then Bal Thackeray declared an all-out war. The pages of his *Saamna* newspaper, popular among poor Marathis, had been filled with tales of shiploads of armaments from Pakistan arriving on the coast. Then, on January 9, at a moment when tensions had increased to a dangerous level, *Saamna* provoked the mob to mass murder, in an editorial apparently written by Thackeray himself: "Muslims of Bhendi Bazar, Null Bazar, Dongri and Pydhonie, the areas we call Mini Pakistan that are determined to uproot Hindustan, took out their weapons. They must be shot on the spot . . . the next few days will be ours."[31]

The next six weeks saw furious Hindu mobs overtaking the city in a reign of terror; a thousand people, most of them Muslim, were killed by burning, shooting, beatings, or drowning; Hindu mobs burned down entire neighborhoods and Muslim-majority industrial districts and drove at least 150,000 Muslims out of the city. When it was over, the geography of Bombay was permanently transformed. No longer could Hindu and Muslim families live comfortably as neighbors, as they generally had for centuries; the Sena-dominated Hindu slums were transformed into "gated communities" to be feared and avoided by Muslims. The riots were followed by a Muslim bombing campaign, the first act of Islamic terrorism within India, and this cycle of reprisal continued for the next decade. Almost overnight, the world's most multicultural city became far more segregated.

The riots boosted the Shiv Sena's fortunes, even though an official inquiry would hold the party responsible for starting them and provoking their most serious acts of violence. (It would not be until 2008 that anyone would be punished, when three Shiv Sena officials, one of them a member of Parliament, were jailed.) In the 1995 elections, a coalition of the Hindu-nationalist Bharatiya Janata Party (BJP) and the Shiv Sena won control of Maharashtra state, ending decades of Congress rule. Among their first acts was to rename the city's capital Mumbai—a pronunciation traditionally used by Hindu speakers of Marathi and Gujarati but not by Urdu-speaking Muslims or by any speakers of English or Hindi (the latter including most religious minorities), who had always called it Bombay. Even in its name, the city became more segregated. And the party used its official power to create physical segregation. Efforts by victims, mainly Muslim, to rebuild their slum homes were blocked by the Sena-controlled municipal and state governments, which launched campaigns of slum clearance that targeted communities, many of them Muslim, that were not loyal to the party. In 1998, the Shiv Sena entered national politics as a member of the BJP-led National Democratic Alliance, whose tolerance for Hindu nationalism gave Shiv Sena greater power and influence in Mumbai and allowed violent acts to take place with impunity.

By the end of the 1990s, the Shiv Sena had taken the place of many forms of government and public service in Mumbai—though only for the city's Hindu residents—with vital public services emerging not from government or public-sector agencies but directly from the political offices and *shakas* of the Sena. "Mid-rung Sena politicians personally living in the slums are respected as patrons by the slum inhabitants," one study observed. "Promises of flats were made by one, not in his capacity as a corporator [municipal official] but as the local leader of the Shiv Sena. His political position was not as important as his status as a Hindu leader in the Shiv Sena. Relief money for constituents came from Shiv Sena funds, not the government treasury . . . the Shiv Sena's social work [provided] daycare centers, schools, and even medical help to its members. Shiv Sena ambulances race sleekly to the rescue through the streets of Mumbai in contrast to the government's ramshackle vehicles."[32]

Sanjay Solkar's move to Mumbai had its impetus in the opening of Shiv Sena offices in his village. At the time of his birth, his family had little or no knowledge of Bombay; the transportation links were poor, and the family was able to grow enough food to keep from starving, though they were malnourished. But when the Sena set up shop there in the early 1990s, as part of its move from being a strictly Bombay-centered movement into Maharashtrian state politics, it forged a tight link with the poor farmers. The *Sainaks* built wells and schools, repaired roads, and provided assistance to the "sons of the soil," all in the name of Marathi and Hindu purity. When a cash economy began to develop in the village, Sanjay's relatives, and many of their neighbors, began seeking work in the city. The Shiv Sena was there to help, its village office tied to the *shakas* of the arrival city. In the name of excluding others, Bal Thackeray's movement ended up making rural-to-urban migration easier and more efficient for some, enabling the further growth of the arrival city.

Nevertheless, the Shiv Sena's haphazard, gangsterish form of organization has meant that, for the past 20 years, Mumbai has done little about the paralyzing housing policies and sources of corruption that stand in the way of successful rural-arrival communities. It has meant that Hindu–Muslim violence is an enduring feature on Mumbai's ideological landscape. In 2002, when Hindu nationalists in northern Gujarat led a massacre that killed 2,000 Muslims, Shiv Sainaks in Mumbai participated in actions that killed 700 people, most of them Muslim. This violence continued during the period of BJP-led government, which lasted until 2004. The movement continues to dominate Mumbai, though it has metamorphosed. In 2006, disgruntled relatives of Bal Thackeray formed a breakaway party, the Maharashtra Navnirman Sena ("Maharashtra Reconstruction Army"), which claims to abandon the *Hinduvta* politics and "bureaucracy" of Shiv Sena and return to the Sena's radical Marathi-rights roots. The MNS quickly won a large following in Mumbai, leading the uprisings against English-language signs in 2008 and 2009, and may yet eclipse Shiv Sena. However, its forms of organization, its tactics and its arrival-city constituency are nearly identical.

This migrant-driven ethnic movement has permanently changed the politics of the world's preeminent arrival-city megalopolis. It has meant that the arrival city is sometimes treated with respect, since the slum-based Shiv Sena has granted land ownership, sewage, and water supplies, and municipal services, such as schools, clinics, and parks, to deserving (Hindu) slums, in ways that sometimes follow the best practices of urban land reform and turn the self-built settlements into truly thriving neighbourhoods. It has also meant that the worst sort of practices—bulldozer slum clearance, high-rise replacement of upwardly mobile arrival cities, complete neglect of the most basic sanitary and health needs, and criminal-gang control of services—have continued, and have even been amplified, in slums that are not part of that privileged group. It is a dangerous, divisive form of politics, one that retains the power to take over the Indian state and one that could have been avoided if governments had kept the needs of the arrival city in mind from the beginning. Its evolution ought to be studied by governments in Africa, South America, and East Asia, for it is precisely the form of politics that fills the vacuum when the rural migrants are taken for granted.

8

THE NEW CITY CONFRONTS
THE OLD WORLD

THE PROBLEM OF SPACE
Les Pyramides, Evry, France

Like the ruins of some lost Martian empire on the cover of a previous generation's science-fiction novel, the dun-and-gray pyramids materialize amid fields and forests along the motorway an hour
south of Paris. Les Pyramides, the product of the largest European
architectural competition of the 1960s, is the most utopian of the
many state-planned utopias that ring the perimeter of Paris, built to
house an expanding French urban middle class who were supposedly
seeking an escape from the postwar congestion of downtown Paris—
and occupied, almost from the beginning, by the precise opposite
group, a rural, non-French working class who are fighting their way
inward. As you get closer, the pyramids look less utopian, their stuccoed walls streaked with rain damage, their shadow-strewn concrete
pathways offering little security for the 12,000 pyramid-dwellers,
their central squares occupied by small clusters of young men with
nothing much to do.

One warm November evening in 2005, on the edge of one of those
squares, Aziz Foon shuttered the doors on his tiny shop, which sits
at the foot of a poured-concrete tower, squeezed between a cell-
phone vendor and a Turkish café, beneath an exuberant sign reading

"NUMBER ONE: Produits Exotiques—Alimentaires—Cosmetiques." Aziz, a very large and indelibly good-humored Gambian man of 46 with a bald pate and deep black skin, spends his days at the back of his narrow shop. Its walls are filled with an amazing range of products: cassava leaf, plantain root, African hair tonics, Islamic wall hangings, cooking pots, Dora the Explorer toys, canned coconut milk, Haribo candies, butane-gas cylinders, hair extensions, baby formula, kilograms of ghee, Argentinean corned beef, tiny tins of *petits pois* and *haricots verts*, prayer beads. "It's all the things that black people need," boasts Aziz's even more ebullient 33-year-old stepson, Yousef, dressed in silver chains and an oversized T-shirt and greeting his customers in Swahili, Mandinka, Hausa, Vai, Lingala, and Bambara, not to mention German, English, and French.

It is the only shop in Les Pyramides that sells these things—in fact, it is one of the very few shops owned by anyone who lives in these buildings. The vital arrival-city practice of starting a shop, or any sort of small business, is exceedingly difficult here. Little space is available for private use in these public-housing districts, and France's bureaucracy makes it extremely difficult for immigrant families to obtain commercial-property leases, business licenses, or lines of credit. It is even harder to buy your apartment: People here pay government-subsidized rent, with few other choices. Those who have a job—perhaps three-quarters of women and men of Aziz's age and probably fewer than half the adults below the age of 30—work outside of Les Pyramides and its surrounding city of Evry, commuting long distances, often to industrial suburbs on the opposite side of Paris, on what the city's mayor calls "embarrassingly substandard" public transit.

On this particular Tuesday evening, Aziz locked his shop and walked across the darkened square, offering nods of greeting to the uneasy clusters of young men, most of them kids of his customers, who hung out here until their parents got home each night. He walked along the vacant pedestrian pathways toward his apartment, which sits midway up one of several hulking pyramids of dull-coloured cubes, on the edge of a stagnant concrete pond.

His screams could be heard across the Pyramides complex. Ahead of him, he saw a vertical black column rising into the purple sky from a familiar spot. He ran and shouted in anguish. Bathed in orange light on the side of the street was his hard-won Renault Safrane four-door, the product of a decade of saving, its hood propped open, flames leaping from its engine and passenger compartment, a dense black cloud of toxic smoke rising hundreds of meters into the air, merging with scores of similar mushroom-cloud plumes that stretched around the Paris outskirts. It looked as if the entire city was ringed with fire that Tuesday night, as a thousand cars and a dozen government buildings burned in the poor high-rise suburbs, known popularly as *banlieues difficiles* or *cités*. During a three-month period in 2005, almost 10,000 cars were set alight by mobs of angry young men, a hundred buildings were burned, the French government declared a state of emergency, almost 3,000 were arrested, and a crisis of national identity threw the government of President Jacques Chirac into terminal disarray and launched the presidential career of Nicolas Sarkozy. Aziz was well aware of the emergency: out here in Les Pyramides, almost every night that season had felt like a military attack, with swooping platoons of police battling youths and clouds of smoke filling the air. Aziz knew this, but he never believed it would touch him.

The circle of young men scattered as Aziz tried to put out the flames. They disappeared into the shadowy spaces beneath the pyramids, but he knew who they were. As he slunk back to his building's urine-scented elevator, Aziz began cursing them. The destruction of a car may not figure highly in the taxonomy of suffering, but what lay behind that act was a sense, felt strongly by Aziz and others like him, that this was no longer a community, that he and his neighbors were no longer moving in the same direction.

When I caught up with him after the attacks, in his large, bright living room dominated by a big-screen TV and an overstuffed couch, he expressed his anger in peculiar terms. He cursed France, the country he fought to join—"Every day I stay in France, it is as if I am living in a big hole with a cover over it." He cursed his neighborhood and its buildings. And he cursed the "immigrants," as he called the young men. "These immigrants do not know how to live here," he said. "They cannot find a way to raise their children properly here, so they turn violent. Their situation infuriates me."

To an outsider, this language seems odd. After all, Aziz himself is an immigrant. A Gambian who had grown up in the center of the capital, Banjul, he arrived here in the outskirts of Paris in the 1990s, after his job in the security department of Gambia's national airline gave him an opportunity to come to France. He was attracted to the towers of Les Pyramides by the generous size of their apartments, and their modern, urban feel, and their rents that would command only a tiny flat in Paris. He is poor by French standards but well off in African terms, and he sends plenty of money home, to his six other children.

The young men he was cursing, on the other hand, are not immigrants at all; almost all of them were born in France, and they all are fluent in the country's language and customs and indistinguishable in most ways, but for their addresses, *banlieue* slang expressions, and complexions, from any French teenagers. Theirs was not the anger of foreigners. France is a country of immigrants—a quarter of its 65 million people either are foreign-born or are the children or grandchildren of immigrants,[1] and this, in itself, has not caused tension.

The anger in 2005 was not Islamic, either. Among the countless chronicles of those months, including the conclusions of the French intelligence service, there are no credible records of any Muslim messages or motives in the riots.[2] Among French-born children of Algerians, only 4 percent say they attend mosques more than once a year, and the largest group is totally non-observant, making them just as secular as white French kids.[3] Almost all of the rioters of 2005 were French citizens, and repeated studies have shown that they share the values and attitudes of native-born French youth, even if their *"banlieue* culture" forbids them entry into mainstream French society—in fact, this was itself the point of the riots.[4] In their mass confrontations with police, the rioters often held their French ID cards in the air. People were mystified by the lack of slogans or messages in this vast (but almost non-lethal) uprising, what the French police intelligence service described as a "kind of non-organized insurrection without a leader or manifesto"—but these ID cards *were* the manifesto, they *were* the message. This was a battle of French against French, a battle for acceptance.

Still, there was something different about these young men. Their parents, unlike Aziz, came to the outskirts of Paris as villagers. By "immigrants," he means that they are rural migrants making their first foray into urban space, the situation faced by the great majority of families in Les Pyramides and throughout the periphery of Paris.

Like some 50 million other Europeans, they live in an arrival city.[5] In those autumn months of 2005, the European arrival city violently announced its presence to the world. France had seen riots and acts of destruction in its *banlieues* frequently, since the early 1980s, when the French children of its North African immigrants first came of age. But this was a terminal moment: France had cut off an entire generation's future, blocking the path forward to the city and backward to the village, and thousands of young people reacted in the only way they knew.

There has long been a tendency to refer to the neighborhoods on the Paris outskirts, and similar neighborhoods across the West, as "immigrant ghettos" or "ethnic enclaves," and to attribute their failings and eruptions to a perceived racial and ethnic segregation. When you examine them as arrival cities, though, the distinguishing thing about Les Pyramides and its even uglier siblings is not ethnic ghettoization but extreme heterogeneity.

The sociologist Loïc Wacquant has built his career on proving that the French *banlieues* and other "neighbourhoods of relegation" across Europe are not at all segregated in the sense of classic American black ghettos but are, instead, "anti-ghettos," places that are, in fact, very multi-ethnic—and this, he argues, is precisely the problem:

these neighborhoods are places of "advanced marginality" that haven't been able to form any sort of community at all, ethnic or otherwise. They "are characterized by their low to moderate levels of segregation and lack of demographic coherence and cultural unity . . . the demands of their residents are fundamentally social, having to do not with difference or 'diversity' but *equality* in treatment by or access to the police, the school system, housing, health care and, above all, employment. They pertain to the *sphere of citizenship and not that of ethnicity*."[6]

The response of Nicolas Sarkozy, who was interior minister at the time of the riots and built his presidential bid on his tough response to the car burnings, was to impose extra policing and attempt to restrict immigration, on the basis, he argued, that such village-based immigrants are fundamentally unassimilable.[7] Yet the experience of tens of thousands of other French Africans who have made good livelihoods outside of France belies this claim. The European arrival city is not a homogenous place; the continent contains some of the world's most effective and flourishing rural-arrival neighborhoods. Even within Paris, the inner-city quarter of Belleville—the sort of place that was demolished or abandoned to build the *banlieues*—is studied today as a place of entrepreneurship-driven advancement, with its prosperous and self-supporting mix of North and sub-Saharan Africans, east Europeans and Asians, and its transition to middle-class success.[8]

France's arrival cities are not ethnic ghettos. Les Pyramides, a fairly typical example, has not only large numbers of Africans but also sizable populations of Indians, Sri Lankans, Turks, Egyptians, and eastern Europeans, as well as a good number of people like the white French woman, who grew up in a village in Brittany, who runs the Turkish café next door to Aziz's shop. She doesn't feel stuck. But a great many people here, from a dozen countries on three continents, have arrived from rural poverty and have found that their children are trapped halfway between the village and the city, with nowhere to move.

Something happens to villagers when they arrive in the French urban outskirts. The culture of transition, that fertile amalgam of village and urban life, is frozen in its early stages, prevented from advancing into permanency, from growing into something that contributes to the country's economy and culture. The parents often manage the first stage adequately, keeping one foot in the village and one in the city, holding down rudimentary jobs and supporting their villages through remittances. But they are prevented from moving to the usual next stage, from launching any kind of small business, from owning their house, from meshing themselves with the larger urban community—they remain isolated. And their children, fully acculturated, find themselves stuck—in part by a well-documented racism that denies them jobs or higher-education postings on the basis of last names or postal codes.[9] But behind that "post-code racism" is the reality of those locations: Because of the physical nature of the *banlieue* and the organization of its institutions, the villagers have no means to move to the next stage. This is often mischaracterized as a clash of civilizations or a failure of assimilation; it is better understood as an arrested rural–urban transition.

"The problem is that these kids are made to see themselves as immigrants," Aziz told me. "France wants them, it needs people who can do this kind of cleaning and building work. And they end up stuck in Les Pyramides, because it's the place where they're made to go. And their kids have nothing. They were born here, they speak the language perfectly, they can work. But they don't have work. They didn't build Les Pyramides with Africans in mind. There are not enough rooms, no place for markets, nothing that people from villages can use to make a start—it's architecturally very beautiful, I think, but the problem is that it's not being respected by the young people here. They turn against it and they turn against the police and the government and now even people like me."

Two towers over, a proud French air force veteran named Badiane Babikan, born in a small village 15 kilometres from Dakar but educated in the great cities of Africa and France, spoke to me with even deeper frustration about the families who form the majority of Africans in Les Pyramides.

"These villagers are as strange to me as I am to a Parisian," he told me in a quiet confession when I visited his tiny office across from the community center. "When people from Senegal hear about what's happening here, the riots, they just don't understand—villagers become successful people there after they move to the city. It's too tight-knit there for something like that to happen. Here, they just stay villagers."

Strangely enough, the young men who burned Aziz's car see it almost exactly the same way—as an interruption of their family's rural-to-urban transition. The rioters of 2005 were overwhelmingly the children and grandchildren of villagers. This point is almost always neglected in analyses of the events of that autumn, but it is a dominant element in the rioters' own understanding of their actions. When I have interviewed rioters in Les Pyramides, Clichy-sous-Bois, and Cité des 4000 in the weeks and years afterward, the transition from village to urban life—and the barriers that prevent them from making that link—are most often mentioned.

After all, the whole thing got started with the deaths of two French children of African villagers—a point absent from most accounts of their demise. The boys who were electrocuted in Clichy-sous-Bois in October 2005, while hiding from the police in an electrical substation, were both immediate products of the great migration. Zyed Benna, 17, was the son of Amor Benna, who had come from an agricultural village in Djerba, Tunisia, in 1966 to work as a sewer cleaner in Paris. And the family of 15-year-old Bouna Traore had come to France in the 1970s from the desert village of Diaguily, in southern Mauritania.

One of the rioters who responded violently to news of the electrocutions, and may have had a hand in Aziz's tragedy that night, was Mafoud, a skinny 15-year-old, whose tough comportment is undercut by his languid air of geniality. His parents came from a Malian village near Cayes, which has been rendered infertile by the encroaching desert; they work at night, as a laborer and a cleaner, and he rarely sees them. He is a self-described lost soul, spending his days listening to Tupac Shakur in the laneway, smoking marijuana, and bantering with other teenagers—often about their geographic nullity. "We come from a small village in the middle of nowhere, and it's like we can't get out of the village here—my whole family, 10 of us is living in two rooms, and my mother and father can't make a living like they did in the village, and I can't make a living like a French man should," he says. "That's our problem—we're not African and we're not European." The burning of cars, symbols of mobility and success, has become a poignant gesture for guys like Mafoud.

A few buildings over, often hanging out in the plaza, is Moussa Sambakesse, a muscular 19-year-old, who says he has cut his ties with the street scene and is preparing to leave France for London, where he's been able to use his trade-school degree to land a job in a big hotel—the sort of entry-level job that youth in the French *banlieues* simply can't get in France. According to Brice Mankou, a sociologist who spent time with the rioters of Les Pyramides in 2005, about half of them are dropouts like Mafoud who have left school and relegated themselves to the gray-market underworld, and half are guys like Moussa, with good educations and real skills, but a great frustration about their ability to thrive as Frenchmen.[10]

Shortly before the riots, Moussa's mother, Alima Sambakesse, took him and his three brothers to visit her village, a tiny place called Marena, in Mali. She had hoped that the boys would feel attached, as she still believes she will move back there someday, when she has been able to earn enough to buy her family a bigger house. Moussa walked around the perimeter of the village, which took just more than an hour. He was introduced to a great number of relatives, most of whom lived in mud huts, but he could find little to say to them. He visited a classroom but didn't understand the language and found the customs disquieting. "These are my people, but I didn't understand them," he says. "It made me realize that it's not my life—I'm a European."

Viewed from the pyramids outward, through the eyes of Moussa and Mafoud, the Malian village and the Parisian metropolis both appear as distant vanishing points. But we should turn our attention to the original perspective, the view from the village inward: How does the *banlieue* look coming in? What are all these villagers doing here? How did the European arrival city become short-circuited? How did France, and Europe in general, end up with such a large number of villagers in its midst?

Alima, Moussa's mother, came here in 1984, 10 years after France officially ended immigration. She was not the first person in her village to leave for the city; that honor went to the man she married, who had come over as a worker during the period of legal immigration. Alima's family, desperate for income, had engaged their daughter, age 20, to a man she had seen only during brief visits; they married in France. Like most women of her generation from African villages, she had never been to school; she was fluent in Bambara but spoke little French. Her husband died in 1991, shortly before her fourth son was born (making her part of a large population of single mothers, almost a quarter of all families in Les Pyramides),[11] and she soon began working as an all-night office cleaner in another corner of Evry. A third of her income goes back to the village, the rest to food and school supplies—there isn't anything left for savings. Her job left her children unattended for much of their after-school time; her older children soon took charge of raising the younger ones. In effect, the children were raised on the streets and concrete squares of Les Pyramides, by a community of other African and Arab children and teenagers in similar circumstances, a parentless world that pulled many of them into delinquency, others simply into bitterness and anomie.

"The thing that it takes a long time to realize, after you come here, is that a village is not at all like a big city," Alima told me one Sunday in her tidy living room, which is dominated by the obligatory large couch and big-screen satellite TV, tuned to Malian shows when she's around and American programs when she's not. "In the village, when

you're raising your children, even if you have to work, you're surrounded by extended family members who can help you. When you
get into trouble, there are people who know and who help you out.
Here, you're really on your own. You end up with your children on
the street, you know it's wrong, and you worry. Every day, every
second, I worry. All the time."

Many in France see this as a case of villagers transplanting their
cultures and folkways directly into the urban sphere without realizing
that these practices are inappropriate, if not dangerous, in the context of the housing project, where there is no immediate community
to watch the children. But the villagers themselves know otherwise.
They fall back on these traditional ways only out of desperation, as
Alima Sambakesse's story indicates, when nothing else is available.

In the winter of 2007, I arranged a meeting with a dozen ex-rural
women at Generation Femmes, a women's center in Evry. They had
come from a dozen countries, including India, Egypt, and all parts
of Africa, and most spoke little French. But all of them expressed a
strong desire not to live like villagers and to raise their children off
the streets, and they shared a sense that their surroundings, both
architecturally and economically, were denying them the connections
and opportunities they needed to cast off the old ways. Desperation
was forcing them back out of urban life.

"There are definitely a lot of problems with discrimination here,
but people don't realize that the bigger trouble is that a lot of the
people who come from the places I do, from the *banlieues*, don't have
a social network that connects them to French society," said Isna
Hocini, 30, the grandchild of Algerian immigrants who runs the
center. "And in France, it's very important to have a network to get
into school or to get a job—it's not enough just to send your résumé
in. That's the major problem with the *cités*, the lack of networks—a
huge problem."

That lack of networks is a product of the *banlieues* themselves,
both in their function and in their physical design. One of the strange
paradoxes of large, high-rise public-housing projects like Les Pyramides

is that they suffer from a low-population density. The neighborhoods that work best as urban neighborhoods and arrival cities—two- to five-story structures with direct access to the road and small businesses below—tend to be very high density. By spreading so few people across such an isolated expanse without room for improvisational construction, the people there are bound to be disconnected from one another. This architectural point is not lost on the *banlieue* residents themselves or on the politician who represents them. "By building Les Pyramides at such a low density with only pedestrian pathways, they basically killed the possibility of having a real city," Evry's Socialist Party mayor, Manuel Valls, told me. "It doesn't have any downtown, there's nothing with shops or small businesses to hold it all together. Look at the way it was built—it's very Cartesian."

It didn't start that way. When African villagers first came to France after the Second World War, they built their own arrival cities. During France's celebrated "three glorious decades" of industrialization and growth after the war, severe labor shortages led to a demand for immigrants, and the government chose to attract as many workers as possible without having an explicit immigration policy. Hundreds of thousands of Africans arrived from lands that had recently been colonies, and to discourage them from settling permanently with their families, the government at first constructed dormitory apartments for single men. As everywhere, these were a moral and practical failure.

Many North African workers ignored the dormitories and built their own arrival cities, shantytown *bidonvilles* in disused parts of some of France's major cities. By 1965, at least 225,000 people were living in such settlements. The most famous product of these self-built slums was Azouz Begag, the author and sometime French cabinet minister, who spent his childhood in a ramshackle dirt-floored settlement by the river in Lyon. Chaâba was a densely populated place that resembled the flourishing arrival cities of the developing world, "a shantytown of shacks made of planks of wood and corrugated iron roofs."[12] His family lived there from 1947 until 1968, when that city, and many others like it, was razed, its residents moved to the new concrete utopias on the edge of town.

Those new buildings went up with astonishing speed. Between 1956 and 1965, at least 300,000 new apartments were built by the French state each year—many to house the expanding postwar baby boom, others to replace *bidonvilles*, others for new workers. Most were featureless rectangles with large empty spaces between them. Les Pyramides was a later development, meant to correct the wrongs of the earlier designs and to attract the middle class out of central Paris and into the new industrial districts on the outskirts. But industry was moving elsewhere, and a new flood of villagers was arriving. The halt of immigration in 1974 actually increased village immigration, because it led to a scramble for family reunification.

The new buildings were clean and orderly and low-rent, more than half the apartments had toilets, and they didn't crowd the major cities of France. But they had been designed with absolutely no contribution from their future residents, without any conception that their occupants might not be fixed commodities such as "factory worker" or "foreign laborer." The point that was missed, the point that planned housing so often misses, is that the occupants might be people *in transition*, on the way from one condition to another. None of the tools were there: no opportunity for home ownership, no chance to start a business, no easy transportation links to the metropolis, no chance for the occupants to build an organic neighborhood with a high-enough population density for mutual self-help.

THE PROBLEM OF CITIZENSHIP
Kreuzberg, Berlin

When Sabri Koçyigit, the Turkish radical-turned-prisoner-turned-bourgeois we met in chapter 6, made the journey from his village in remote Sivas, Turkey, to the ramshackle outskirts of Istanbul, he was to experience three decades of sometimes painful advancement. For more than two million of his erstwhile rural neighbors, the journey has been equally arduous and the distances even greater, taking them not to the edge of the Bosporus but even farther westward, into the very heart of Europe. The Turkish villagers of outer Istanbul and the Turkish villagers of inner Berlin began from the same location, at the same time, with the same ambitions, but their contrasting arrival cities have shaped them into very different people.

Alara Bayram was 15 in 1979, the youngest of nine children born to the baker in a poor village near Sivas. Her father took her aside one Friday afternoon and told her that she had been engaged to marry a neighbor 10 years her senior. Erhan, her absent husband-to-be, wasn't especially prosperous or talented, and he came from a family known for its brusque and violent ways. But he possessed something more valuable than any dowry—a German working visa. With this, it did not need to be said, her family could gain its first foothold in the West, a possible escape from the severe economic and political deprivations that continually plagued their mainly Alevi and Kurdish village. While dozens of their neighbors were moving to the *gecekondu* outskirts of Istanbul, Alara was to join the 2.6 million Turks and their children who would spend those same decades establishing themselves in the arrival cities of Germany.

Her journey was not to be a quick one. While she toiled at the bakery for the next eight years, Erhan shuttled between Germany and Istanbul and the village, ostensibly securing a better job and saving money, before finally returning to turn their religious wedding into a legal marriage in 1987. "I didn't want to marry him," Alara told me, "but I was afraid for my family." Later that year, she followed him to Frankfurt, where he had landed a job in a car-parts factory. She was four months pregnant when she got there and learned that he had, until the previous year, been married to a Turco-German woman and fathered a child with her. That explained both the mysterious interval and the rare German visa. Somehow, she came to terms with this secret history and moved into the spartan workers' dormitories with him. For the next few years, life was austere but stable—he drank heavily in the evenings, but the tight-knit community of Turkish migrant workers kept his worst instincts reined in. Alara stayed home, raised the children, watched Turkish TV shows on the satellite TV, obeyed his orders to stick to the housework, and didn't learn German.

Then, when she was pregnant with their fourth child, Erhan decided it was time for them to progress to the second stage of arrival, to make their break from the dormitory compounds and move to the Turkish enclave of Kreuzberg, in what was then still known as West Berlin. Beginning in the 1960s, Turks had flooded into this run-down neighborhood adjoining the Berlin Wall, drawn by its large apartments, its low rent, and the fact that its landlords would rent to Turks—something that was far from guaranteed in most German neighborhoods. After the Wall came down, shortly after their move, Berlin's center of activity shifted to the East, neatly leapfrogging Kreuzberg and leaving parts of it poor and neglected, home to anarchists, pacifists, ecologists, and other members of the urban subaltern—and to the largest urban population of Turks in the Western world.

Erhan had come to Kreuzberg because he had some relatives there and hoped to make more money. Alara had looked forward to the less stifling urban surroundings. Instead, she says, "as soon as we got there, everything began to fall apart." Freed from the scrutiny of Frankfurt neighbours, her husband's drinking got out of control. "He tortured me, beating me with whatever he could get his hands on, and then he'd threaten to end my life, very seriously," she remembers. He started a small, unlicensed, and mostly unsuccessful moving company, paid no taxes, and had an affair and a child with his secretary.

In 1998, their eldest daughter was permanently disabled in a car accident. Erhan wanted nothing to do with this "cripple"—the girl spent a year in treatment in Hamburg, and he didn't visit her once. She now lives in a clinic in Berlin. In 2000, Alara left her husband, taking the children with her. They lived in a hospice, in single rooms, with friends. He regularly threatened her life. In 2003, she divorced him. Two years later, in the culmination of a long-simmering family feud, he murdered his cousin on the street outside her apartment, then shot himself in the head. "I wasn't shocked. I was relieved," Alara says. "I knew he had a pistol—he had threatened me with it many times. He often told me who he wanted to kill—first the cousin, then me, then himself. My two decades with him had been a nightmare."

I am using Alara's story not because it is shocking and extreme, but because—with the possible exception of its bloody climax—such tragedies are a familiar part of the Turkish experience in Kreuzberg and in similar Turkish arrival cities across Germany. Physically, these neighborhoods should not be scenes of deprivation and violence. Compared to their French counterparts, these would seem to be ideal locations: in the center of the city, closely tied to the broader German community and economy, generously provided with social services. But Kreuzberg is not a functioning arrival city by any means. Rather than becoming urban and German, many of its residents seem to become more rural and Turkish and increasingly further removed from the center of society.

The marriage-breakdown rate among Turks in Kreuzberg, according to neighborhood officials, is around 80 percent. And no wonder: An extraordinary 49 percent of Turkish women in Germany say they have been subjected to physical or sexual violence by their husbands, according to a study by the German Ministry of Foreign Affairs; a quarter did not meet their husbands until their wedding day, and 17 percent said their marriages were forced—a practice that is dying fast in Turkey but was revived in Germany in response to immigration policies. Rates of alcoholism and violent crime are far higher than elsewhere in Germany. And the German language isn't spoken. One survey found that 63 percent of children born to Turkish parents in Berlin do not speak any German when they enter their first year of school, and 80 percent of Turks cannot participate in parent-teacher meetings, because their German is not good enough. A 2003 educational survey found that Turkish children are two years behind their German classmates. More than half the Turks in Kottbusser Tor, the Turkish-dominated area of central Kreuzberg, are unemployed; jobless rates for Turks of all ages in Kreuzberg are at least twice the rate for Germans. And Turks are retreating into religion: Fully 29 percent of adult Muslims (the majority of whom are Turks) in Germany attend mosques regularly, higher than the rate for Turks in the rest of Europe or in urban Turkey.[13]

It has become a commonplace in the German media to refer to Kreuzberg as a "parallel society" or an "urban village," where non-integrated Turks preserve their traditional village ways—sacrificing sheep in their bathtubs, covering their heads, forcing their wives into marriage, and sometimes engaging in the lurid honor-killing murders of miscreant women that frequently occupy the German media. This image has, to a large degree, turned the German public and its leaders against "Turkish culture" and persuaded many people that Turks are conservative traditionalists who cannot be made into good European and, more broadly, that Turkey ought not to enter the European Union.

But Kreuzberg, like most arrival cities, is not a reproduction of the homeland. The Turks in Berlin are forced into a grotesque caricature of their home country's life, one built on primitive traditions that no longer exist in much of Turkey, one that is as alien to most citizens of Turkey as it is to Germans. The figures cited above, both for spousal abuse and for forced marriage, are significantly higher than those reported in surveys of Turkish women in Ankara, even though a sizable part of Ankara's population has migrated from the same regions of Turkey.[14] The Turkish writer Dilek Gügö reports that Turkish women moving to Berlin are "shocked to find themselves forced to wear headscarves by their mothers-in-law, sharing a flat with their husband's family, and to see that Turks in Germany were 20 years behind those in Istanbul." The Ankara scholar Mehmet Okyayuz, who lived in Berlin for 33 years before returning to Turkey, finds that Berlin's Turks are "caught in a time warp."[15]

Women have fared better in the squatter outskirts of Istanbul than they have in the Turkish neighborhoods of Berlin. While both neighborhoods tend to be more religious and conservative than their larger cities, the Turco-German scholars Şule Özüekren and Ebru Ergoz Karahan made a detailed study of both and found that women in the outskirts of Istanbul are more likely to be employed, educated, and in contact with the larger world: Turkey's arrival cities are often pathways to liberation, helping their residents "change their sides from losers to winners."[16] The German neighborhoods often lead in another direction.

Something happens to Turks when they come to Kreuzberg, freezing them in a now non-existent Turkish rural past. This is not the intrinsic nature of Turkish society or the inevitable fate of Turkish villagers arriving in the West. In France, almost all second-generation Turks are fluent in French. In the Netherlands, home ownership and upward social mobility are far more prevalent. In London and Stockholm, Turkish neighborhoods blend successfully into the city's mainstream.[17] A major comparison of Turks in Britain and Germany found that, even though they have the same back-grounds, unlike their German neighbors the British Turks soon fall into the same career paths as native-born Britons, melting easily into the working population.[18] Another study found that Pakistanis in Bradford, England, have a far easier time entering mainstream soci-ety through small-business accomplishment than Turks in Kreuzberg, where licensing and bank policies often prevent them from starting businesses.[19] It isn't Turkishness that is preventing success here nor is it the physical nature of the neighborhood. Kreuzberg has none of the physical or logistical problems of the French *banlieue*. And like many arrival cities, its arrivals are a minority, accounting for only 18 percent of the population. In short, segregation is not the problem here.

What is missing from the German arrival city, what prevents most of its citizens from experiencing any kind of arrival, is citizenship, in both the legal and the cultural sense. Turks, even into the third generation, are perpetually treated as temporary visitors or "foreigners" in German society, and, in return, see themselves that way, so neither group tries to improve the arrival city. That attitude is a reflection of actual citizenship, which has historically been unattainable by Turks. In 2002, after Turks had been coming to Germany for 41 years and numbered 2.5 million, only 470,000 had managed to attain German citizenship. The proportion of Turks who become naturalized Germans has never exceeded 3 percent each year, an extraordinarily low number by European standards. This means not only that a large majority of Turks in Germany don't become citizens, even after four decades, but that a substantial number of their German-born children and grandchildren also remain Turkish, even though most of them have never seen their country of citizenship. The German experience provides a bracing lesson in arrival-city politics to those countries that believe they can fill their unskilled-labor needs with temporary-worker programs.

From the beginning, German policy seemed almost hard-wired to produce a failed arrival city, one whose residents can neither establish themselves in a meaningful way nor realistically expect to move permanently back to their villages. This exclusion began in 1961, when the German economy was booming, creating large-scale labor shortages; the erection of the Berlin Wall had severely curtailed the supply of workers from within Germany and eastern Europe. That year, the Federal Republic of Germany set up a recruitment office in Istanbul to hire labor for the Telefunken transistor factory, in Berlin, and the automotive plants of the Rhineland. The workers, under the 1961 Recruitment Agreement for Labor, would initially be known as *Fremdarbeiter* (alien workers) and then, in a better reflection of the policy's goals, as *Gastarbeiter* (guest workers). About 10,000 came in the first year, arriving at a special segregated rail terminal in Munich and housed on factory sites by their employers, who were expected to provide return tickets.

The Turkish "guests" were meant to be employed for a short but indefinite period and then return. This was a popular view among both Germans and the Turkish men themselves, a majority of whom intended to move back within four to six years, ideally to buy some property or start a shop or a small business.[20] But employers needed to teach the workers specialized skills and basic German language, which took months, and they discovered that workers isolated from their families were less productive, so, within a few years, employers were attempting to bypass the system and settle the workers. At the same time, many of the Turkish men discovered, as arrival-city pioneers so often do, that returning was not so easy. Their villages had become dependent on their remittances, they had developed personal relationships in Germany, and they had become the social and economic enablers for future waves of men from their villages.

In 1974, Germany abandoned the guest-worker system and officially ended all immigration. At that point, 910,500 Turks were living in Germany. About half the *Gastarbeiter* had returned to Turkey, and the rest had formed complex lives in the nascent arrival cities. They were not encouraged to become part of German society; indeed, the government did nothing to aid their transition to urban or European life, since they did not officially exist.

By not having any immigration policy at all, Germany virtually guaranteed that all of its immigrants would be family-reunification migrants, and thus mainly villagers. Over the next 30 years of "non-immigration," more than a million more Turks would legally enter the country, a great many of them from even more rural, more conservative, and more deprived backgrounds than the original guest workers. Most of them would occupy the handful of urban neighborhoods where they could obtain housing. By 2002, there were 2.6 million Turkish citizens living in Germany, yet only 30 percent of them had immigrated as workers. More than half were spouses and children brought over by those workers, and fully 17 percent—more than 440,000 people—were the German-born children of those families, who had never seen Turkey, except perhaps on brief trips, but were denied citizenship in Germany.

What happens to people when they are pushed into an irreversible rural–urban transition in a country that does not allow them to exist as citizens? The economic and material effects can be seen on the streets of Kreuzberg. On its bohemian, ethnic-German edges, it is teeming with shops and cafés, driven by an architectural layout that seems ideal for the best forms of urban life. In its Turkish core, though, those same streets are strangely barren, devoid of activity—a forlorn kebab shop here, a charity storefront there, a distinctly un-Teutonic amount of garbage on the street. Because so few Turks are allowed citizenship, they are prevented from forming businesses by German laws, so their rate of entrepreneurship is lower here than among Turkish communities in other European countries.[21] To make matters worse, between 1975 and 1990, Turks who were in Germany legally were subject to indelible stamps in their passports, known as *Zuzugssperre*, which officially forbade them from settling in Kreuzberg and other Turkish enclaves. That policy was a failure, as discrimination prevented Turks from renting apartments elsewhere, but it did guarantee that a larger part of Kreuzberg's economy would be underground and informal, unable to grow roots in German society.[22]

One of the most astute observers of this phenomenon is Kazim Erdoğan, an Alevite Turk from another Sivas-area village. He arrived in 1973 with a backpack and no work permit, spent some time in jail pending deportation, then used a university admission to remain in the country, and ended up thriving academically. He now runs a social-psychology practice that helps Kreuzberg residents adjust to German life. "I would estimate that 95 percent of the Turks living here have come from rural backgrounds and have stayed rural in their minds—because they were told they'd be going back, that they'd have to go back, so they never saw a reason to learn German and to adapt," he told me. "The only thing that kept them going was the notion that this was temporary. They just didn't see any reason to adjust—they were told they could save money and move back and join the middle class in Turkey. I would assume it was that hope that enabled them to endure circumstances that otherwise would have been intolerable. But it also prevented them from becoming citizens here . . . Those who migrated to the cities in Turkey are closer to achieving their goals, whereas here I'm constantly being confronted with the living dead."

Alara Bayram entered Germany during a period, beginning in 1976, when between 50 and 60 percent of all Turks entering the country were under 16 years of age; the rest were almost entirely women, brides who had seldom met their grooms.[23] Today she lives in a small apartment on a barren street in Kreuzberg with her four children. She wears a headscarf, though her three daughters, who are fluent in German, don't. Her oldest son, 17, has dropped out of school and speaks little German, and Alara worries that he's becoming an alarming duplicate of his father. None of her children are German citizens. "Three of them want to become German, but I tell them not to lose their Turkishness—they should think about their home," she says, referring to a country they have only visited on beach vacations. "This is no place for them to start a life, I tell them. I'll go back someday, and I hope they follow me."

The German arrival city took its shape and character as a direct result of citizenship policies, and Alara's life, too, has been shaped by them. In those years, naturalization was available only to adults who had lived in Germany for 15 years. Citizenship was defined, strictly along blood lines, to ethnic Germans and their descendants (despite the dark historical resonances of such policies). So most Turkish workers were denied any access to German society or to many public benefits. The possibility of becoming integrated, or of marrying a German, or becoming a part of the local school community, was remote.

In Berlin, as in much of Europe, the alien-seeming practices that arose from those policies often came to be seen as "Muslim"—including symbolic matters, such as women wearing headscarves, and more ominous acts, such as forced marriage and honor killing. But this behavior, to a large extent, was being created within Europe by

European policies: It was a Western-manufactured Islamic conservatism. For instance, the rise of forced marriages in Germany just as
they were on the decline in Turkey is an inevitable and understand-
able result of Germany's ceasing all immigration just as immigrants
had become integral to the economy. "These people aren't naturally
conservative or religious," says Dr. Erdoğan, "but they're often put
in situations where they have to adopt conservatism and religion."
Half of all Turkish men living in Germany look for their spouses in
Turkey, even today. He adds: "Many young men who grow up here,
they have to go to Turkey to look for wives because there is just no
hope of looking for a wife here, without citizenship. And the kind
of wife you can find who is going to satisfy that need, she is inevitably going to be coming from the more religious and conservative
families." It was those women, least equipped for the task of urban
arrival, who ended up bringing children, themselves without citizenship, into the world.

In the first years of the twenty-first century, the German government began to awaken to the problem in its midst. It became apparent that Turks, and other immigrants, would have to be permanent:
With its low birth rates, the German population would fall from
82 million to less than 60 million by 2050, leading to the collapse of
the country's pension and social-security system and a dramatic
decline in living standards for everyone. The government realized that
the "guest" Turks, many of them with German-born grandchildren
by now, were both a problem and a solution. In 2000, after 20 years
of fruitless parliamentary debate, Germany finally amended the
Foreigners Act of 1965, introducing the possibility of naturalization
for German-born children of immigrants. A path to citizenship was
now available to their parents if they had stayed for eight years with
legal employment. And, for the first time, Germany introduced *jus
soli*, the right of citizenship to those born to parents who resided
legally in Germany.

This well-intended policy ended up having the opposite of its
desired effect. Studies show that the naturalization rate of Turks in

Germany peaked in 1999, a year before the new citizenship law, after which the number of Turks becoming German actually declined. [24] Through two seemingly innocuous clauses in its law, Germany had created an awkward Catch-22 for its Turks. First, it required those seeking citizenship to have been employed in formal, legal jobs—a reasonable policy if it had been in effect in 1961, but one that, after Turks had spent almost four decades building gray-market economies within their arrival cities, forced them either to abandon their livelihoods or to avoid citizenship. Second, it required that naturalized Turkish Germans abandon their Turkish citizenship after the age of 23. This ignored the cultural reality of the arrival city, the importance of its links to the village, both for the social security of the residents and for the village itself through remittances. Rather than bringing their status in line with their actual lives, Germany ended up forcing the Turks to choose between their established, precarious, but workable lives of non-citizenship or complete abandonment of those networks and institutions in exchange for legal citizenship.

This is not just a problem in Germany. It is even more acute in the states and cities of the Persian Gulf, notably Dubai, where only 17 percent of the emirate's 1.4 million people are citizens. The remainder, three-quarters of whom come from the Indian subcontinent, include some short-term workers but also large numbers of people who have been residents for years or decades, who have formed families and deep ties to the economy but have no legal right to own property or seek health care, pensions, or other benefits and no incentive to become taxpayers and participants in the culture and development of the city. As the economy has slowed and unemployment has risen, there have been signs of a pending German-style crisis.

German policy is still changing, and the pressure of a growing bloc of successful Turks—a group that includes members of the Bundestag and prominent cultural and media figures—may end up transforming the German arrival city into a functioning reality, at least for the third generation of Turkish Germans. It is hard to avoid the sense that places like Kreuzberg could have played a far more important role in German society, rivaling famous arrival cities like Brick Lane, Belleville, the Lower East Side, or even the outskirts of Istanbul. It's a contrast that German Turks are well aware of. "Those migrating to Istanbul shaped their residential areas," Şule Özüekren writes. "Investing in their own housing and using their political power, [they] improved their living conditions . . . to show an upward mobility, while their counterparts in Berlin moved from barracks or hostels to multi-family blocks during the same period."[25] For Alara Bayram and her non-German, not-really-Turkish children, stuck in their gray rented apartment and unsure of their futures, that comparison is a constant insult.

SPACE AND CITIZENSHIP
Parla, Spain

Even compared to the difficult experiences of the Malians of Paris and the Turks of Berlin, Lisaneddin Assa's journey to Europe was a truly tough ordeal, an arrival that should not have worked.

When he left his tiny mountain village in the Rif region of northern Morocco, in 1999, there were only the vaguest rumours of an employment boom across the Strait of Gibraltar in Spain and of men who were willing, for a fee equivalent to almost a year's earnings for a villager, to help Moroccans make the perilous 13-kilometer trip between the beaches of Tangier and the Andalusian coast.

Lisaneddin was the first member of his extended family to make that crossing, and the whole village was counting on him. At that time, despite more than a dozen centuries of interchanges between Morocco and Spain, the crossing was a novelty—Spain had been a closed society, a net exporter of emigrants, until the very last years of the twentieth century. The men on the beach who loaded each of the ill-constructed wooden rafts with several dozen migrants knew nothing of navigation, seamanship, currents, weather, or immigration. They took the money and, if the men were lucky, sent them off with an unreliable outboard motor and little else. Hundreds drowned every year, more starved or baked to death at sea or drifted until they landed, ruined, somewhere farther along the northern coast of Africa. Corpses washed ashore with alarming regularity.

Lisaneddin was lucky. But after he pulled himself off the beach and begged a ride northward to Spain's central plain, things would get tougher. In a country whose language he did not speak, he found himself not just a minority but a real rarity: In the 1990s, the number of Moroccan citizens numbered in the tens of thousands in a country of 45 million.

For Lisaneddin and many other new arrivals, the only work available was picking strawberries. He slept outdoors, in alleyways and ravines, during the months when work was thin, and his Berber roots offered little help in sheltering him from the weather. "It was like being an animal," he remembers. "In those years, we were the first wave to come, and we knew nothing. There weren't even slums for us, nothing. We had to survive by our wits and eat what we could find and send everything back to the village."

The arrival city would change his fortunes. When this soft-spoken, cheery man first recounted his story, we talked in his large butcher shop and supermarket at the foot of a small apartment building in the city of Parla, on the far southern outskirts of Madrid. He and several of his fellow villagers and family members live around here, where they have become homeowners, active citizens fluent in Spain's language and culture, and poor but thriving participants in the European economy, as entrepreneurs, employees, or students.

In its physical appearance and original design, Parla seems a southern twin of Les Pyramides: a sprawling island of low-rise apartments that loom like a mirage above the dusty plain, linked by commuter train lines to the larger city. It is a postwar bedroom suburb that was soon overwhelmed by villagers moving inward. In 1960, it was a dusty agricultural village of 1,800; by 1978, it contained 31,000 Spanish

factory workers; today it has almost 130,000 people, a large proportion of them South American or Moroccan immigrants and their
children. As in Les Pyramides, over 80 percent of Parla's citizens
travel to other places to work.

Yet there is something different about Parla. Its streets do not have
the barren, empty look of those in Evry or Kreuzberg; they are lined
with busy Moroccan-owned shops and cafés, the young people seem
to be going somewhere, and the bright colors and haphazard development of a thriving arrival city add piquancy to the ground level in
a landscape of five-story apartment buildings. In many of its busy
streets and squares, it feels as though the best aspects of a Moroccan
town and a Spanish city have been fused.

The underlying difference between Parla and its French and
German counterparts is that the town's government realized early
on that it was becoming an arrival city and understood the implications of this change. So did Spain's national government, in part
because the Spanish immigration experience followed the French and
German precedents by 40 years. So, when its economic boom around
the turn of the century caused the immigrant population to expand
at record-setting rates—from 0.2 percent of the population in 1990
to 9.6 percent, or 4.5 million people, in 2008—Spain did not respond
by blithely assuming that its rural-to-urban migrants would automatically become functioning urban citizens, as France did, or that
they were simply non-citizens who could be ignored, as Germany
did. Instead, it made investments in their citizenship and prosperity.
And when economic crisis ripped across Spain, these investments
may have prevented a catastrophe.

This long-term investment in the arrival city did not happen
immediately. During its first years of immigration, from 1991
onwards, Spain attempted to close its borders and ban immigration (even as its economy was beginning to demand large numbers
of skilled and unskilled workers). During the 1990s, Spain's arrival
cities began to take the shape and to develop the problems of
those in other parts of Europe. Parla's residents in those years were

overwhelmingly non-citizens, and they often lived marginal lives. There was an underground economy and high crime rates, and the town was attracting the politics of the Spanish far right and of North African nationalism.

Beginning with the election of Prime Minister José Luis Rodríguez Zapatero and his moderate-left Socialist Party government in 2004, Spain embarked on Europe's first policy initiative aimed specifically at the arrival city. First, in 2005, it tackled the dangerous obstacle of citizenship with an amnesty program that put almost 700,000 undocumented but fully employed immigrants on the path to full Spanish citizenship. This wasn't a new policy. Beginning in 1986, Spain had issued at least four amnesties, culminating in a 2000 law that created a permanent mechanism to incorporate full-time employed immigrants into citizenship. (That law was opposed by the right-wing Popular Party government but passed by Parliament against its will.) Zapatero's 2005 law was in a way a mopping-up, designed to ensure that all the residents of Spain's arrival cities would be legal, tax-paying citizens.[26]

It was followed, in 2007, by an even more ambitious program, engineered in cooperation with the government of Senegal, designed to deter dangerous illegal sea crossings by migrants and end illegal immigration to Spain. While amnesties offering regularization of "illegal" immigrants have been used throughout the Western world in the postwar decades, Spain's program was part of a new approach designed to make regularization an option in advance, incorporating rural-to-urban transition into the employment system. Under this program, tens of thousands of Africans every year were granted work permits, allowing them to enter the country legally and work for a year; if their employment contracts were extended, they were allowed to bring over their families and so embark on a path toward citizenship—an effort to prevent the fragmented families and underground lives of the European arrival city and to allow Spain to add half a million immigrants to its economy each year without creating a marginalized class on the outskirts.

This had an immediate and dramatic effect. Suddenly, the occu-pants of arrival cities could buy their apartments, lease shop spaces, start small businesses, and form families that weren't hampered by ambiguous national status. Children of migrants attended school as Spaniards. Moroccan neighborhoods (and many South and Central American ones) could become, in practice, Spanish neighborhoods with polyglot cultures. It meant that the boom created active citizens rather than rootless foreigners scrambling for money—and it meant that the subsequent Spanish economic collapse and unemployment crisis would be faced in a sensible and humane way, without turning the outskirts into disaster zones.

"It changed everything when that happened," Lisaneddin Assa told me as he packaged meat for his customers one Tuesday. When regu-larization happened, Moroccans across his neighborhood rushed out to buy their flats. "It leveled the playing field—it gave us equality with the Spanish citizens of Parla. Suddenly we could do things like start a business or buy a flat or even put up a building."

But the Spanish government was farsighted enough to realize (or more precisely to learn from the precedents of its neighbors) that simply registering citizenship or allowing property ownership, though a crucial step, is not adequate to make the arrival city work in the long term. They realized that actual material assistance would be required, a strong presence of the arrival nation's government in the communities of its new ex-villagers. So the Zapatero govern-ment, beginning in 2008, launched a program costing two billion euros over two years to make the rural-to-urban transition work, a fund that would pay for special education, immigrant reception and adjustment, and employment assistance. It also included programs in arrival cities devoted to finding and building homes, obtaining access to social services and immigrant-targeted health care, inte-gration of women, equal treatment, community participation, and community building. This is in some ways an even more controver-sial program, since it creates the impression that immigrants and their offspring receive more personalized and higher-quality social services than those offered to native-born Spaniards, no matter how poor or deprived, and the inequality became an issue in the 2008 national elections. In the years of economic devastation that followed that election, though, Spain's arrival cities avoided crisis. While migrants suffered very high unemployment after the collapse, places like Parla did not become centers of social unrest, because the larger communities had firmly established business networks and support systems. Because they were citizens rather than outsiders, the Moroccans did not become an underground threat.

"We realized that in Germany and France there are these marginalized areas where the migrants don't feel part of the society, and we realized that we have time to address this issue in advance," says Antonio Hernando, the Zapatero government's immigration spokesman. "We're spending this money to strengthen social public services where there are high immigration levels and to create services to mediate between the host society, the city of arrival, and the migrants themselves . . . There may be some services that Spaniards don't agree with, but as long as they comply with the law, that's the only condition we put on them. These migrants are working legally now and paying the taxes that finance the pensions for a million Spanish people. They are the financial foundation of our country's welfare programs, so we need to make sure that in return, they have the same rights and livelihoods as other Spaniards."

When the Spanish economy entered recession in 2008—and it was an earlier and more dramatic downturn than elsewhere in Europe, owing to a speculative property bubble in Spain's coastal regions and suburbs—the response was a novel inversion of the asylum policy. With the majority of its arrival-city residents legally in place, Spain offered those who were unemployed and not yet citizens cash payments to return home for at least two years, with guaranteed legal residency upon return. With five million in-place immigrants allowed to bring over family members without penalty, it was much easier for Spain to crack down on illegal immigration (because legitimate family reunification was not falsely identified as "illegal"), and sending countries, notably Morocco, were eager to cooperate, since remittance flows were secure. In 2009, Spain saw a 70 percent decline in the numbers of Africans arriving illegally by boat, while Greece, without such citizenship policies, experienced a 40 percent increase.[27]

Parla has become, unusually for Europe, an arrival city that recognizes itself as an arrival city. Its city hall, an airy modern structure grafted onto the sleepy clapboard building that served the town until the end of the twentieth century, effectively functions as a center for managing immigrant arrival and rural-to-urban transition. Its integration office offers legal services, job and housing help, translation and interpreting services, women's services and shelters for Moroccans, and language education. Its urban works have not been the pretty but disconnected parks and pavilions of other outskirts-cities but a popular tramline that connects dozens of points in Parla and a high-speed train that links it to central Madrid in less than 20 minutes—a link that has visibly opened Parla's economy to the wider city. The city has built a large residential development of mid-sized apartment buildings and ground-level row houses, designed with the direct involvements of the city's migrant communities, which provides ground-floor space for small businesses and pathways to home ownership, all at a high enough housing density to keep streets busy and to provide a flow of customers into small businesses. This is still a poor place, and it has all the social problems associated with poverty and immigration, but even in the midst of the crisis there is a sense of optimism and opportunity: People here are not trapped.

A major study found that the Spanish-born children of Moroccan immigrants are becoming fully integrated into Spanish language and customs far better than South American and Central American migrants to Spain, whose parents would seem to lack the disadvantage of a foreign language. This difference is attributed to the fact that Spanish immigration policies for Moroccans and other Africans, which were formulated a decade later, made it possible for entire families to migrate and become citizens, so that children are not raised in single-parent families or in families assembled through immigration-driven forced marriages. The Latin American migrant process was more likely to split up families.[28]

Lisaneddin and his wife have five daughters, aged from four months to nine years, all born in Spain, all citizens. The older ones are fully acculturated Spaniards in identity, behavior, and self-description and are respected as such by their peers. "The children born here, in general, are treated like Spaniards, not like Moroccans," he says. "Most people here really don't notice the difference, not with the kids who were born here. It's very mixed, very open. You can afford to get a start here, and the government gives you help, so if you work hard you can become successful in this city. We really do feel like we have arrived, and we belong."

9

ARRIVAL'S END:
MUD FLOOR TO MIDDLE CLASS

THE NEIGHBORHOOD THAT CAME IN FROM THE COLD
Jardim Angela, São Paulo, Brazil

Each weekday morning, Pedro and Denise Magalhães wake in their whitewashed bungalow on the southern outskirts of São Paulo, make a quick espresso, check the headlines on the web, drag their two teenagers away from their TVs and computers and usher them off to school, and open the front gate to begin their drive to work. As they back their Peugeot sedans into the street, Pedro glances across the road to a spot he has spent his entire life watching: a small park in the middle of their boulevard, one of the few scraps of green in this extremely dense neighborhood. These days it is occupied only by a lone drunk, an old school friend of Pedro's who fell on hard times and sleeps on one of its benches. Two decades earlier, when Pedro attended the secondary school at the top of the street, he would pass this park each Monday morning and frequently see that at least one bullet-punctured corpse had been dumped there, very often the bodies of his schoolmates, sometimes one of his friends. For a number of years this was almost a weekly occurrence. Murder, for everyone living here, was a staple of daily life, and horrific poverty and isolation its backdrop.

In 1996, Jardim Angela became known as the most violent community on earth.[1] This was the wider world's confirmation of something that had been evident to residents of this *favela* for years. In 1976, it was empty parkland with a few migrants' shacks strung along its snakelike main street. By the end of the century, this hilly strip of land had a population exceeding 250,000 and an astonishing 309 homicides per year.[2] Almost all the victims were teenagers, caught up in local gang struggles. Its murder rate, which was the highest in Brazil through the 1990s and peaked at 123 per 100,000, made it more deadly than most war zones.* Some of the killings were carried out by warring teenage gangs. Others were conducted by the military police, who staged raids every few months, shooting up parties, capturing and torturing teenagers, and conducting clandestine assassinations. There were also private-sector death squads, made up of current and former police hired by local businessmen to kill troublesome gang members. Property values were below zero: The neighborhood was a degraded pile of shacks, almost uninhabitable after most shops and services moved out and crime became the main business. Drug abuse and alcoholism were default modes of coping, and the infant-mortality rate was one of the highest in the country. Jardim Angela was synonymous with dangerous slum life. Pedro Magalhães was caught in its center, in his most vulnerable years, with a dead father, an impoverished family, a pregnant teenage girlfriend, and no useful education. It seemed certain that he would become one of the lost arrivals.

Pedro was born in 1971, the youngest son of a farming family in the poor north of the inland Minas Gerais state, just as Brazil's great migration was approaching its peak. In 1976, his family abandoned the village and took advantage of the father's seasonal-migration links to São Paulo to participate in a land invasion on the city's far southern boundary. It was a risky move. The land was near the edge of one of two lakes that provide most of São Paulo's drinking water, and the city had a history of violently evicting squatter communities

---

* By comparison, the most murder-prone city in the United States, Detroit, has a homicide rate of 46 per 100,000.

from water-supply areas. But Brazil's military dictatorship was under stress and had few resources to fight urban battles. The sheer mass of people converging on the city made a sustained resistance unlikely. Pedro's family cobbled together a wood hut, pressed tightly against its neighbors, on the lower slope of the *favela*'s main hill, on far less desirable land than their current residence. Although his family's wood shack would be bulldozed by São Paulo authorities more than once in the land battles of the 1970s, they were able to stay, penned in by a city that would neither completely evict them nor formalize their ownership, leaving them in a limbo with neither services nor official citizenship.

In its earliest years, there was a mood of optimism in Jardim Angela. It was far better than the village, and there was work. "It was quite a deserted place then," Pedro told me. "Lots of empty spaces, big areas for kids to run around." And jobs for the adults, in the local metalworking industry and a big bicycle plant. There was pirated electricity, but no water, sewage, paved streets, bus service, or any other connections to the urban surroundings, and the city did not recognize ownership of the *favela* huts. In 1976, just as Pedro's family was arriving, Oliveira Viana Municipal School opened, a one-room classroom at the top of the little park. For the next 20 years, the school would be the only permanent face of government in the *favela*. In 1982, Pedro's own life took a difficult turn when his father died, and his mother was forced to work as a dinner lady at the school, a job that provided hardly enough to support her three sons. And as their family life foundered, the fast-growing neighborhood seemed to collapse around them.

The great 1970s wave of rural–urban migration had been built around an industrial economy controlled and usually owned by Brazil's military dictatorship in a closed economic system. In the 1980s, this all fell apart. The artificial economy collapsed in simultaneous currency, fiscal inflation, and banking crises, just as the military regime was launching a stumbling transition to democracy. For the entire decade, Brazil had very little economic activity and no government with the fiscal resources to support an emerging urban community. It was a time of decay. For Jardim Angela and hundreds of other new-formed *favelas* and squatter enclaves around São Paulo and Rio de Janeiro, this proved a disastrous combination. The new migrants, who had just begun to build their houses, often using money they'd borrowed, suddenly found themselves without any means of employment or any resources with which to start their own companies. The communities had not yet become linked to the larger city in even the most rudimentary way, so there was no way for the suddenly jobless migrants to find work outside the *favela*.

"It became very bad very quickly—we had the fathers unemployed, so mothers had to become the primary breadwinners," says Jucileide Mauger, who was a schoolteacher at Oliveira Viana in those years. "The dads started drinking, and we could only give kids four hours of school a day, so the second-generation kids were unsupervised, with nothing to do, and they were becoming teenagers. There became a huge problem with poverty, and there was no government at all to help. Kids would come to school without having eaten, with no uniforms; we had to provide for them. The families were falling apart, everyone was unemployed, and the situation kept getting a lot worse."

Pedro Magalhães was one of those kids. He watched his classmates turn to crime. At first, it was mainly theft: They would rob the drivers of trucks that delivered water and fuel to the neighborhood—just about the only outsiders to enter the *favela*. Then, by the end of the '80s, it became more serious: The older teenagers formed gangs inspired by American movies, the Bronx and the Ninjas, and they got involved in cocaine and went to war with one another. It became increasingly brutal. They were strictly local gangs, without links to international cocaine trafficking, and perhaps because of this they were both less organized and more violent than the big gangs. They would, and often did, kill for an outstanding debt worth a few dollars. "For a number of years, starting in 1992, we had kids killed every week, sometimes every day—their bodies would be dumped out in that square, and I'd see that they were our students," says

Ms. Mauger, who became head teacher of what was a 2,500-student school at the height of the violence shortly after her predecessor lost her teeth in a beating by gang members inside the school. "One family with seven brothers, five of them were killed one year. I knew something had to be done. I'd keep the school open in the evenings so they could play in the courts . . . I thought just keeping them in the building was important—never mind keeping them in classes, never mind what we were teaching, it was a matter of having them in here and not out shooting one another. The government wasn't present, the police weren't present, it was just us."

Pedro hovered on the edge of the gangs, never quite joining but tempted. One morning on the way to school, his friend Chico approached him, feverish and excited: "I had a dream," Chico said, "I'm going to kill Carlos." Chico had become a paid killer. He murdered Carlos and dropped his corpse in the small park. He killed 30 more people in the next year, mostly classmates, before he, too, wound up in the park. As the violence reached world-record levels, Pedro repeated a year of school because of bad grades and, he says, incompetent teaching. Then, at 18, he learned that his girl-friend, Denise, was pregnant. He was unemployable, without any prospects. He was about to drop out of school. The only possible source of employment was the Bronx gang. "I didn't want to join," he says. "I'd have to kill for them and they were all on drugs, but it was the only thing there was. They were trying to recruit me, and I didn't have any choices."

Pedro and Denise recounted this story to me one Saturday morning as they drove their family, crammed into the back seat of her Peugeot, from their house in the middle of Jardim Angela to the nearest indoor shopping mall. It has become a family custom to spend Saturday mornings shopping at the mall's department stores, then to have lunch in the food court. Their daughter, Kassia, 17, a freshman at a private college who wants to major in fashion design, gets her lunch from Panda Express. Vitor, 14, enrolled in a private high school, eschews the usual McDonald's for heartier Brazilian fare. They practice their English, learned from private tutors, on me, discussing their favorite brands of mobile phones and preferred social-networking sites. Tuition for the two of them costs $800 a month, eight months a year. Denise talks about the family's next big move: She and Pedro have just put a one-third down payment on a $63,000, three-bedroom condominium on the eighth floor of an 18-story building beside this mall, on the edge of the *favela* cluster that includes Jardim Angela. The development contains government-funded "*favela* rehousing" apartments, squat, turquoise-painted blocks with small windows, as well as large flats like theirs, in modern, glass-walled towers with broad balconies, marketed to people who want to stay in their original *favela* surroundings, near their friends and relatives and businesses, but with modern amenities and more security. For the next few months, they will continue to live in the whitewashed shantytown house on the edge of the park, which belongs to Denise's mother. There is a property boom taking place within Jardim Angela, as the people at the top of the *favela* move into new apartments and people living lower on the hill purchase their vacated houses. The proceeds of this boom are financing business start-ups.

Pedro is a member of Brazil's new arrival-city middle class. For the past decade, he has owned and run an information-technology consulting firm, based out of Jardim Angela, which currently provides network-hardware services to a multinational branding company. His earnings, combined with his wife's pay, amount to between $30,000 and $35,000 a year—a comfortable middle-class income by the standards of the developing world. It is a salary that allows them to send both their children through private education, to have two cars and all manner of modern appliances, clothes, toys, and a broadband connection, and to save enough money to become property owners. Like many arrival-city dwellers, they managed this by moving in with relatives during their child-rearing years to save housing costs.

I have not chosen Pedro and Denise because they are rare and miraculous exceptions but because they are fairly characteristic of a sizable minority of people in Jardim Angela today. In the years since the *favela*'s collapse into violence, a thriving middle class has emerged; depending whom you believe, between a fifth and a third of the neighborhood's population have "made it" enough to become home-owners. It remains a poor neighborhood, with most of its population employed informally as delivery drivers, domestic servants, builders, or call-center operators (there is little unemployment), and drug abuse remains a visible problem in some quarters. But there is a fundamental change now. The main street, once a strip of forlorn drinking establishments, now teems with furniture and appliance stores, restaurants, ice-cream parlors, and home-improvement outlets. Households here have an average of 1.5 televisions each, and a third have DVD players; half have cell phones; a third have family cars; and 14 percent own computers, half of them with broadband internet. All the houses are now made of brick; two-thirds have invested in expanding or improving their houses, and about a third have stuccoed, painted exteriors (stucco and paint are worldwide badges of disposable income).[3]

Beneath all this are more important changes. First, violent crime and gangs are no longer dominant features. Between 1999 and 2005, Jardim Angela's homicide rate fell by 73.3 percent and continued to plummet to levels comparable to a South American middle-class neighborhood. The Bronx and Ninja gangs have by all accounts faded into irrelevance. While a larger statewide gang has taken control of the city's entire cocaine trade, reducing gang rivalries, most informed observers believe the disappearance of gangs from this neighborhood is a direct result of economic development. Cell-phone theft and armed robbery are now the prevalent crimes, and the major cause of teenage mortality is motorcycle accidents. Second, the neighborhood is today tightly linked into the city, with bus services running through the *favela* to a nearby commuter-train link, as well as offices of numerous government agencies. Third, since 2003, the people here have legally owned their homes, thanks to a forward-looking São Paulo mayor who made land-titling a priority.* As a result, almost two-thirds have invested in improvements. Fourth, there are now the means to start and run a small business, and the neighborhood is packed with shops, department stores, credit agencies, and small workshops. People here remain poor, and there remains a large population of young people (mainly male high-school graduates) who are stuck in a netherworld of casual employment. But a notable and sustainable middle class is emerging within the *favela*, turning it into a much better neighborhood and improving the living conditions of even the poorest residents. The process of arrival, dramatically interrupted in the 1980s and '90s, has returned.

It is worth examining Jardim Angela's transformation closely, for it offers answers to a key question of our age: What does it take to make the journey from a rural shack to the center of middle-class urban life within a generation? Or, for that matter, even in two generations? This is, after all, the core function of the arrival city, the sole objective of all those hundreds of millions of journeys from village to city. It is a wonder, then, that we know so little about how this can be accomplished. It is clear, from our tour of the world's arrival cities, that this transformation often does not take place within a generation and that grim and violent repercussions can take place when it doesn't. Yet it should also be clear that rural migrants consider this transformation to be the norm. In fact, they expect it. In Jardim Angela, we can see what obstacles can block their path and what can be done to remove them.

In 1996, there did not seem to be any paths at all. Jardim Angela, built by soy farmers and sugar-cane planters to be a platform for their dreams, had turned into a deadly, isolated antechamber for their children. The second generation had no purchase in urban life and no connection to the village. They were culturally city-dwellers, with a

---

* Some Jardim Angela residents have had titles since the 1980s, but in 2003 it became possible to own property on protected water-supply land.

standard of living and expectations far higher than those of their parents, but they were trapped in a world that treated them as no more than the unwanted offspring of villagers. Lost and without support, they consumed one another. "There wasn't a day that would go by, when I walked around the parish, that I wouldn't step across two or three bodies," says Father Jaime Crowe, the *favela's* priest, who found himself with the task of burying an entire generation. "To step over a body in front of a door with a newspaper thrown over it to have a drink—you'd think nothing of it. Children, small children, would tell me that their life was not worth living. It had to stop." To most Brazilians, it seemed as if some evil had overtaken Jardim Angela, as if its people were genetically predestined to violence, poverty, and inactivity.

Yet it was becoming abundantly clear to a group of committed people living in Jardim Angela that this was not its natural or inevitable state. They had the desire and the will to do better, but there was nothing to provide the capability. As the violence peaked in 1996, and with no sign of an improvement, people began to meet and came to a shared conclusion: that Jardim Angela's problem wasn't the presence of evil; it was the absence of normal city institutions and functions.

Pedro Magalhães learned this earlier than most. At 18, with Denise pregnant and his school career jeopardized, he teetered on the edge of gang life. He had no interest in crime—in fact, it inspired a moral revulsion—but he would do anything to secure his daughter's future, and no other options were presenting themselves in the barren economy of Jardim Angela. Then his oldest brother stepped in with an offer: a job cutting hair in his barbershop, which he had opened in the better years and was one of the few arrival-city businesses still standing (in large part because haircutting requires little capital and no links to the city outside). "That job saved me," Pedro says. "It allowed me to keep out of trouble, and it gave me enough savings that I could borrow the money to study computers." Through the dense network of mutual connections that defines the arrival city,

Pedro was able to weave a new sort of life, one built on education, financial credit, and entrepreneurship. He found his pathway to the middle class, and it led through the middle of the arrival city.

Was it possible that all the residents of Jardim Angela were attempting something similar? That was the question the *favela*'s community leaders began asking as the violence peaked and they began holding emergency meetings at the school to talk about the neighborhood's grisly problems. After having been ignored for years by the larger municipal, state, and national entities outside, the *favela* developed its own grassroots municipal government, at first as an emergency response to the deaths of hundreds of children and then as a larger, more potent institution. The meetings at the school became known as the Forum for the Defence of Life. As the *favela* became infamous for its violence, these meetings were first attended by school officials, some police, and Father Jaime (who was the first to organize the meetings); then by members of international aid organizations, which took up the *favela* cause as news of the violence spread; and, finally, by representatives from municipal and state governments. Soon, hundreds of residents were attending. The citizens of Jardim Angela were unanimous in their descriptions of the neighborhood's needs: first security, then education, then a proper link to the larger city, physically and economically.

"The school became the first really neutral territory, the first public space," says Jucileide Mauger. Before, her school had offered four hours per day of the most basic sort of teaching—like many arrival-city schools, which are either private or minimal, it offered few handholds for social mobility. Lobbying the government and the aid organizations for funds, they engineered a school better attuned to arrival-city needs. "We had to cultivate the idea that the school is a government body, that it's an authority, that you have to come and follow rules. We made it part of the community. Then we started evening classes for adults and older teenagers with a seventh- or eighth-grade education who wanted a new start." These were so successful that the school had to open all 15 classrooms at night.

Education proved popular, not just to the kids who wanted to avoid the life of gangs and drugs but to those who lived that life. "Many kids had dropped out, started drug dealing at 12 or 13—then, at 20 or 21, realized that it's not such a good living, so they come back here looking for a future."

Most dramatic and visible, and most often praised by Jardim Angela residents, was the change in security. Before, the police had literally been heavily armed military platoons traveling in armored vehicles invading from fortresslike bases outside, treating the entire neighborhood as "enemy territory" and the whole population as potential combatants. They would raid at night, arrest, kill, then leave. Drug crime was their only priority. The police were feared as much as the gangs—often more so, since at least the gang's killers were neighbors and relatives. There were good reasons to distrust them: In the early 1990s, hundreds of military police were implicated in thousands of revenge slayings and contract killings in the *favelas*.

As the violence peaked, some of the *favela*-born members of the police began to feel that they were partly responsible for the poverty and isolation. By treating the arrival city as a quarantined zone subject to periodic invasions, they were pushing the neighborhood inward, against itself. In 1998, after years of pressure from the Forum for the Defence of Life, the police embarked on a truly bold experiment. They built a station inside Jardim Angela, with big windows and an open door, reduced their vehicle count to two cars for 200 officers, and devoted themselves to foot patrols, going door to door in the style of beat cops—something Brazil had never seen before. They developed a philosophy of "community-based policing," a worn catchphrase in the wealthy world but a very new idea in Brazil.

"For my first 15 years as a cop, I approached crime in an aggressive manner, because that's all I knew," says Davi Monteiro da Conceição, known to everyone here as Sergeant Davi, a former military police strongman who began attending the Forum for the Defence of Life meetings in the 1990s, became captivated by the ideas circulating, and now commands the Jardim Angela community force. "There were many confrontations—I took part in the exchange of gunfire . . . But I changed the way I acted. Now I have more involvement with the people around me. They still don't completely trust us, so we have to keep things at the personal level. We need to go into their houses and explain to them that the police aren't just for beating up and being violent, which is all we'd done before, but that there are other uses for police—it's slow going."

It was too late for most members of Pedro's generation, but his children's neighbors and classmates have entered a very different world, one in which Jardim Angela is an integral part of São Paulo. The years of political organizing within the *favela* changed things, as did the realization by more enlightened city and state governments that these neighborhoods were an important investment. It helped that São Paulo passed a comprehensive gun-control law in 2003, which the Jardim Angela community police enforce aggressively. It helped that a farsighted mayor the same year recognized the social and economic value of giving the outlying *favelas* comprehensive bus and commuter-train service and an affordable transit pass for poor workers. It helped that medical clinics and street lighting were installed. It helped that micro-credit agencies established themselves here and offered loan guarantees and that small-business laws were liberalized, making it easier for *favela*-dwellers to use the value in their real estate to start a company. And it helped that entrepreneurs and agencies built venues to popularize and profit from the music and dance that had been an underground part of the *favela*'s culture. For the arrival city's third generation, there were suddenly reasons to stick around and improve the place.

"The second generation grew up without a past—they didn't have their parents' rural backgrounds, and they didn't have futures, either," says Bruno Paes Manso, a São Paulo scholar and writer who has analyzed the economics behind *favela* violence.[4] What he discovered in his investigations was that São Paulo's dramatic reduction in crime rates during the 2000s was due not primarily to police enforcement or gang organization but to economic development. The emergence of legitimate jobs in the *favelas* encouraged thousands of gangsters to abandon the life. "They went into crime, but there was an attitude of 'I don't want this destiny for my son.' You never had an ideology of maintaining this way of life—it was just a circumstance the second generation found itself forced into. It felt like a prison for them. There was no self-valorization. The third generation is much more integrated into the economy and the culture of the city. The transportation, the jobs in the city, the hip hop music movements—these gave them a past and a tradition, an ability to talk about their roots and their future. You always hear them saying, 'I come from village roots, I come from slaves, native communities, and I have no interest in dying before I'm 25, because I'm a Paulista' [São Paulo citizen]. They're creating a new identity."

The children of Pedro and Denise Magalhães have no sense of fear or desperation: They are aspirational teenagers of São Paulo, attached to the music and culture of Jardim Angela but utterly unconcerned with the economics or folkways of migration or the battle that was required to give them normal lives. Looking over the string of apartment towers that she will soon call home, I ask 17-year-old Kassia about the prospect of living in a high-tech castle of former neighbors, eight stories up: Does she look forward to the view? "No," she tells me, "it's not such a great view. There's a park, but there are *favelas* in the way."

This is fundamentally a book about social mobility. The move from village to city, we have seen, is always a calculated effort to raise a family's living standard, income, and quality of life, using the arrival city as its main instrument. Urban poverty, despite its crowding and frequent humiliations, is an improvement on rural poverty, and no arrival-city resident considers poverty anything but a temporary necessity. But the creation of an arrival city is only the first step in a journey planned carefully by the migrant. Nobody invests their entire life, and a generation's income and peace, simply to move from one form of poverty to another. The residents of arrival cities do not consider themselves "the poor" but rather successful urbanites who happen to be passing through a period of poverty, perhaps for a generation.[5]

The arrival city, if it is to function at all, must create members of a middle class: Families with enough earnings and savings to start businesses and employ others, to own and improve dwellings, to send children to university, to have a sustainable quality of life capable of moving them, and their neighbors, beyond merely surviving. An arrival-city middle class is important for a number of reasons. It creates social and political stability, because the middle class ties the neighborhood to the institutions of the wider city and thereby opens a pathway to something other than crime, marginal informal-economy employment, and dependency. The presence of an arrival-city middle class shows new arrivals and their children that the process of migration is not a journey into perpetual injustice, that sustainable prosperity is available to those willing to study and invest. It tends to generate employers and political leaders within the arrival city, improving the quality of life for others. And research has shown that the presence of a middle class raises living standards for those neighbors who remain poor.[6] The economist Steven Durlauf has shown that a middle class, even a small one, within a poor community can generate "neighborhood feedback effects" in which investments in the higher education of children become a behavioral norm.[7] And, significantly, the presence of a middle class within the arrival city helps improve the standards of living in the originating villages, financing non-agricultural industries in rural areas and creating a parallel rural middle class. By equalizing village and city, the middle-class arrival city puts an end to rural–urban migration.

Middle-class status is not an unrealistic expectation for rural arrivals: It has been the historic norm. It is what occurred in the cities of Europe and North America throughout the late nineteenth and twentieth centuries. As we have seen, it is widely attainable in the more successful Western arrival cities today. And it can be observed in the arrival cities of the developing world. Turkish *gecekondu* neighbor-hoods have cultivated a new, internal middle class that now domi-nates the nation; former shack-town *favelas*, like Rio de Janeiro's Rocinha district, have evolved into desirable middle-income enclaves, and their São Paulo cousins have spawned a consumer and industrial boom and a new form of national politics. The more established slums of Mumbai, like Dharavi, now have internal economies worth hundreds of millions of dollars, and within their labyrinthine walls I have encountered slum-based factories employing 40 or 50 people and financing computer-science educations for extended families.

Jardim Angela today is a good example of just such a middle-class arrival city. According to the five-band Brazilian measure of house-hold wealth and consumption, in which band A are the country's wealthiest 20 percent and band E the poorest fifth, at least 14 percent of people living in the *favela* district encompassing Jardim Angela now fall into the comfortably middle-class B band, and only 31 per-cent into the second-poorest D band, with more than half the *favela's* population living within band C, the lower bounds of the middle class, a massive change from the 1990s.* It is a pattern repeated across the arrival-city *favelas* of São Paulo.[8] You can see it in the colorful array of shops, services, and small businesses that fill the streets.

Still, these places remain the global exception rather than the rule. Many arrival cities are failing to give members of their second generation, no matter how hard they work or school themselves, the chance to enter the middle class. And that is jeopardizing eco-nomic growth and political stability in many countries. David Rothkopf, a scholar with the Carnegie Endowment for International Peace, described this neglect as a large-scale mistake: "With the notable exceptions of India and China and a few others, which show some heartening middle-class growth, we are doing a very bad job of building the middle classes, which are the foundation

---

* Significantly, only 0.5 percent of people in Jardim Angela are in the poorest E band. Today, only rural residents in most countries are poor enough to fall into the bottom 20 percent of the population.

of stability and the antidote to the boom-bust cycles that bedevil much of the emerging world."[9]

To explain the nature of this challenge, it is important to understand what we mean—and what rural-to-urban migrants mean—by "middle class." One way to define a middle class is by identifying the middle-income range: you pick out those families that earn between 75 percent and 150 percent of a country's median income. The economist Branko Milanovic did this for the entire world, dividing all 6.7 billion people into a "lower class"—which turned out to be those whose annual family incomes were below $4,000 annually, the median income of Brazil—and an "upper class," those families with more than $17,000 a year, the median income of Italy. The lower class made up 78 percent of the world's population, the upper class 11 percent, and the worldwide middle class, those families living on between $4,000 and $17,000 a year, another 11 percent.[10]

The middle class can also be identified by their role and self-identification. Even if much of the "middle class" today are better-paid factory workers and computer operators rather than the traditional bourgeoisie, an important identifying characteristic is their ability to deploy savings and investments to alter their future status. The middle class, by almost universal consensus, are those who can easily take care of all their food, housing, and transportation needs in a sustainable way across generations and who also have a consistent ability and willingness to borrow (and repay) money for investments in future growth, to accumulate savings and capital, to put their children through any level of education, and to gather enough resources to start a business, expand a house, or buy a vehicle without sacrificing living standards.* As it happens, in the developing world this level of security and comfort tends to be attained at almost exactly the income level defined by Milanovic in his study. With regional variations, somewhere between about

---

* The word *sustainable* is important here: As the 2008 credit crisis demonstrated in many countries, a middle-class illusion can be built on unsupportable levels of private debt.

$5,000 and $15,000 per year in family income is the gateway to the middle class.

The middle class should have grown a lot more in the two decades after the economic crises of the 1980s and the liberalization of the world's economies. Based on the extraordinary economic growth of that time, along with the increases in per capita incomes and boosts in living standards that occurred in those years, there should have been far more social mobility. In 2006, economists working for MasterCard predicted a "deluge" of a billion new middle-class consumers, with family incomes of more than $5,000 annually, emerging from Asia, with 650 million such consumers appearing in China and 350 million in India by 2020. At the time, there were exactly 12 million people with such incomes in India and 79 million in China, so the projected growth was exponential, with equivalent rewards to industry: "As soon as income exceeds the $5,000 threshold, marginal expenditures shift quickly to discretionary spending such as dining out, personal travel, auto purchases, etc., and these have a huge business and economic impact," the MasterCard report claimed. The estimate has been echoed in similar studies.[11]

Something went wrong, though. While living standards did improve, especially for the very poor, many who had sat on the brink of the middle class at the beginning of the long boom ended it, 20 years later, still sitting on the brink, unable to get in. These frustrated people were, overwhelmingly, the children of rural arrivals.

In one of the most important studies of the middle class in the developing world, three economists from prominent U.S. think tanks examined large banks of income statistics from around the world and found that the turn to market economics had been generally positive for income groups on the extremes—the poor and the very rich saw their fortunes rise dramatically in the 1990s and early 2000s (the poor, in large part, because of urbanization). But they concluded that "the middle has had very mixed rewards: increased upward mobility for some sectors . . . but increased uncertainty and downward mobility for others." In Latin America, for example, liberalization brought income gains for most people but "increasing economic insecurity for middle-income households." It described large segments of the middle class—broadly those without post-secondary education or family connections (that is, the arrival-city second generation) as "stalled in the jam."[12]

In too many places, this "stalled" condition has left a large part of a generation out of the middle class. In his study of social mobility in Mumbai, the geographer Jan Nijman found that "the upper-middle income classes have grown relative to the total, the lower-middle income classes have shrunk, and that the ranks of the poor have expanded slightly" during the 1990s—that is, the numbers entering the middle class in that decade were smaller than the numbers of poor people entering the city every year. His detailed examination of new home buyers found "little upward mobility"—in other words, the majority of home buyers were children of homeowners, not children of migrants. People who should have been stepping into the middle class, those earning $5,000 to $8,000 a year, were finding themselves barred from home ownership.[13] Entry to the middle class, in India and elsewhere, had become difficult in a time when other forms of growth were widespread.

The problem had little to do with markets and much to do with the way governments responded. At the precise moment when governments should have been stepping in to help the newly secure poor find entry points to middle-class success, many governments seemed to vanish from the scene. It was a vast fiscal miscalculation. In the aftermath of the 1980s, when countries opened to markets, many adopted exceedingly tight spending policies—sometimes because these were required by international lending agencies as conditions for bailout loans, in many more cases because the countries were opening themselves to international capital markets for the first time and wanted to demonstrate their macroeconomic discipline. In either case, the result was that a large part of the world was failing to invest in the development of its middle class (and the functioning of its rise from poverty through arrival cities). They would pay the price well into the twenty-first century.

"These societies ignored a couple key dimensions of middle-class development," says Sherle Schwenninger, the U.S. economist who co-authored a major study in 2007 that found that the global middle class had stagnated. [14] "They'd been slow to develop home mortgage markets that would have helped develop middle entrepreneurial industries; they have ignored state spending on infrastructure," he told me. "Too much of the economy was ignored, partly under the pressures to pay attention to public finances."

The parts of the economy that were being ignored by these governments were precisely those that had their locus in the arrival city. In analysis after analysis, the site of failed mobility turned out to be the institutions and functions that are most needed to make the arrival city work.

Janice Perlman, whose work with South American rural–urban migrants in the early 1970s was the first to recognize the economically central and dynamic nature of the arrival city, returned to revisit her subjects and their children. "The move from an illiterate rural life in agriculture (or fishing) to a literate urban life in manual labor was a great leap in socio-economic mobility for the original interviewees or their parents," she concluded, and "there have been major improvements in collective consumption of urban services and in individual consumption of household goods over 35 years." But, while "significant gains were made in education by the children of the original interviewees . . . these gains are not fully reflected in better jobs." Notably, she found "a striking lower rate of return to educational investment" for those living in arrival cities: Paying to send your kid to a private secondary school or college, as the Magalhães family are doing in São Paulo, does not guarantee that they will enter the middle class. Perlman did find that large numbers of children of Brazilian rural migrants are becoming middle class, but only by leaving the arrival city behind. Of the original migrants, 34 percent are now living outside the arrival city in "legal" homeowner neighborhoods that would qualify as middle-class, and 44 percent of their children and 51 percent of their grandchildren are. In order to break out of the types of jobs their parents held, though, they needed university educations, and few were able to get them.[15]

Another large-scale study, directed by the U.S.-based Council on Foreign Relations, found that those developing countries that experienced middle-class growth had done so because they had stable currencies and had attracted long-term capital flows, but also because they had cultivated a number of things directly aimed at the arrival city: financial institutions capable of supporting small businesses plus "access to reasonably priced, long-term credit" for poor consumers to finance home ownership, post-secondary education, and infrastructure development.[16]

Even more significantly, a United Nations study of earnings in the developing world, which examined the factors behind failed middle-class growth in this century's first decade, found that developing countries are investing in post-secondary education at the expense of primary and secondary schools for the poor, causing educational benefits to be biased toward the existing middle class, thereby cutting off migrant families and reducing social mobility. And it found that the primary and secondary schools for the poor were not delivering the same results: The best teachers and educational resources were outside the arrival city.[17]

It was the economist Amartya Sen who first recognized that poverty is, fundamentally, not the dearth of money or a lack of possessions or a shortage of talent or ambition but the absence of *capacities*—the lack of tools or opportunities needed to function as a full citizen.[18] This concept has become widely used in the field of development, but it finds its most pointed and obvious truth in the arrival city. For it is here, where there is the most will to reach out for betterment, that people are most dangerously deprived of capacities, those knobby handholds in the otherwise smooth vertical face of the economy. As we've seen, most needed are the capacity to start a business and the capacity to be educated: When these are provided, a whole new class can develop. Those capacities suddenly material-ize, as they did in Jardim Angela, when people have effective self-government, when they have good security and access to credit and urban amenities, when the government takes an active involvement in the neighborhood. And in the eyes of arrival-city residents and many observers, another key to realizing these capacities lies in the full ownership of the land beneath your feet.

A HOUSE FOR MR. AND MRS. PARAB
Mumbai

I met the Parab family on the day they joined the middle class. They had awoken in the soupy lassitude of a late-spring Mumbai morn-ing, the four of them curled together on the floor of the dimly lit, one-room *chawl* that had been their home for the past six years. It was a concrete-block cube of 200 square feet with a corrugated-metal roof, its neat main floor beneath an elevated cooking plat-form. They greeted their neighbors in the narrow passageway outside, packed their last possessions into a waiting minivan, and made the bumpy half-hour ride to an adjoining, heavily treed neighbourhood.

As they approached Om Shanti Apartments, a gray and somewhat weather-beaten 22-year-old poured-concrete tower, Subhashini Parab, 36, enthusiastically reassured her children about their new surround-ings. "You are only a five-minute walk to the railway station in one direction, and there is a very good temple five minutes the other way," she told 18-year-old Prateek and 11-year-old Rohan, though there was no need for such reassurances. She had spent the 18 years of her marriage to Manohar, a quiet man 16 years her senior, push-ing the family to make it out of the slums and into the genuine middle class. This, long deferred, was their moment of arrival. It had taken far longer than they expected, and it succeeded only by dint of the booming slum property market.

Moments later, they discovered the silent isolation of the middle class. There seemed to be endless expanses of polished-marble floor space, the novel prospect of separate rooms for different functions, of thick walls between families, of having one's own toilet. In the *chawl*, water was available for two hours in the morning, a short walk away; here it is available all the time, out of the wall. This apartment is known in the arcane language of Mumbai property listings as a "1bhk," or one-bedroom-hall-kitchen, a basic 450-square-foot space divided into three rooms, well lit by big windows. To the Parab family, the most astonishing thing about it, and the most deeply unnerving, is its silence. No longer would they hear every word and movement around them; no longer was the air constantly vibrating with the parry and banter of their entire community. When they stopped talking, sound died away. Alarmed, Manohar switched the new 26-inch TV to a Bollywood musical, turned up the volume, and left it on while he talked.

They had bought the place a month before but had decided to stay in the slum an extra four weeks before moving in for a reason that would seem, to almost anyone in the world, characteristically middle class: Subhashini had cashed in her life's accumulation of gold jewelery, a trove valued at $10,000 and traditionally saved for the marriage of children, and spent it on renovations to the dingy old apartment. A wall was ripped out, new kitchen counters installed, floor tiles replaced with marble, impressive new ceiling mouldings and lights installed by her carpenter cousin. The couple talked about the comfort and self-respect these improvements would bring them—and domestic self-respect is not a value to be neglected among slum-dwellers—but they also talked about the equity value. These improvements would raise the resale price of the apartment they had just bought for $42,500.

It is an elegant home. It is also barely theirs. Their family income had crossed the middle-class threshold three years earlier, when Manohar had landed a job driving executives' cars for a company that makes electronic instruments. He had come to Mumbai from his village in central Maharashtra at age 14, making the transition from pavement to slum using his network of fellow villagers. Subhashini was the child of a veteran arrival-city family, a gregarious woman of singular self-confidence, and she made it a well-organized project, from her marriage at 18, to get her family out of the slum.

His annual salary of $6,600 was not going to be enough to do it. The Parabs encountered two problems that are endemic across the world of arrival cities: an illiberal property market rigidly reined in by zoning and rent-control regulations and ownership restrictions, and an underdeveloped credit market that makes proper mortgage loans available only to the very highest-income groups. One set of restrictions discouraged anyone from building or selling homes affordable to the lower middle class (or to almost anyone, as millions of Mumbai home buyers have discovered); the other made it impossible for the Parabs to get a home loan of any sort, even with a sizable down payment. Or as Dinanath Berde, the estate agent who sold them the house, told me: "There are a great many poor people in this city who want a three-room house, but all too often either they are not available because nobody is able to build them, or their household budget is not matching the supply. There just are not entry-level homes here."

So it would take the Parabs three more years to turn their savings and income into a home, during which Subhashini spent months visiting bankers and estate agents, researching government regulations, and finding work. In the end they did it by taking advantage of another, very different side of Mumbai's property market. The Parabs, like many arrival-city residents around the world, had bought their slum shacks as they moved up from the lowest level of housing. They had held on to both their previous properties and had used both their earliest 110-square-foot shack and their more recent 200-square-foot *chawl* as sources of rental income. They get $35 a month for the first home and $70 for the second; combined with Subhashini's earnings working part-time at a costume-jewelery workshop, this was enough to boost their income to just under $8,000 a year—the point at which a loan became feasible. They discovered, as people trying to enter the middle class all over the world are discovering today, that the line cannot be crossed on one income alone: it is necessary to become a two-income, and sometimes a three-income, family. This has given considerable economic and social power to women in many otherwise traditional communities; it has also, in turn, made child-care services a desperately important commodity in the arrival city.

Even with all those income sources, it was not a simple matter of buying a house. The Parabs were not eligible for any kind of actual mortgage. India's banks are extremely conservative in their lending practices, a fact that saved the country's economy from ruin in the credit-crunch crisis of 2008 but that also has frozen millions of people out of the housing market. Instead, as millions of other families in the developing world do, they took out a consumer-purchase loan, ostensibly for buying appliances and at a far higher interest rate than most mortgages. Even that was not quite enough: As is customary in Mumbai, off the books they had to pay several thousand dollars in "black money" cash payments directly to the sellers, above and beyond the official purchase price.

For this family to get a middle-class berth required a network of property enterprises and a highly leveraged financing arrangement of staggering complexity. It has left them with a home, but in a fragile way: Their monthly expenses, including $200 for the loan, $15 in maintenance fees, $80 for Prateek's college tuition, and $12 for Rohan's secondary-school fees, are about the same as Manohar's salary; they have absolutely no leeway for disasters or setbacks. "It's difficult to get by—we have had to borrow so much, and our income barely meets our expenses," says Manohar. "We are really counting on our sons for everything." At this, Prateek, practicing his Java programming on the computer in the corner of the room, looks over nervously.

The secret to a successful urban arrival for the Magalhães and Parab families, as for Sabri Koçyigit in Istanbul and the Tafader family in

London, has involved full and legal ownership of property. This gave them not only a secure place to live but also a source of equity. The arrival city's middle-class transition is very often built on real-estate values.

And if those values prove to be illusory, social mobility can grind to a halt. While most people living in the world's arrival cities have paid someone for their property and believe themselves to be the full owners, many of them are not legal or secure owners: They could be evicted by government authorities or private-sector agents at any moment, and their property carries no official financial value, so it cannot be leveraged for other uses. One study estimates that in the developing cities of Asia, Latin America, sub-Saharan Africa, and the Arab states, between 25 and 70 percent of the urban population is living on land with no clear title.[19]

For a great many politicians and economists during the past 20 years, the major issue surrounding arrival cities has been the question of property ownership. That, they believe, is the beginning and the end of the social-mobility issue. The debate began in the 1980s, when a Peruvian economist began a drive to turn that country's millions of rural-arrival squatters into property owners. Hernando de Soto established a network of formalization committees, which turned the jumble of arrival-city land titles into proper deeds and allowed people to form small businesses in a few days with a couple of forms, rather than the hundreds of days and scores of forms previously required. It was an exercise in immersing the very poor in a real economy. In 1989, de Soto described this process in a book provocatively titled *The Other Path*. Its title was a reference to the Shining Path guerrillas, the extreme Marxist-Maoist group that had become Peru's principal oppositional force in politics. As with so many other movements, they threatened the integrity of the state by mobilizing the frustrated and trapped arrival-city second generation into violent action. His book argued that the simple granting of property ownership to rural-migrant squatters in the outskirts, and easing the process of forming businesses for them, was a far better method of ending poverty and creating a middle class than the radical collectivizations offered by the Shining Path or the more bureaucratic state-driven solutions offered by populist governments.[20]

De Soto's message had a dramatic effect, not just in South America but especially in Washington. His methods became orthodox among governments across the developing world, and it is likely that hundreds of millions of people in the periphery have received secure land title because of his influence. It helped that de Soto, in his early works, was opposed to most forms of state redistribution, a message that appealed to the U.S. Republican administrations of the time. It also helped that his ideas came to be championed by Alberto Fujimori, the conservative, Washington-friendly president of Peru.

For a time in the 1990s, largely thanks to *The Other Path*, the word "formalization" was the mantra of the World Bank, the U.S. Agency for International Development and other bodies devoted to alleviating poverty. They had finally turned their attention to the arrival city and found a single remedy: home ownership. De Soto's think tank, the Institute for Liberty and Democracy, advised numerous developing-world governments, spreading the message of formalization, and dozens of poor countries used its advice to grant title deeds to squatters in the 1990s. In 2000, de Soto published an even more successful work, *The Mystery of Capital: Why Capitalism Triumphs in the West and Fails Everywhere Else*, which contained the shocking assertion that "the total value of the real estate held but not legally owned by the poor of the Third World and former communist nations is at least US$8.3 trillion."[21] If this capital could be unlocked by giving the poor formal ownership of their houses, he wrote, the result would be an economic equivalent to nuclear fission, instantly freeing up a great quantity of untapped capital to build a new middle class in the world's South and East.

In some places, his ideas were highly successful. In Brazil, as we have seen, the titling of squatted land has worked extremely well in alleviating poverty and building a middle class.[22] In Turkey, the massive legalization and titling of self-built *gecekondu* houses on the outskirts was the beginning of the birth of a new middle class and an economic and political renewal. Likewise, a great number of studies have found that titling has improved lives, by giving the poor more money to invest and by reducing the burdens of holding and securing their land, in Thailand, Ecuador, Nicaragua, and Peru.[23] Indian cities have had some success with such programs when they are applied.

Yet, in other places, the simple granting of land titles did little to improve lives. In Colombia and Mexico, it was found that land ownership didn't give people better access to credit (or if they had it, they didn't use it). In Jordan, it was found that property rights neither gave people more secure tenure nor created more investment.[24] A study of such programs in sub-Saharan Africa found that ownership had actually weakened the security of the new landowners, turning their entire lives into defensive postures against government and business.[25] Other studies, in Ghana and Nigeria, found that the poor sometimes did better if they remained squatters within an informal, non-taxpaying economy.[26] Still other studies pointed out that formalization, while helping the mass of the poor by giving them a step into the middle class, in fact hurts the poorest of the poor, who don't have the resources to reach even this bottom rung and end up getting jettisoned back into homelessness or rural poverty.[27]

Even the original Peruvian experience did not, at first, offer a great example. Although a tentative middle class was originally created in the slums, Fujimori's monomaniacal application of economic reforms led to a phenomenon known as "Fuji shock." Hyperinflation was ended and fiscal balance returned, but Peru's people suffered from dropping wages, increasing food costs, and rising poverty. While some arrival-city residents gained a hold on the middle class, even more middle-class urbanites were plunged into poverty.

Clearly, the simple ownership of land was not the route out of poverty. There had to be something else involved. It is obvious, from the experiences of dozens of arrival cities I've observed, that land ownership is invaluable and widely desired by rural migrants and their descendants, but it accomplishes little without a wide and expensive range of government-funded services and supports. This conclusion is backed by research from around the world, which shows that active state spending and involvement, and not just title-granting actions and the goodness of the market, are needed to create social mobility. Arrival cities, one analysis notes, "require a welfare-oriented political will and strength in which a formalization of economic relations makes up a perhaps important but far from sufficient foundation."[28] Or in the words of a U.S. study: "Real security in housing is buttressed by local schools and jobs, health care facilities, water and sewer services, and transportation networks. This whole complex of necessities and amenities gives value to property. Without auxiliary services and infrastructure, title alone has little meaning."[29]

What comes from this work, and from the experiences of families like the Magalhães in Brazil and the Parabs in India, is a conclusion that is unlikely to please ideologues on the socialist left or the free-market right: To achieve social mobility and a way into the middle class for the rural-migrant poor, you need to have both a free market in widely held private property and a strong and assertive government willing to spend heavily on this transition. When both are present, change will happen.

10

ARRIVING IN STYLE

INTENSITY, SPONTANEITY, AUTONOMY
Slotervaart, Amsterdam

Mohamed Mallaouch stepped off the flight from Marrakesh at Schiphol Airport, took the train into the western outskirts of Amsterdam, and marveled at the green, geometric patterns before him. After the low clay villages of his mountainous home in northern Morocco, after the helter-skelter enclaves of Marrakesh, this was an altogether different way of living.

To his eyes, it looked like a child's model city, full of artificial-looking leafy spaces, built from Lego and green felt. In deliberate contrast to the densely packed hodgepodge of the canal city's famous inner districts next door, the planned enclave of Slotervaart was an orderly grid of broad, low apartment buildings with wide expanses of parkland between them, each building separated from a meandering, quiet street by a thick verge of lawn and trees, all isolated from the bustle of the central city by a large, forested park pierced with elevated roads. When it was created in the 1960s to replace a bombed-out industrial district, Slotervaart and its larger district of Overtoomse Veld was a bedroom community for Dutch workers. Its small apartments were served with only a few shops on the main boulevard, to keep domestic life quiet and free from the ravages of commerce and capitalism. Between the buildings were numerous public squares, built for pedestrians. Like many urban-outskirts neighborhoods across Europe, it was inspired by the ideas of Le Corbusier and the Congrès Internationaux d'Architecture Moderne, which held that the key to good life was a strict functional separation of working, living, and recreational areas. Strict zoning was applied. On the architectural renderings, the public squares were decorated with small clusters of pale-skinned people, conversing and appearing to enjoy standing around outdoors.

"It seemed like a perfect place at first," Mohamed says, "and in many ways it is a good place to live, but after only a few weeks in Slotervaart I knew there was something seriously wrong. It had become a dumping ground for migrants, cut off from everything." Mohamed had come from Morocco to work as a schoolteacher. In 1992, when he arrived, about half the 45,000 residents of Slotervaart were Moroccan migrants (as well as a significant minority of Turks), most of them from the remote, thoroughly rural Rif Mountain region he called home. They'd been arriving since the 1960s, filling labor shortages in a country known for its low fertility rate and an economy prone to high-employment boom periods.

"The biggest problem I faced, right from the beginning, was that so few of the children spoke Dutch—there was nobody helping them learn the language, and no reason for them to want to learn it." The next thing that struck him, as it does most people who visit, was the dense foliage of satellite dishes sprouting from the apartment balconies. This is what the Dutch call a "dish city," an isolated urban island linked by television to the cultures of the Maghreb and the larger Arab world, with little connection to the Netherlands. Mohamed was shocked by the terrible quality of the state school and its teaching: Only the very worst teachers were willing to work out here, and this had led to a decline of education standards and the flight of the neighborhood's non-migrant residents to outside schools. A third of young Moroccan-born men were high-school dropouts, unemployed and unemployable, prone to substance abuse and criminality. They clustered in the barren public squares and glades between buildings, making the neighborhood a source of fear. The crime rate was appalling. People felt trapped and alone: It was a long and frightening walk between buildings, never mind between Slotervaart and the larger city, and Mohamed was disturbed to find that the very shape of his neighborhood kept it out of contact with Dutch society. He was even more alarmed by the religious subcultures that this system had seemed to produce. Radical, ascetic, Saudi-style Islam, which had not been part of Moroccan village culture, had become widespread. When Dutch visitors came here, they looked at Slotervaart's Arabs, with their diets of calves' brains, their chador-wearing women, and strict piety, and assumed that this was a stubborn holdout of village life, a fixed and primitive alien culture superimposed on the city.

Mohamed knew otherwise. The cultural conservatism of Slotervaart was not rural Moroccan culture or urban Dutch culture; it was a new hybrid, a culture of arrival created by trapped people. "These are the problems when you have a system that forces people to live outside of it, to see the system only from the outside and never participate," he told me as he tended to crowds of Arabic children at his school. "The people here live the contradictions between the two cultures, without being a member of either one. They are not welcome to the culture of their parents, and the school fails to do anything to make them part of the society around them. My students and their parents really wanted to be Dutch, but there was no way to be Dutch here; there was no contact with the Netherlands, so they invented this new culture. It was not good for them or anyone." In the twenty-first century, this bitter isolation would rise to threaten the core of Dutch society and state.

The threat emerged from one of those young second-generation men whose aimlessness and isolation had so worried Mohamed Mallaouch. Born in Slotervaart in 1978 to rural-migrant parents, Mohammed Bouyeri left high school to find himself disconnected from the economy, alienated from parents whose marriage fell apart, lost in the echo chamber of Slotervaart's internal obsessions. In 2003, still living in Slotervaart, he had turned to radical Islam, organizing a deeply fundamentalist group of self-proclaimed martyrs. On November 2, 2004, he took action, ambushing the filmmaker and provocateur Theo van Gogh, shooting him eight times, slashing his throat, and using a dagger to pin to his corpse a five-page manifesto calling for the death of several senior government figures. This eruption from Slotervaart transformed Dutch society and politics in a dark and lasting way, launching anti-immigrant and far-right political parties to high office and becoming the dominant issue in Dutch politics for many years. Mohamed Mallaouch watched in disapproval as his neighborhood became the most feared place in western Europe. His students were still falling into the traps that had captured Bouyeri. They joined criminal gangs or angry mosques or simply hung around the big open public squares and empty green spaces of Slotervaart in menacing packs that seemed to mock the city's utopian design.

Mohammed Bouyeri's crime provoked a new sort of politics at the local level, too, and spurred the creation of a different type of arrival city. Amsterdam mayor Job Cohen, whose life was threatened in the note pinned to van Gogh's corpse, realized that these were the politics of failed arrival. At the same time a number of Slotervaart's ex-migrants realized that their arrival city had, for far too long, been planned and managed from outside. They began to govern themselves. Their first Slotervaart City Council chair from within their ranks, Ahmed Marcouch, was elected in 2006 and immediately shattered preconceptions by doing a number of things that the rural arrivals had long wanted: making police and security more intensive and engaged, including anti-gang patrols and a bicycle-borne truancy force dedicated to making sure teenagers were all in school; cracking down on rogue mosques and extremist organizations; and lobbying for improvements to the dismal schools and services. He met up with Cohen,* and this unlikely bond between a former Moroccan villager and a Dutch Jewish lawyer resulted in an

---

* Job Cohen and Ahmed Marcouch both entered national politics in 2010.

astonishing transformation of the neighborhood, one that sought to demolish everything it had been.

Five years after the van Gogh slaying, Slotervaart had become a sea of construction cranes, diggers, and wrecking balls. Gone was the neat, orderly plan. Gone were the quiet, meandering lanes. Gone were the green spaces between buildings. In their place were noisy, shop-filled market plazas, straight streets designed for vehicle and pedestrian traffic, and blocks of buildings, all in different plans and designs and heights, packed tightly together in a solid wall facing the street, with apartments on top and commercial spaces below, playgrounds and shopping courts behind. This vertical canyon of buildings, the most radical corner of the new development, resembles an industrial warehouse district from the 1920s, just the sort of high-density urban neighborhood that grassy utopias like Slotervaart had been designed to replace.

Before, Slotervaart had been a place that looked good from a helicopter or from the vantage of a downtown planner. In a radical departure, Amsterdam decided to make it into a place that looked good to someone arriving from a village. People were moved much closer together, not just because they wanted it—and they very much did, for reasons of safety, convenience, and commerce—but also because of the belief that higher population density is better for social cohesion and prosperity. Zoning restrictions were all but eliminated, so that retail, light-industrial, and commercial services could be mixed up with housing. Business and licensing laws were relaxed, so people could open shops and companies without much paperwork and without full citizenship status.

And to the social-housing apartments that had dominated the neighborhood were added condominiums, unaffordable to most first-generation Moroccans and Turks but within reach of young Dutch couples and some children and grandchildren of immigrants. This was a deliberate effort to create an interface with the established city culture by attracting a middle class who wanted to "buy in," in hopes that mixing and mutual influence would occur. To make this work, some of the housing blocks introduced very low-cost studio space for creative businesses on the ground floors, in hopes of attracting young downtown entrepreneurs and artists and thereby creating, from scratch, the sort of mix of immigrants and artists that has brought life to Spitalfields in London or the Lower East Side in Manhattan or to inner Amsterdam districts such as De Pijp or De Jordaan. This was, in short, a brute-force effort to accomplish what urban felicity had done in the former warehouse and industrial quarters of major cities: By making the failed arrival city of Slotervaart look and feel like one of those successful places, the hope was that it would become one.

This was not an obvious solution to Islamic radicalism. But Job Cohen tells me that he believes, from an important earlier experience with dangerous immigrant enclaves, that a violent or threatening ethnic culture is nothing more than the temporary product of an ill-designed urban form or economic structure. "I am convinced," he tells me, "that if the socio-economic component was not at stake, then the ethnic component would be less interesting and significant . . . I believe, in Amsterdam, that the issue of segregation is related to income levels and access, not just to ethnic backgrounds—among migrants, low income forces them to live in places that are the lowest price, and only that makes them segregated." He is guided by a strong form of environmental determinism—the belief that ideologies and attitudes are shaped by the physical nature of the surroundings. Fixing the shape and form of the neighbourhood—making it less orderly, less planned, less preordained—will not only create a greater physical and economic bond with the wider city but it will solve a number of other root-cause problems of arrival-city failure. It will create an internal economy, at first based on low-level shops and services, but eventually developing a lower middle class. It will develop a functioning property market for those migrants whose businesses succeed enough to let them buy their apartments. This, in turn, will attract an "outside" middle class from the original city, who ideally will blend with the emerging migrant middle class. And this, in turn, will solve one of the most significant problems of the arrival city, the terrible state of schools. By becoming a place with successful, ethnically integrated student groups with influential parents, the schools will be driven to perform better and attract the best teachers.

It is far too early to tell whether this ambitious project, known as the New West Plan, is succeeding. Crime rates have fallen in Slotervaart, but there are still many problems of gang membership, Islamic fundamentalism, and poverty. Yet there is reason to trust this major investment in de-planning. In Amsterdam, it has worked before. In fact, it has worked on an even larger scale, transforming another dangerous neighborhood.

Bijlmermeer, on the opposite side of Amsterdam in the city's southeast, was subject, under Job Cohen's watch, to what has been described as the most dramatic and violent act of arrival-city transformation in modern history.[1] Built in the late 1960s as an even more ambitious project in utopian design than Slotervaart, it was a huge honeycomb of 31 very wide 10-story apartment towers with wide spaces between them, housing 60,000 people in a commerce-free expanse of parkland and public spaces, separated from the city by a greenbelt. It never really even began to succeed. Isolated physically and psychically from the urban society and economy, it attracted a great many rural arrivals from the former Dutch colony of Suriname as well as populations from the Netherlands Antilles and sub-Saharan Africa, with a large section becoming the first black-majority town in the Netherlands and the whole place having only a 20 percent Dutch-born population. These ethnic groups, and their neighborhood, became bywords for murder, drug addiction, idle poverty, and casual violence. It was an epic instance of failed arrival. Bijlmermeer was often described in the 1970s and early 1980s as the most dangerous neighborhood in Europe. Over the decades, various efforts were made to improve the appearance, the management, the sanitation, or the policing of Bijlmermeer, but none of these efforts recognized the rural-to-urban dynamics at work in the neighborhood, its need to have handholds in the proper city.

Finally, beginning in the mid-1990s, in a farsighted gesture of radical urban de-planning, Amsterdam demolished all the apartment towers in two waves and replaced them with a tighter arrangement of mid-height structures, which gave each apartment its own garden and "ownership" of a section of street, with loosely zoned spaces for shops and businesses in between, allowing teeming and haphazard markets.* This decade-long job was accompanied by a new, active government role in the city's southeast; its cornerstones are a powerful local security patrol and a municipal corporation dedicated to providing support to entrepreneurs and job-related training to youth. A new Metro link to the neighborhood flowered into a prosperous business and entertainment hub. By the turn of this century, Bijlmermeer was being described as "a national hot spot" and "the core of a network city."[2] This rebuilding was combined with a targeted effort to improve education and job opportunities for the Dutch-born children of migrants. As a result, the second-generation Surinamese now have rates of university education and income similar to the ethnic Dutch, and their children, the third generation, are broadly accepted as full-fledged Dutch citizens with little controversy.

Behind Slotervaart's forest of wrecking balls is an effort to repeat the success of Bijlmermeer. There is solid reason for optimism, despite the apparently dire state of the Moroccan and Turkish village migrants. The arrivals themselves have remained stuck in a cultural and economic netherworld—but their children have the characteristics needed to turn the arrival city's fortunes around, if the physical and political changes have an effect. True, about a quarter of Slotervaart's second generation are high-school dropouts (somewhat less than the rate among the Moroccan-born first generation), likely to face a lifetime of unemployability, benefit dependency, and social housing. But more important is the impressive size

---

* The change in approach was precipitated in part by a 1992 disaster, in which an El Al Boeing 747 crashed into an apartment tower in Bijlmermeer, killing 43 passengers and 39 people in the building and drawing attention to the neighborhood's plight.

of the second-generation population who have carried on to post-secondary education: Fully a third of ethnic-Moroccan youth in the Netherlands (most of whom live in arrival cities like Slotervaart) are either enrolled in or have finished university, a rate twice as high as with "white" Dutch citizens from non-immigrant backgrounds.[3] This educated population is almost certain to form an arrival-city middle class, turning Slotervaart into a radically different place within two decades—so long as it can become a place where successful people want to stay and help the next generation of arrivals.

What is it that the Dutch are doing with their arrival cities? First, they are increasing their *intensity*. In urban-planning terms, intensity refers to the amount of human activity allowed on a given piece of land. Until very recently, most urban officials believed that the greatest threat to the poor was crowding, density, and confusion. "Low-intensity development" was considered crucial to creating happy residential neighborhoods. The solution, for many cities, was rigid zoning, division of uses, and the use of roads and public spaces to create lower densities and intensities of land use.

The concepts of zoning and land-use permission remain dear to the hearts of urban planners, who often still believe that cities should be sharply divided into residential, commercial, and light-industrial enclaves, with little overlap. Yet the most successful urban neighborhoods in the world are neither low density nor highly zoned: The best sections of Manhattan, the London neighborhoods of Kensington and Chelsea, the sixth and seventh arrondissements of Paris, for example, are extremely high-density, very mixed-use districts. In less desirable neighborhoods, the poor arrivals are stuck with low-intensity, high-division planning that forbids spontaneity.

These were the principles behind the urban redesigns of the post-war years, the rebuilding of Europe's great bomb-ravaged cities, and the rise of planner-driven redesigns in the United States and Britain in the 1950s. But beginning in the 1960s, it became apparent that this urban vision was failing badly. Low-intensity urban housing-project neighborhoods were falling behind, and failing to develop economically. The timing of their construction coincided with the beginning of the great rural–urban migration across the developing world, and those migrants, when they reached the West, ended up living in these failed developments.

As well as a high concentration of human activity, the successful arrival city needs to provide space for *spontaneity*. In a new-migrant community, a given patch of land might need to be a residence, a shop, a small factory, a gathering-place, a place of worship, or any combination of these from time to time, and it needs to change and evolve. Most Western urbanites nowadays understand that downtown-core neighborhoods need to be spontaneous, organic, and flexible. Unfortunately, the neighborhoods where newcomers arrive are rarely allowed the same creativity, and their planners remain devoted to rigidly separated uses of property and land.

We have learned what is wrong with this zoning approach from hard experience. The urbanist Jane Jacobs, who spent the 1950s studying and admiring the works of these big-project planners, was sent in 1958 to report on a huge slum-redevelopment high-rise project in Philadelphia, built using rigid zoning, low housing density, and broad public squares. "The drawings looked wonderful with all these little people in them," she told me years later. "And I went down to see it. It was just like the picture—except all those little people weren't in it. The only person in it, in the whole thing, for blocks, was a little boy—one lone little boy who was sort of disconsolately kicking at a tire." The rest of the new residents had wandered back to the last remaining stretch of the old "slum" neighborhood (a failed African American arrival city) to sit on the front steps of the nineteenth-century row houses. Such social gatherings were no longer possible in the new apartments or the useless, anonymous public square.[4] Despite its poverty, the old neighborhood's density, its mix of business and residences, and its privately owned space and access to the street gave it a potential for human mixing, mutual security, and entrepreneurship that could never exist in a low-density project. From the beginning, its residents knew it would become "the projects," a place without hope of arrival.

Jacobs was inspired by this shock of realization to write *The Death and Life of Great American Cities*, which argued that urban neighborhoods should be treated as organic entities, permitted to grow, change, and develop functions as their residents desire, without restrictions on usage, intensity, or change. This liberal, organic view of urbanism was shared by the sociologist William Whyte, who demonstrated the importance of density and concentration, and the architect-planner Oscar Newman, whose 1972 study, *Defensible Space*, demonstrated that dense, privately owned spaces with access to the street created a community sense of self-surveillance and security.[5] These ideas influenced a generation of urban thinkers and played a huge role in the revitalization of the urban cores of Western cities in the 1970s and '80s.

The urban core can take care of itself nowadays. The place where these liberating ideas are most needed today is in the migrant-packed margins. "The task," Jacobs wrote of those downtown neighborhoods, "is to promote the city life of city people, housed, let us hope, in concentrations both dense enough *and* diverse enough to offer them a decent chance at developing city life."[6] Density, spontaneity, and diversity of use are hard to find in the *banlieues difficiles* of Paris, the apartment-block housing projects of North America's outer-ring suburbs, the council estates of many British cities or the *Plattenbau* quarters of German cities. And these, sadly, are precisely the sorts of districts where rural migrants arrive. Changing this rigid thinking is expensive and difficult, but the stakes are high: It can make the difference between a new middle class and a violent, angry outcast community. Today, a few cities are beginning to spend the money. After the British writer Alice Coleman observed the damage done to social mobility and the "social malaise" caused by the isolating design of Bijlmermeer and other European housing projects in her large-scale 1985 study, *Utopia on Trial*, the governments of Amsterdam and London began demolishing projects and replacing them with more organic and connected designs.[7] In these new districts of Amsterdam, in the revitalized East London, in the new outskirts of Madrid, in the public-housing districts of downtown Toronto, and in a handful of other neighborhoods across Europe and North America, the change is being made to denser, more fluid, and spontaneous neighborhoods.

Finally, Slotervaart is becoming *self-operational*. Once it came to be governed by its rural-migrant majority, it changed. Its first priority was security. Ahmed Marcouch, the first rural-migrant council chair, established "street nuisance patrols," plainclothes community-police groups who confronted the petty criminals and gangs of idle young men who spread fear and deterred small-business creation, and enforced truancy laws. Their second priority was schooling. Vitally, the new internal government put pressure on the larger city to end the segregation of primary and secondary schools (caused mainly by ethnic-Dutch residents sending their children out of Slotervaart but also by migrant residents retreating into insular Muslim schools). Higher-quality schools are meant to be magnets for a mixed population. "We're trying to make a system where people can feel pride about their city, their country, their neighborhood, about themselves," says Mohamed Mallaouch. "Everybody here wants their child to become better, to become Dutch, and now you are no longer trapped between two cultures, you can take the aspects of each one that works for you, to make a business or an education. It is a start."

Around the world, arrival cities transform themselves from destitute poverty traps into pathways to success when they develop effective and well-connected internal governments. A major study of slums by World Bank economist Deepa Narayan and her colleagues found that things begin to improve in the most important areas— security, medicine, health, transportation—when slum communities develop effective, non-corrupt, democratic government from the inside.[8] The beneficence of a national or big-city government, they found, is less important than the development of sources of "personal agency" among the slum residents, who, after all, have been trying from the beginning to find a way to govern their own affairs.

LAND, LINKAGE, SECURITY
Karail, Dhaka, Bangladesh

Maksuda Begum makes a pungent journey before dawn from her tiny tin-and-wood shack, through a labyrinth of narrow mud passageways, to the shore for ablution, then onto a narrow bamboo canoe packed with standing people and across a sewage-filled lake to the city's mainland, followed by a long walk along endless car-packed roads to the concrete-bunker sweatshop where she sews clothing for 10 hours. And back again after nightfall, to the dense and noisy squalor known as Karail. Each night, after her return, Maksuda, an attractive and serious-looking woman of 32, lies in bed, stares at the corrugated-metal slats of her ceiling, and sobs with yearning for her daughter.

She came here, nine years before, from the poor villages of the southeast, carrying a pocketful of her family's savings, with dreams of mobility and success and a good job in a garment factory. Karail provided it: Far denser and more chaotic (and flood-prone) than other Dhaka slums, its access to the city and thriving economy proved a base for a new life. All went well until her husband, a rickshaw driver, left her. Even though she had been the main breadwinner, without his presence and income she could not find a way to raise her young daughter here and earn enough to feed her and have her cared for during the day. So she was forced to deliver her eight-year-old, who had become her sole companion, to a "charity school"—in essence, an orphanage. They see each other once a month. "I'll continue to live and work like this only because I must find a way to get my daughter back and send her through school," Maksuda told me, knitting her hands. "She is my only hope, my only thought, my only dream. All I think about is what I've done to her."

Maksuda's whole life, her whole scaffolding of success, turned out in an instant to be built of tissue and vapor. There are too many people around her making similar discoveries. Jotsna Ujjal, in the adjoining hut, was doing well until, a few years before, a sudden flood ripped through their house. She and her family were forced to cower in the ceiling beams as they watched their possessions float away and sewage-laden water inundate their world. The children still have nightmares of poisonous snakes floating into their house, all the more real because it actually happened. Jotsna and her husband have a worse nightmare, having lost all their savings (poor Bangladeshis are in the habit of keeping years of dowry savings under the mattress).

From the high-rise apartments of Gulshan, Dhaka's most desirable district, Karail fills the horizon, a shimmering plane of corrugated-metal roofs covering a thin peninsula in the middle of an inner-city lake. When I first came, nobody in Gulshan seemed to know how to reach the squatter enclave, though they spent all day looking at it. Karail appeared, to these better-off Bangladeshis, as an impossibly tight nest, or perhaps an infestation: hundreds of human silhouettes dangling their children into the lake to wash, or fishing, or lighting fires to cook. Packed into this dense space are between 16,000 and 20,000 people, living so close together that there are no gaps between their roofs.

After some exploration, between Gulshan high-rises I found a hidden mud-shore inlet, where dozens of narrow bamboo canoe ferries awaited. Once I had handed over a coin and made a precarious standing journey across the fetid lake and stepped onto the litter-crusted shore, the solid gray wall of Karail opened into a rabbit warren of tight passages, little more than a meter across, between walls of wood and tin. These alleys opened into wider dirt streets, invisible from outside, lined with shops, services, and small factories. I walked past a barbershop, a couple of DVD-rental huts, one crowded video arcade, hundreds of street-food fires, entire districts of ironmongers, dry-goods shops, ceramic kilns, woodworking shops, metalwork mills, plastic-moulding factories, and garment shops with dozens of employees, all tossed together from pieces of detritus and waste. Thousands of children run barefoot along the streets, pack into the two dirt clearings to play, and fill the lone video arcade. They are the unattended consequence of thousands more adults heading out into the garment-sewing jobs and domestic-service positions across the lake in the proper city. Child care and primary school are woefully scarce here.

In a shallow gutter in the side of the lane snakes a haphazard mess of a dozen half-inch plastic garden-hose pipes, the backbone of an improvised fresh-water system, connected to a distant water main and interlinked with handmade junctions and duct-tape repairs, which spray a fine mist of water every few meters and create a constant mysterious hiss. Each hose serves between five and 10 families, linked through a complex payment system. There are similarly chaotic webs of electricity (which everyone has) and cable and satellite TV (received by two-thirds of families). In the back laneways or inside the thin-walled huts, there is a round-the-clock background sound of livestock, music, television, cooking, children playing, people bartering and arguing, babies crying, small engines and sewing machines, family feuds and splashing water. It is delicately organized and alive with activity, fragile but substantial.

Karail seems uninhabitable. Yet it is eminently inhabited by people who have actively chosen and worked hard to get there. It was formed in the early 1990s on protected state land owned by the city's Power and Water Development Board, and its residents have profited from Bangladesh's decade-long political power vacuum at the beginning of the twenty-first century. They used that anarchic period to pack into this dense island relatively free from government interference. People pay comparatively high rents to live in its rooms. Most of the residents I interviewed told me they had moved to Karail from other arrival-city neighborhoods, often ones with nicer shacks, because Karail is close to excellent sources of employment. Most people here work in the garment industry or as domestic servants in the middle-class apartments of Gulshan, and there are factory and electronics jobs to be found.

Sometimes those trajectories lead to quick success in Karail. Ujjal Mia, a tall, skinny 21-year-old man with a mop haircut and a patient air, came here 11 months before with his mother and father from poor, flood-prone Khulna district on the Ganges River Delta to the southwest. Their family was in deep trouble: Their paddy land had been rendered largely infertile by increasingly frequent saltwater floods.* Ujjal had made earlier, seasonal migrations to Dhaka to bring the family cash income, during which he had learned some basic wiring skills at an office. Once a fellow villager had led his family to Karail and found them an abandoned two-room hut around a communal fire, Ujjal quickly found a job in a nearby data center, assembling bundles of Ethernet cables. It pays 5,000 taka ($75) a month, more than most of the garment workers earn. His father sold their farmland and used all their savings to set up a tiny vegetable shop in the slum, which earns between $75 and $100 a month. Rent for the two rooms is $25, and utility costs are two or three times that much (once again, slum-dwellers pay the highest rates in the city for utilities), and the family no longer needs to send money back to the village, so they are able to save money. Ujjal says he hopes to learn more advanced electronics skills, though he is unsure of the means, as most of his co-workers are fellow ex-villagers with little urban experience. "I'd like to do other things, but I don't know the way to get there," he tells me over the cooking fire. "But even if we have more money, we'll keep living here the next few years. It's a peaceful place to live now, compared to earlier days when there was crime. Now this is a really good place to be living."

---

* Rising ocean levels caused by the ice-cap melting of global warming are already having effects on Bangladesh, which has one of the largest rural populations at or below sea level. This has led governments and agencies to describe hundreds of thousands of people as "climate migrants." But experienced observers agree that climate and flooding is usually just an incentive effect on a migration pattern already in play, and the rural poverty that makes families vulnerable to climate change is usually a far greater motive to migrate than the climate change itself. The migration scholars Ronald Skeldon and Cecilia Tacoli have both concluded that even intense climate-driven migration in this century will be swamped by the far larger numbers of people making rural–urban migrations for economic reasons.

But too many people in Karail are falling into traps like those that cost Maksuda Begum her daughter or her neighbors their savings. Karail has the potential to be a successful arrival city, but the lack of support makes it tragically precarious. Government has almost no visible presence here, with the exception of water wells drilled by aid agencies and ubiquitous campaign posters during election season. (The slum supported the victorious Awami League in the 2008 ballot, which portends well for its future.) Those children who manage to get a formal education are sent across the lake to a school inside middle-class Gulshan; there are no formal child-care facilities or nurseries. Without the presence of the state or the secure tether of property ownership, small mishaps can ruin lives and create treacherous instability. Many have been forced to return to the village empty-handed, despite good employment.

Karail, like so many other places around the world, may be the beginning of a successful arrival city, but there is no question that it is in urgent need of outside help. It lacks vital amenities that can be delivered only with some significant infrastructure. Many of these are expensive: secure and flood-proof foundations for the houses and paving for the streets; institutions for schooling and child care; sanitation, sewage, and drainage. Delivering such things to an existing slum is much more expensive than laying them in the ground before construction (the usual path in the West). For a poor and corruption-riddled country like Bangladesh, this is an inconceivable expense.

The traditional response of governments and agencies to places like Karail has been to bring in the bulldozers, often at dawn, and tear them down. Luckily for the people of Karail, the city of Dhaka now appears to be pursuing a more informed route. In 2009, it was announced that Karail would be part of a $5.2-million project, financed by Britain's Department for International Development and delivered by Bangladeshi non-governmental organizations, which will try to improve life and reduce poverty in the slums through infrastructure and small-business development. But the specific nature of the project still hasn't been determined; depending how it works, it could help Karail's residents turn their surroundings into a thriving center for arrival and success, or it could contribute to its further isolation and misery.

In an era when the value and effectiveness of foreign aid has fallen into question,[9] one of the few truly effective, sustainable, and life-transforming channels for international assistance is the arrival city. Turning these neighborhoods around (or providing their own networks and self-government bodies the tools to do so) can be an unusually productive and secure aid investment, since a well-functioning arrival city will serve several generations of arrivals and produce multiplying benefits among both urban and rural poor communities. This reduces both village and city poverty, improves fertility rates, and provides the ecological benefits that arise from more urban, dense populations. In many ways, the arrival city is the one channel that can make foreign aid work.

But around the world there is confusion about what should best be done about these neighborhoods. Much of it is rooted in a lack of understanding of their function. Yet, once they are seen as arrival cities at the center of a set of dialectically related rural and urban functions, it becomes easier to devise policies to make them work.

There is an essential paradox in any effort to improve arrival-city housing. In doing so, by injecting money and official recognition into poor, informal communities, you are making them more valuable. And in being more valuable and better serviced with utilities, you are making them appealing to people who are not rural arrivals—notably, to lower-middle-class people from the established "core" city. To some extent, this can be beneficial: The resulting social mixing can attract entrepreneurial capital and lucrative consumer markets, making the arrival-city process easier. But there is a risk that the neighborhood will become inaccessible to any future arrivals. Upgrading rehousing projects to legal minimum standards, as we saw in Kibera, Nairobi, in chapter 2, can price them beyond the rural-arrival market. But, today, a number of approaches to slum improvement do not distort the market unduly (or, more to the point, they permit the poor residents to benefit from the rise in property values). Most of these involve the direct participation of the arrivals themselves.

One approach begins with land. Most slum-upgrading plans are expensive because they involve installing infrastructure and solid foundations beneath existing neighborhoods, never an easy task. Turning illegal, informal, self-built housing into title-holding, legal, sustainable, and sanitary housing is an enormous job, as we saw with Rio de Janeiro's Santa Marta project in chapter 2. Many of the lauded slum-upgrading schemes in Asia and South America are covering little more than token patches of land, so large are the public investments needed. Key to any arrival-city project is to find mechanisms that *use the increase in land values to pay for the project itself and to support the rural arrivals.* Even better, most of the problems can be solved in advance, at much lower cost, with considerably better lives for the arrivals, if the interventions can be made *before the rural–urban migration occurs and the houses are built.* This requires honesty and foresight on the part of governments and an admission that the arrival of large numbers of new residents from villages is both inevitable and, in many ways, desirable.

To see this in its most dramatic and effective implementation, it's worth visiting the southeastern edge of Bogotá, Colombia, where low, rolling hills on former farmland at the edge of a ravine are being lashed with roads, electrical poles, and utility trenches, the interstices divided into tiny lots. This project, known as Operación Urbanística Nuevo Usme, is creating future arrival cities for villagers who have not yet made the move. This approach, known as "sites and services," was popular with World Bank officials in the 1970s but was largely abandoned because the pre-servicing of the land made it so valuable that the village-migrant poor could no longer afford it; the Bank and other institutions switched to costlier slum-upgrading projects. But the Bogotá project (and others like it in Porto Alegre, Brazil, and Pereira, Colombia) has turned this approach on its head by employing a sort of land-development judo, in which the resistive pressures of property speculation are flipped around and turned in favor of the arriving villagers.[10] The project will provide foundations for 53,000 homes self-constructed by 200,000 newly arrived people over 900 hectares of land. The location has been chosen for its proximity to the city, easily served by fast and low-cost transit lines that already exist and sewage and water lines that do not need to be extended far.

Rural migrants will be provided with serviced and fully owned foundations, at prices similar to what they were paying for bare patches of non-legal land in places remote from the city. The owners of the land, in return, will be paid nominal prices for their farm fields but will be given housing plots they can sell or use, so they can participate in any increase in land value. It is somewhat less money than they'd make by developing the land themselves, but it exposes them to less risk. The state pays the up-front cost of development but will recoup it by participating in the land-value increase by building shopping, commercial, and housing facilities on some of the land. As a result, a better quality of arrival city, one that is capable of growing into a thriving high-access center with its own middle class, is built using the proceeds from its own future success.[11]

It is too late to employ such techniques in a place like Karail, but other value-capture instruments can be employed to help the poor in existing urban areas. One reason so many slum-rehabilitation plans fail is because they are based on moving people into what seems to be higher-quality housing while ignoring the larger function of the arrival city. The original slum houses in places like Karail, however squalid, offer the considerable benefit of being *flexible*: rooms and floors can be added as family needs change, and portions can be turned into shops or small industries to provide entrepreneurial income. They are also *connected* to networks of families, transportation routes, and relationships that are crucial to building prosperity and permanence. In a serviced apartment block, however intelligently designed, this is often lost, and residents are reluctant to move into a home that is merely a house.

But this, too, can be turned on its head. In Mumbai, several apartment-block rehousing projects have been supported (and even proposed) by slum-dwellers for a number of reasons: because the existing slum housing is in a dangerous, small, steep, or flood-prone location; because it is poorly connected to transportation or laid out in inaccessible ways; because it is adjacent to danger-ous or smelly industries, like leather-tanning. In all these cases, researchers have found that slum-dwellers prefer to move not just because it is a tangible improvement in the quality of housing but, more important, because it is an improvement in the *resale value* of the housing. Slum occupants, as we have seen, are as eager to leverage their housing investment into business equity or better future housing as any middle-class Westerner (in fact, sometimes more so, because property is often their only asset), and Mumbai slum-dwellers, 85 percent of whom "own" their housing, legally or otherwise, are eager to take part in a calculus of improvement.[12] Indeed, in some instances, slum-dwellers have willingly partici-pated in schemes that require them to put up down payments of $200 per family (a sizable sum of several months' income) on apartments in slum-redevelopment projects, in order to move into housing that has future financial value.[13]

Often, the size of the building makes the difference, and there is a reason why poor neighborhoods in the developing world, when they turn into more prosperous neighborhoods, so often evolve into long rows of five-story buildings with shops on the ground floor. This is an almost ideal arrangement for self-managed neighborhoods. Aprodicio Laquian, the Filipino-Canadian scholar who has advised governments of most major developing countries on slum improve-ment, says the five-story walk-up apartment is the ideal design to increase density and maintain a tightly networked community. "You are going to reach a point where you will need to provide accept-able housing, not just services, and the solution to that is the five-story walk-up," he says. "The moment you go above five stories, you need elevators, electricity, sanitation, which is beyond your reach. But with five stories, you end up with 80 percent more land you can use for economic development."

Nevertheless, many of the most successful slum-improvement projects today are based on the expensive but reliable combination of rebuilding, legalizing, and adding services to existing slum housing. This can be done in an incremental fashion, adding sewage in one project, street lights in another, bolstered foundations in a third, and so on—this is how the more successful Brazilian *favelas* and Turkish *gecekondus* have improved, as subsequent governments found small amounts of money for specific projects. But there is a case to be made for the approach we saw in the Santa Marta neighborhood of Rio de Janeiro, in which President Luiz Inácio Lula da Silva launched fast, expensive, total interventions in which several branches of government, led by security forces, come in and remake the entire slum. The changes are mutually supporting, and doing them all at once allows ownership to be secured among the existing residents, without wealthier outside intervenors buying up property between improvements.

It should be apparent that property value alone is not enough to make a rural–urban migration work. Unless the rural migrant has large pools of savings from a successful agricultural business (which is sometimes the case, and should be encouraged through rural development), people who arrive in cities need the help of the state. And what arrival cities need most—and what the market will almost never provide—are the tools to become normal urban communities.

Sewage, garbage collection, and *paved roads* are, for obvious reasons, vital, and can be provided only from outside. But even more important, in the well-informed view of slum-dwellers, are *buses*: affordable and regular bus service into the neighborhood is often the key difference between a thriving enclave and a destitute ghetto. One might think that the next priority would be electricity and running water, but, in fact, these are often not considered priorities at all by slum-dwellers. They have typically arranged their own utilities, and full-price utility bills can be debilitating for poor households. Equally important, and far too often neglected, is *street lighting*. This makes a tangible difference in both security and property value, at a low operating cost. The experience of entering a *favela* in the evening in São Paulo, which has fully street-lit its informal communities, is far more inviting, for visitor and resident alike, than the dark, menacing spaces of so many other slums.

Smart municipalities employ cost-recovery mechanisms to finance these improvements, developing a small part of the now-valuable land into commercial, retail, or middle-class properties to finance the new services. Still, up-front investments are required to turn slums into healthy arrival cities. As a means to bringing a permanent end to world poverty, there is perhaps nothing better and more effective than investing in the future of supposedly uninhabitable places like Karail.

SURVIVAL CITY OR REVIVAL CITY?
Thorncliffe Park, Toronto

The elevator journey remains a strange and slightly disturbing experience for Adinah Heqosah, even after several months. She prefers the stairs. Today, as she heads out to buy meat at Iqbal's, her husband, Hillal, joins her, places his hand gently over hers, and guides her fingers to the buttons. Until she moved into this ninth-floor apartment a few months before, her only experience with electricity was the bare incandescent bulb that illuminated their mud-and-sand enclosure, casting its pale beams through the house and into the basement pit beneath the kitchen where the large animals slept. Today, in this dense high-rise neighborhood on the other side of the earth, checkout terminals, cash machines, and city buses remain intimidating.

Iqbal's market, on the other hand, is a comfort. The heavy sacks of rice and grain on the floor and the racks of raw spices in the big fluorescent-lit shop remind Adinah of home, and familiar phrases of the Dari tongue are often heard in the aisles. She and her husband both come here frequently. Hillal has learned enough English to get by in the city, but Adinah is only in beginner classes at the neighborhood center and sticks to the familiar streets of Thorncliffe Park, where nearly everyone's an Asian villager. Her seven children are fast becoming fluent in a language she barely understands. They demand pizza rather than *pilau* and won't attend mosque; they talk of moving out when they turn 18, a North American custom the parents don't appreciate.

Hillal, at least, had experience living in a city. There had been only four houses in the village of Varna, near the Tajik border in the far northeast of Afghanistan, when he was a child there in the late 1960s. After years working seasonally in Peshawar, Kabul, and Tajikistan, he returned to Varna to marry Adinah in 1990. By then, there were 15 houses, surrounded by dust and grit. By 2001, when warring Taliban factions had turned the village into a menacing place and they were forced to flee overseas, Adinah had never lived anywhere else. But Hillal had heard, from friends in Kabul, of a place on the edge of a city called Toronto. After fleeing to Tajikistan and Pakistan, they made an urban move across the ocean.

Adinah and Hillal make their way awkwardly, in snow boots, along the oval boulevard that forms the center of Thorncliffe Park, a forest of postwar apartments and one-story shopping plazas. This neighborhood, easily accessible to the downtown core, was built on a former horse-race track beside a well-treed ravine on the far fringe of Toronto, initially for soldiers returning from the Second World War. Adinah adjusts her headscarf as they cross the broad parking lot of Iqbal's, whose kebab counter is packed with Pakistanis, Bangladeshis, and Indians. Among the rice bags, Adinah is stopped by a 30-year-old woman named Maryam Formuli, a fellow Dari speaker, who arrived here from Peshawar just a few weeks earlier. Maryam, a younger, childless woman, who had learned decent English in Kabul, has been hanging around the shop, nervously approaching fellow Afghanis. She greets Adinah warmly and asks if they can talk.

Maryam explains that she has lived for a month here in a two-bedroom apartment with her mother, her brother, his wife, and their three children—a conventional arrangement in Thorncliffe Park, where the Afghani families typically fill the living room with a large Persian rug, a periphery of cushions, and a couple of endlessly refilled tea urns, the family sleeping on the floor in the bedrooms. Maryam has been unable to get her husband into Canada. "Your husband is here?" she asks in a disarmingly abrupt fashion. "How did he come here?" They agree to have tea. The Afghani network is beginning to form. Adinah envies the Pakistanis and Indians, who have taken over multiple floors of her building, replicating whole villages in the vertical plane, and seem able to use their connections, happily crossing the Muslim–Hindu divide, to lever their children into the best schools. For now, figuring out the immigration papers and English classes is enough work.

Maryam thanks them and heads out for an afternoon working at New Circles, a strip-mall storefront containing several rooms full of used clothing organized by size, sex, and season, a popular spot with immigrants from the Indian subcontinent struggling to prepare themselves for the Canadian winter. The real function of New Circles, though, is to train people like Maryam in small-business practices: bookkeeping and inventory, retail-space rental and licensing, incorporation and taxes. Run on government subsidies, it employs dozens of immigrants at a time in its business-training programs. For Maryam, it is the first link into the city's core economy. Like most of the 25,000 people who live here, she hopes to learn a trade or start a business, buy a house, and get out.

For now, though, she has no desire to leave Thorncliffe Park, not even to make the bus-and-subway trip to visit Toronto's core. Though she is fluent in English and is educated, she agrees with the far less urbanized Adinah that this is not the time to venture beyond the oval boulevard. "When we are in Thorncliffe, we feel like we are in Pakistan or Afghanistan, but when we go downtown, we are in Canada," Maryam says, uttering the last phrase with a tone of awe and mystery. "For now, people are very kind to us here, and I prefer to have immigrants around me—if there are problems, they can help."

What kind of place is Thorncliffe Park? It is, depending how you view it, either a successful antechamber to urban life or a place of dangerous isolation and poverty. It is certainly a poor neighborhood, one of the poorest in the largely wealthy city of Toronto. One study reports family incomes averaging around $20,000 a year; another, a poverty rate of 44 percent. Virtually all of its high-rise apartments are private-sector rental units, with no possibility of being purchased by their occupants, and, at around $1,100 a month each, they aren't cheap to rent. It is also ethnically segregated, with as much as 51 percent of its population speaking an Asian language at home and only a small minority of white-skinned Euro-Canadians in its buildings.[14] Based on static observation, then, Thorncliffe Park can only be described as an impoverished ethnic ghetto.

For governments in Europe, North America, and Australasia, this is the central question of the arrival city: Why pour money and support into districts that seem to function as places of perpetual poverty and ethnic isolation? If integration and prosperity are the goals, then arrival cities, these kingdoms of the marginal, would seem to produce the opposite result. Yet Thorncliffe Park is not seen that way at all, not by its residents, not by the agencies and government officials within its circumference, and not by the city beyond its borders. It remains a popular place, with vacancy rates close to zero and long waiting lists for apartments; the people who enter, often from village backgrounds, have an amazingly consistent record of entering the middle-class urban mainstream within a generation. Like many other successful arrival cities, Thorncliffe Park seems to benefit from its tight clustering of poor, rural, foreign residents: This helps it function as an instrument of integration, a platform for urban inclusion.

Thorncliffe Park is the place where networks are developed, where the transition to middle-class city life is made—but the success often leads elsewhere. Jehad Aliweiwi is the Palestinian-born Canadian who runs the Thorncliffe Neighborhood Office, which is this arrival city's de facto self-government institution, a busy facility that provides a wide range of services for poor migrants. "Historically," he says, "Thorncliffe has been a springboard or gateway community, where people settle for a couple years while they get a job, and then they move on. They go to another area where they can buy a house or larger apartment. Now people are laying anchors and staying here. It's not as mobile or transient as it used to be. This is not a place where people feel stuck. It's a place where they feel very comfortable. You don't just pass through it, you go to it."

Aliweiwi points out the paradox of gateway cities like Thorncliffe Park: The more successful they are, the higher their apparent poverty rate. If people are able to leave within a generation for more prosperous middle-class homeowner districts, the neighborhood will be constantly refilled with new migrants from poor rural regions. It appears unchangingly poor and segregated only if you fail to observe the trajectory of each resident. And, for half a century, those trajectories have generally been upward. Almost as soon as its soldiers' bungalows were replaced with high-rise apartment towers in the 1960s, Thorncliffe Park became a pure arrival city. First came Greeks and Macedonians, spending a generation living here, building Orthodox churches (some of which still stand), then buying houses in the inner-city Greek districts or in outer suburbia and moving on. Then came Gujarati Indians and Ismaili East Africans, the latter building the neighborhood's first mosques in the late 1970s. They were joined by Colombians and Chileans, who lived here in the 1970s and 1980s before buying houses downtown. Today, there is a sizable Filipino community and several large groups from the Indian subcontinent. The most recent arrivals are Afghanis, products of Canada's intense military involvement there, beginning in 2006.

"Everyone in Thorncliffe, all are beginners, all are struggling," says Seema Khatri, 42, who recently moved out of the neighborhood to rent a low-rise apartment in nearby suburban Don Mills, closer to a more desirable secondary school for her children. She came from a village in Haryana, in northern India, urbanized herself, and got a university education in India before moving to Canada. She spent several years in Thorncliffe Park working at rudimentary jobs in a cosmetics factory while trying to get her credentials recognized. The neighborhood's networks, she says, helped her to do this. "In Thorncliffe, when you go out, you meet with people who are also struggling. You talk to your neighbors at the deli. They exchange information."

What makes immigrants settle here (and, despite Canada's efforts to limit immigration to educated elites, a significant proportion of people here are village-born) is not its isolation but rather its very accessible pathways to the city around it. It is well served by public-transit routes, it has a large primary school within its borders, and there are good jobs and places to launch small businesses with low rental and start-up costs—though not so good that people want to stay here for more than a generation before moving on. The Neighborhood Office run by Jehad Aliweiwi offers language, acculturation, tax and small-business assistance in many languages, aimed at making the transition to urban success work. This is an arrival city that understands itself.

Thorncliffe Park did not become a successful arrival city by accident. It works, while other high-rise, suburban immigrant enclaves don't, because it has been the subject of significant investment and attention by the state. One major survey of Thorncliffe Park residents by U.S. and Canadian geographers found an almost unanimous high degree of satisfaction among its residents. Other Canadian immigrant gateways, especially those in the farther-flung outer suburbs with poor transportation and economic links to the main city, reported far more pessimistic responses. In Thorncliffe Park, though, there was evidence of "the good segregation of the urban village," the survey found: "[A] spirit of hope provided a basis for building local social capital. Immigrant careers were launched, integration trajectories bore promise, and the sense of citizenship and belonging became more hopeful." The geographers concluded that the ethnic clustering (some would say segregation) gave the arrivals the benefit of "differential citizenship," allowing them to participate in what I have described as a culture of transition.[15]

This highly organized, intentional arrival city is a new kind of place, a half-solution to a crisis in North America, in which the neighborhoods most amenable to receiving new migrants—the dense, poor neighborhoods of the urban core—have become sufficiently developed and improved by previous waves of arrivals that the newest migrants are being pushed to the outer suburbs. In cities like Toronto the process of urban acculturation was, for a century, a largely spontaneous and migrant-driven experience. As a result, governments are only now learning that they need to take a role in urban transition—and often learn this too late.

Toronto may be the world's most complete collection of these old-style arrival cities. Its metropolitan area of 6.5 million has one of the highest immigrant intakes in the Western world: Of the approximately 300,000 foreigners who immigrate each year into Canada (population 33 million), more than 40 percent set down in Toronto. For a century, this immigration was strictly village in origin and followed a classic North American pattern of chain migration. Immigrants from specific villages and regions would move into certain streets, blocks, neighborhoods, and districts, colonizing undesirable low-rent quarters filled with Victorian row housing, building networks of mutual support, setting up strings of shops and small factories, buying and improving the housing stock, using mortgages and property as sources of capital, then moving uptown into more expensive enclaves, ethnic or otherwise, and servicing the next wave of arrivals as landlords and entrepreneurs. I lived for decades among these enclaves of Chinese, Indian, Italian, Portuguese, Caribbean, Korean, Greek, and Pakistani villagers; within their ethnic districts, they built entire class structures and webs of business, their own finance, travel, and media institutions, their own influential elites.

Those who succeeded would sometimes stay and improve their housing and sometimes move out of the ethnic downtown districts into
ethnoburbs, forming "wedges" of ethnic concentration extending
outward from the arrival point. This cycle of mutual assistance has
created a true arrival-city middle class whose interests tend to dominate political policy at the provincial and federal levels, making the
process of arrival a central and continual issue of Canadian politics,
regardless which party is in power, as much as it is in Brazil or Turkey.[16]

That old pattern of settlement is no longer dominant. Some new
waves of migrants do continue to move into the old arrival cities of
the urban core, which still offer much rental accommodation:
Portuguese neighborhoods develop enclaves of migrants from
Angola and Mozambique; the Chinese owners rent to the Vietnamese,
who, in turn, build up their own enclaves farther north. But the greatest share of migrant arrival, including large numbers of rural-origin
groups, is now in the fringes of the city, in neighborhoods built to
be 1950s-style bedroom suburbs for car-borne commuters. Studies
show the city becoming an island of established-immigrant prosperity, surrounded by thick bands of physically isolated poverty.[17] These
neighborhoods often suffer from all the physical-design, zoning, and
transportation problems of Slotervaart, with the potential for similar
social problems (an elaborate Islamist terror plot was intercepted by
police in 2006 centered in Meadowvale, Mississauga, one such isolated arrival-city bedroom community). Thorncliffe Park offers one
solution to this problem: a high-rise neighborhood engineered to be
a place of rapid, well-managed transition, at considerable expense.
It is, unfortunately, an exception.

We can no longer expect the Western arrival city to form and
manage itself spontaneously. The immigrant waves of the early twentieth century and the postwar years—the last waves of the first great
flood of rural–urban migration, mainly from Europe—coincided
with a great expansion of public spending on education, local government, mass transportation, and urban infrastructure. The retreat
of heavy industry created neighborhoods of low-cost housing that

could be bought and improved as a source of family capital. Today, neither the preformed desirable neighborhoods nor the floods of public investment are certain to be there. As the economy opens up again, demographic growth slows, and new waves of low-skilled immigrants are needed in coming years, it is important that North American and European cities pay attention, *in advance*, to the needs of the villagers entering their perimeters.

Arrival-city neighborhoods, however successful, raise some disquieting questions. Are we wise to spend public money on creating and maintaining such enclaves, rather than on efforts to integrate new immigrants directly into the core society? Do low-cost urban neighborhoods packed with village migrants really provide the best pathway to inclusion, integration, and arrival? Should they be encouraged and promoted, or should governments find ways, if they can, to prevent the great migration from forming enclaves of newcomers in their less-popular urban spaces?

To embrace the arrival city is to put aside generations of thinking, which held that success is measured by dispersal. The original theory of urban assimilation, developed by the sociologist Robert E. Park and his colleagues of the Chicago School, beginning in the 1920s, is built around the earliest understanding of the arrival city. Based on an analysis of U.S. cities (especially Chicago) during a period of heavy rural-origin migration, Park concluded that immigrants start out in highly concentrated populations in rented quarters in poor inner-city areas with low property prices but become integrated and successful only as they leave the ethnic enclave behind and disperse into integrated mainstream society. In this theory, the uni-ethnic nature of these inner-city neighborhoods and their separation from the more established city were the cause of their poverty. "Social relations," Park wrote, "are inevitably correlated with spatial relations."[18]

But it is equally possible to become fully integrated, economically and culturally, *within* the confines of the original arrival city.

Indeed, a sizable new body of scholarship shows that ethnic "clustering" can be the most effective pathway to social and economic integration. The most challenging examination of supposedly segregated neighborhoods comes from the British scholars Ceri Peach, Nissa Finney, and Ludi Simpson, whose detailed examinations of notorious arrival-city enclaves, such as Tower Hamlets and Bradford, have found that these neighborhoods are no more prone to poverty or social isolation than non-clustered neighborhoods, and that such places—that is, arrival cities—"disperse" approximately the same number of their ethnic group outward into ethnically mixed middle-class neighborhoods as they take in from abroad.[19] That is, they remain poor only because they are constantly receiving new (poor) arrivals.

And segregation, contrary to media stereotype, may actually deter violent extremism. Peach and Finney looked at Islamic terrorism among immigrant groups and found it far lower among arrival-city inhabitants. Of the 75 alleged al Qaeda members arrested in Britain on terrorism charges between 2004 and 2009, only 17 came from neighborhoods with more than 18 percent Muslim populations; a majority of 42 lived in places with fewer than 6 percent Muslims.[20] While extreme religious-fundamentalist movements can and do form among disenchanted second-generation youth in dysfunctional arrival cities like Slotervaart and Beeston, Leeds (which produced three of the four suicide bombers who carried out the July 2005 attacks on London), there is no correlation between ethnic concentration and terrorism—that is, it is just as likely to arise, if not more so, in places other than arrival cities. Anecdotally, there are strong suggestions that the tight-knit networks of arrival-city culture tend to deter the worst forms of extremism. In fact, it seems to be universally true, in both the Middle East and the West, that rural-arrival enclaves are not the main places where radical Islam arises. The Dutch sociologist Asef Bayat, in a detailed study of such neighborhoods in Iran and Egypt, found that arrival cities are very rarely "the breeding ground for violence, crime, anomie, extremism and, consequently, radical Islam."

Rather, he found, they are "a significant locus of struggle for (urban) citizenship and transformation in urban configuration." The centers of Islamism, he found, were predominantly the lower-middle-class neighborhoods that had benefited from the state-run economies of the decades before the 1980s, then lost out to informal-economy competition from these new arrivals. Religious fanaticism has little to do with rural–urban migration.[21]

The crucial paradox of the arrival city is that its occupants all want to stop living in an arrival city—either by making money and moving their families and village networks out or by turning the neighborhood itself into something better. Some arrival cities, like Thorncliffe Park, are self-renewing, constantly attracting new waves of arrivals, often from different cultures. But most, if they succeed, tend to produce their own obsolescence. The arrival city is now the favored new residential neighborhood in many North American and European cities, with districts like Rampart in Los Angeles, the Lower East Side in Manhattan, Spitalfields in London, Belleville in Paris, and Ossington in Toronto becoming desirable for young graduates (some of them the children of the original arrival-city tenants) seeking homes precisely because of the presence of dynamic, city-transforming arrival-city communities. The first wave of arrival, up to the First World War, created the core neighborhoods of most Western cities; the second, postwar wave is now creating the next set of places to live—and the next set of cultures. This reverse attraction (critics call it "gentrification") is taking place, in exactly the same way, in the arrival cities of Chongqing, Mumbai, Istanbul, Cairo, and São Paulo, just as the arrival cities of the West are equally prone to the arrival-city failures seen in those cities. It is the same process, involving much the same people; the only difference is in wealth and resources. The great migration of the twenty-first century has the advantage over its nineteenth-century precursor, in that it is taking place in a world that understands what a good arrival city looks like. The last time around, these desirable quarters took shape by accident, with too many humanitarian disasters along the way. This time, we will need to plan, anticipate the inevitable arrival of villagers, and invest in their urban futures.

For the ultimate lesson of the arrival city is that it does not simply add itself on to the edges of the city; it *becomes* the city. Whether it does so creatively or destructively is a matter of engagement. The philosopher Kwame Anthony Appiah has described this process of collision and grappling-on of villagers to the city as the heart of a vital cosmopolitanism, an embrace of what he calls a life-giving contamination: "We do not need, have never needed, settled community, a homogenous system of values, in order to have a home. Cultural purity is an oxymoron." He completes his argument by citing the self-defence made by the author Salman Rushdie at the hands of the same Iranian cultural purists who gained power by manipulating the polyglot arrival cities of Tehran. Rushdie, facing the fatwa, defended his novel *The Satanic Verses* by describing it as an arrival city, like the arrival cities that fill its pages, like the arrival cities throughout the world: a place that "celebrates hybridity, impurity, intermingling, the transformation that comes of new and unexpected combinations of human beings, cultures, ideas, politics, movies, songs. It rejoices in mongrelisation and fears the absolutism of the Pure. Melange, hotchpotch, a bit of this and a bit of that is how newness enters the world. It is the great possibility that mass migration gives the world, and I have tried to embrace it."[22]

This is the way of the world. The functioning arrival city slowly colonizes the established city (just as the failed arrival city is likely, after festering and simmering, to invade it violently). The city discovers, confronts, and, in fortunate circumstances, embraces the arrival city. Yesterday's alien villagers and immigrants become today's urban merchants and tomorrow's professionals and political leaders. Without this metamorphosis, cities stagnate and die. Beneath the sterile debates about multiculturalism and globalization are the specific experiences of waves of rural migration striking the soft points of the world's cities. It is, as each family's experience shows, an accumulation of people who want more than anything to become an accepted part of the whole. These families are taking calculated risks, betting on property and education and the largesse of friends and strangers. It costs governments money to make those gambles pay off: The arrival city is an expensive place in the short run, absorbing more public revenue than it produces at first. Yet three centuries of urban history have surely shown us that the investment is well worth it, both for the huge gains it produces and for the terrible tolls it averts. If these families are driven out or trapped on the margins or denied citizenship or an ownership stake in the larger city, they will turn into a far more expensive threat. In the coming decades, during our lifetimes, more villagers will take these risks than at any previous time in human history. This will be the world's final century of urbanization, no matter how it plays out. This is our opportunity, now, to turn this final migration into a force of lasting progress, an end to poverty, a more sustainable economy, a less brutal existence in the village. It will work only if we stop ignoring those awkward neighborhoods on the edge of town.

NOTES

1 ON THE EDGE OF THE CITY

1 From Cardoso's introduction to the first edition of Janice E. Perlman, *The Myth of Marginality: Urban Poverty and Politics in Rio De Janeiro* (Berkeley: University of California Press, 1976), xii.

2 This was the message most commentators took from one recent popular book on such districts, Mike Davis's *Planet of Slums* (London: Verso, 2006). Davis provides a more nuanced view of the transformative potential of the arrival city in an earlier work, *Magical Urbanism: Latinos Reinvent the US City* (New York: Verso, 2000).

3 UNFPA, "An Overview of Urbanization, Internal Migration, Population Distribution and Development in the World," in *UN Expert Group Meeting on Population Distribution, Urbanization, Internal Migration and Development* (New York: United Nations Population Division, 2008).

4 UNFPA, "State of World Population 2007: Unleashing the Potential of Urban Growth" (New York: United Nations Population Fund, 2007); UN Population Division, "World Population to 2300" (New York: Department of Economic and Social Affairs, 2004).

5 UN-HABITAT, "State of the World's Cities 2008/2009" (Nairobi: United Nations Human Settlements Programme, 2008).

6 Suketu Mehta, *Maximum City: Bombay Lost and Found* (New York: Knopf, 2004), 15. Mehta's memoir offers one of the most detailed and important chronicles of the modern arrival city.

7 Jerry White, *London in the Nineteenth Century* (London: Vintage, 2007), 107.

8 UN-HABITAT, "State of the World's Cities 2008/2009."

9 UN Population Division, "World Population Prospects: The 2008 Revision" (New York: Department of Economic and Social Affairs, 2009), "World Population to 2300."

10 Dilip Ratha, Sanket Mohapatra, and Zhimei Xu, "Outlook for Remittance Flows 2008–2010" (Washington: The World Bank Development Prospects Group, 2008); FE Report, "Wb Study Forecasts $10.87b in Remittance Earnings this Fiscal," *Financial Express*, July 30, 2009.

11 This nadir of Tower Hamlets was chronicled in detail by Keith Dovkants, "The Betrayed: An *Evening Standard* Special Investigation," *Evening Standard*, January 1995.

12 Divya Sunder and Layli Uddin, "A Comparative Analysis of Bangladeshi and Pakistani Educational Attainment in London Secondary Schools," *InterActions: UCLA Journal of Education and Information Studies* 3, no. 2 (2007).

13 A good comparison is found in Irena Kogan, "Labour Market Careers of Immigrants in Germany and the United Kingdom," *Journal of International Migration and Integration* 5, no. 4 (2004).

14 Nissa Finney and Ludi Simpson, *"Sleepwalking to Segregation"? Challenging Myths About Race and Migration* (Bristol: The Policy Press, 2009), 127.

15 Geoff Dench, Kate Gavron and Michael Young, *The New East End* (London: Profile Books, 2006), 134.

16 Lucinda Platt, "Migration and Social Mobility: The Life Chances of Britain's Minority Ethnic Communities" (Bristol: The Joseph Rowntree Foundation, 2005).

17 Joachim Brüß, "Experiences of Discrimination Reported by Turkish, Moroccan and Bangladeshi Muslims in Three European Cities," *Journal of Ethnic and Migration Studies* 34, no. 6 (2008).

2 OUTSIDE IN

1 Sudha Deshpande, "Migration to Mumbai: What Do the Census Data Show?" *Loksatta* (2003). English translation provided by Deshpande.

2 Johannes Jütting and Juan R. de Laiglesia, eds., *Is Informal Normal? Towards More and Better Jobs in Developing Countries* (Paris: OECD, 2009).

3 An excellent comparison of life under a "formal" work economy versus an almost completely informal one in Mumbai—and the benefits of the latter—is found in Sudha Deshpande and Lalit Deshpande, "Work, Wages and Well-Being: 1950s and 1990s," in *Bombay and Mumbai: The City in*

Transition, eds. Sujata Patel and Jim Masselos (Oxford: Oxford University Press, 2005).

4 Deepa Narayan, Lant Pritchett, and Soumya Kapoor, *Moving Out of Poverty: Success from the Bottom Up* (Washington: The World Bank, 2009).

5 Cecilia Tacoli, "Rural–Urban Interactions: A Guide to the Literature," *Environment and Urbanization* 10, no. 1 (1988).

6 Ronald Skeldon, "The Evolution of Migration Patterns During Urbanization in Peru," *The Geographical Review* 67, no. 4 (1977): 405.

7 Charles Tilly, "Migration in Modern European History," in *Human Migration: Patterns & Policies*, eds. William H. McNeill and Ruth S. Adams (Bloomington: Indiana, 1978), 53.

8 Saad S. Yahya, "Unmaking the Slums: Emerging Rules, Roles and Repertoires," *Stetson Law Review* 36 (2006): 131.

9 Patrícia Mota Guedes and Nilson Vieira Oliveira, "Braudel Papers 38: Democratization of Consumption: Progress and Aspirations in São Paulo's Periphery" (São Paulo: Instituto Fernand Braudel, 2006).

10 UN-HABITAT, "The Challenge of Slums: Global Report on Human Settlements" (Nairobi: United Nations Human Settlements Programme, 2003), 9.

11 Martim O. Smolka and Adriana de A. Larangeira, "Informality and Poverty in Latin American Urban Policies," in *The New Global Frontier*, eds. George Martine et al. (London: Earthscan, 2008), 105–107.

12 L. Jellinek, "The Changing Fortunes of a Jakarta Street Trader," in *The Urbanization of the Third World*, ed. J. Gugler (Oxford: Oxford University Press, 1988); Alan Gilbert, "Urban and Regional Systems: A Suitable Case for Treatment?" in *Cities, Poverty and Development* (Second Edition), eds. Alan Gilbert and J. Gugler (Oxford: Oxford University Press, 1992).

13 Perlman, *The Myth of Marginality*, 1, 15, 243.

14 Jorge Rodriguez and George Martine, "Urbanization in Latin America and the Caribbean: Experiences and Lessons Learned," in *The New Global Frontier*, eds. George Martine et al. (London: Earthscan, 2008), 362.

15 The World Bank, "World Development Report 2009: Reshaping Economic Geography" (Washington: IBRD, 2009).

16 UN-HABITAT, "World Urbanization Prospects: The 2005 Revision" (New York: United Nations Population Division, 2006), 24.

17 Chen Hong, "Disgruntled Workers on the Move," *China Daily*, Jan. 18, 2008.

18 Xinhua, "Tsinghua Professor: Big Chinese Cities Need Slums for Migrant

Workers," *People's Daily*, Apr. 15, 2008; Fiona Tam, "Mayor Aims to Put Shenzhen at Top of Mainland's Welfare League," *South China Morning Post*, Apr. 15, 2008.

19 Soutik Biswas, "India's 'Biggest Slum Demolitions,'" BBC News http://news.bbc.co.uk/1/hi/world/south_asia/4222525.stm.

20 Amnesty International, "The Unseen Majority: Nairobi's Two Million Slum-Dwellers" (London: Amnesty International, 2009).

21 Marie Huchzermeyer, "Slum Upgrading in Nairobi within the Housing and Basic Services Market," *Journal of Asian and African Studies* 43, no. 1 (2008): 22.

22 Gary Duffy, "Brazil's Battle for Shanty Town Residents," BBC News, http://news.bbc.co.uk/1/hi/world/americas/7870395.stm.

3 ARRIVING AT THE TOP OF THE PYRAMID

1 "West Adams—Mapping L.A.," *Los Angeles Times*, http://projects.latimes .com/mapping-la/neighborhoods/neighborhood/west-adams/.

2 Ibid.

3 Dowell Myers, "Demographic and Housing Transition in South Central Los Angeles, 1990 to 2000: Working Paper" (Los Angeles: USC School of Policy, Planning and Development, 2002).

4 Dowell Myers, Julie Park, and Sung Ho Ryu, "Dynamics of Immigrant Settlement in Los Angeles: Upward Mobility, Arrival and Exodus" (Los Angeles: The John Randolph Haynes and Dora Haynes Foundation, 2005), 8–9.

5 Dowell Myers, "Demographic Dynamism and Metropolitan Change: Comparing Los Angeles, New York, Chicago and Washington, DC," *Housing Policy Debate* 10, no. 4 (1999): 924.

6 Myers, Park, and Ryu, "Dynamics of Immigrant Settlement in Los Angeles": 4.

7 Mike Davis, *Magical Urbanism: Latinos Reinvent the US City* (London: Verso, 2000), 51–55.

8 Rickard Sandell, "Immigration: World Differences" (Madrid: Real Instituto Elcano, 2007); UNDP, *Human Development Report 2009: Overcoming Barriers: Human Mobility and Development* (New York: Palgrave Macmillan, 2009); OECD, "International Migration Outlook" (Paris: OECD, 2007).

9 AFP, "Apec Warned of Critical Labour Shortages," Nov. 10, 2009.

10 VECCI, "Task Group Report: Workplace Futures" (Melbourne: Victorian

Employers' Chamber of Commerce and Industry, 2009); ABC News, "Business Group Warns of Labour Shortage," 2009; Mark Pownall, "It's Not Plain Sailing on Skilled Migration," *WA Business News*, Nov. 5, 2009.

11 CFIB, "Business Barometer," *Canadian Federation of Independent Business*, Nov. 4, 2009.

12 Christian Joppke, "Why Liberal States Accept Unwanted Immigration," *World Politics* 50, no. 2 (1998): 266.

13 AFP, "Apec Warned of Critical Labour Shortages."

14 Jason Gilmore, "The 2008 Canadian Immigrant Labour Market: Analysis of Quality of Employment" (Ottawa: Statistics Canada, 2009).

15 Garnett Picot, Feng Hou, and Simon Coulombe, "Chronic Low Income and Low-Income Dynamics among Recent Immigrants" (Ottawa: Statistics Canada, 2007).

16 CIC, "Annual Report to Parliament on Immigration, 2005" (Ottawa: Citizenship and Immigration Canada, 2005).

17 Jeff Dayton-Johnson et al., *Gaining from Migration: Towards a New Mobility System* (Paris: OECD Development Centre, 2007), 20.

18 Picot, Hou, and Coulombe, "Chronic Low Income and Low-Income Dynamics Among Recent Immigrants."

19 Dennis Broeders and Godfried Engbersen, "The Fight against Illegal Migration: Identification Policies and Immigrants' Counterstrategies," *American Behavioural Scientist* 50, no. 12 (2007): 1592.

20 Audrey Singer, "Twenty-First Century Gateways: An Introduction," in *Twenty-First Century Gateways: Immigrant Incorporation in Suburban America*, eds. Audrey Singer, Susan W. Hardwick, and Caroline B. Brettell (Washington: Brookings Institution Press, 2008).

21 William H. Frey, "Melting Pot Suburbs: A Census 2000 Study of Suburban Diversity" (Washington: Brookings Institution Press, 2001).

22 Ivan Light and Michael Francis Johnston, "The Metropolitan Dispersion of Mexican Immigrants to the United States, 1980 to 2000," *Journal of Ethnic and Migration Studies* 35, no. 1 (2009).

23 Robert A. Murdie, "Diversity and Concentration in Canadian Immigration: Trends in Toronto, Montreal and Vancouver, 1971–2006" (Toronto: Centre for Urban & Community Studies [University of Toronto], 2008).

24 Marie Price and Audrey Singer, "Immigrants, Suburbs and the Politics of Reception in Metropolitan Washington," in *Twenty-First Century Gateways*, 150–51.

25 Neal Peirce, "Outreach to Immigrants: A Suburb's Exciting New Way," *Nation's Cities Weekly* 32, no. 19 (2009): 2.

4 THE URBANIZATION OF THE VILLAGE

1 Martin Petrick and Ewa Tyran, "Development Perspectives of Subsistence Farms in South-Eastern Poland: Social Buffer Stock or Commercial Agriculture?," in *IAMO Forum* (Halle, Germany: 2004).

2 Poland achieves only 21 percent of the EU average gross product per hectare of utilized agricultural land for crops. See Hilary Ingham and Mike Ingham, "How Big Is the Problem of Polish Agriculture?" *Europe-Asia Studies* 56, no. 2 (2004): 215.

3 Robert R. Kaufman, "Market Reform and Social Protection: Lessons from the Czech Republic, Hungary and Poland," *East European Politics & Societies* 21, no. 1 (2007).

4 Ingham and Ingham, "How Big Is the Problem of Polish Agriculture?" 222–23.

5 Dilip Ratha, "Revisions to Remittance Trends 2007," in *Migration and Development Brief 5* (World Bank, 2007).

6 For a moving account of the psychological effects of this mass family displacement, see Fan Lixin's film *Last Train Home*.

7 A new social security system launched by Beijing in December 2009 will take many years to implement and may prove fiscally impossible to apply fully. See Howard W. French, "Pension Crisis Looms for China," *International Herald Tribune*, Mar. 20, 2007; Ariana Eunjung Cha, "In China, Despair Mounting among Migrant Workers," *The Washington Post*, Mar. 4, 2009.

8 James Kynge, "China's Workers Enable Village Consumer," *Financial Times*, Feb. 26, 2004.

9 Rob Young, "China's Workers Return to Cities," BBC News, Sept. 8, 2009.

10 Michael Lipton and Qi Zhang, "Reducing Inequality and Poverty During Liberalisation in China: Rural and Agricultural Experiences and Policy Options" (Brighton: PRUS Working Paper no. 37, 2007); OECD, "Review of Agricultural Policies—China" (2005).

11 Ran Tao and Zhigang Xu, "Urbanization, Rural Land System and Social Security for Migrants in China," *Journal of Development Studies* 43, no. 7 (2007): 1,309.

12 Srijit Mishra, "Farmers' Suicides in Maharashtra," *Economic and Political Weekly*, Apr. 22, 2006.

13 Debarshi Das, "Persistence of Small-Scale, Family Farms in India: A

Note," *The Journal of International Trade & Economic Development* 16, no. 3 (2007); Srijit Mishra, "Agrarian Scenario in Post-Reform India: A Story of Distress, Despair and Death" (Mumbai: Indira Gandhi Institute of Development Research, 2007).

14 Katy Gardner, "Keeping Connected: Security, Place and Social Capital in a 'Londoni' Village in Sylhet," *Journal of the Royal Anthropological Institute* 14 (2008).

15 Tasneem Siddiqui, "Migration as a Livelihood Strategy of the Poor: The Bangladesh Case," in *Regional Conference on Migration, Development and Pro-Poor Policy Choices in Asia* (Dhaka: RMMRU, 2003).

16 Katy Gardner and Zahir Ahmed, "Place, Social Protection and Migration in Bangladesh: A Londoni Village in Biswanath" (Brighton: Development Research Centre on Migration, Globalisation and Poverty, 2006). A revised and expanded version appears in Gardner and Ahmed, "Degrees of Separation: Informal Social Protection, Relatedness and Migration in Biswanath, Bangladesh," *Journal of Development Studies* 45, no. 1 (2009).

17 Deboarah Fahy Bryceson, "Deagrarianization and Rural Employment in Sub-Saharan Africa: A Sectoral Perspective," *World Development* 24, no. 1 (1996); Vali Jamal and John Weeks, "The Vanishing Rural–Urban Gap in Sub-Saharan Africa," *International Labour Review* 127, no. 3 (1988).

18 See, for example, Robert Fishman, "Global Suburbs," in *First Biennial Conference of the Urban History Association* (Pittsburgh: 2002); Elisabeth Rosenthal, "Chinese Town's Main Export: Its Young Men," *The New York Times*, June 26, 2000.

19 Roger Ballard, "A Case of Capital Rich Under-Development: The Paradoxical Consequences of Successful Transnational Entrepreneurship from Mirpur," *Contributions to Indian Sociology* 37, no. 49–81 (2003): 41.

20 The most comprehensive exploration of the farm-size issue is found in Michael Lipton, *Land Reform in Developing Countries: Property Rights and Property Wrongs* (Abington: Routledge, 2009), 65–120.

5 THE FIRST GREAT MIGRATION

1 Jeanne Bouvier, *Mes Memoires*, ed. Daniel Armogathe (Paris: Editions de la Découverte, 1983), English translation from Mark Traugott, ed., *The French Worker: Autobiographies from the Early Industrial Era* (Berkeley: University of California Press, 1993), 367–81.

NOTES

2 Tilly, "Migration in Modern European History," 58.

3 William H. McNeill, "Human Migration: A Historical Overview," in *Human Migration: Patterns & Policies*, eds. William H. McNeill and Ruth S. Adams (Bloomington: Indiana University Press, 1978), 6.

4 Mary Dorothy George, *London Life in the Eighteenth Century* (Chicago: Academy, 1985), 25–26.

5 William H. McNeill, *Population and Politics since 1750* (Charlottesville: University Press of Virginia, 1990), 9–10.

6 Olwen H. Hufton, *The Poor of Eighteenth-Century France 1750–1789* (Oxford: Oxford University Press, 1974), 99–101.

7 George Rudé, "Society and Conflict in London and Paris in the Eighteenth Century," in *Paris and London in the 18th Century* (London: Wm. Collins, 1974), 35–36.

8 Rudé, "The Social Composition of the Parisian Insurgents of 1789–91," in *Paris and London in the 18th Century*, 104–109.

9 McNeill, *Population and Politics since 1750*, 11.

10 Rudé, "Society and Conflict in London and Paris in the Eighteenth Century," 53–55.

11 S. L. Popkin, "The Rational Peasant: The Political Economy of Peasant Society," *Theory and Society* 9 (1980); Patrick Svensson, "Peasants and Entrepreneurship in the Nineteenth-Century Agricultural Transformation of Sweden," *Social Science History* 30, no. 3 (2006).

12 Jonathan David Chambers and G. E. Mingay, *The Agricultural Revolution, 1750–1880* (London: B.T. Batsford, 1968), 104.

13 Eugen Weber, *Peasants into Frenchmen: The Modernization of Rural France, 1870–1914* (Stanford: Stanford University Press, 1976), 10. This is also very well documented in Graham Robb, *The Discovery of France* (London: Picador, 2007).

14 For claims of Britain's superior living standards, see Tom Kemp, *Economic Forces in French History* (London: Dobson, 1971); Charles P. Kindleberger, *Economic Growth in France and Britain, 1851–1950* (Oxford: Oxford University Press, 1964). For more recent, nuanced arguments about this distinction, see Patrick Karl O'Brien, "Path Dependency, or Why Britain Became an Industrialized and Urbanized Economy Long before France," *Economic History Review* XLIX, no. 2 (1996): 213.

15 Karl Marx, *The Eighteenth Brumaire of Louis Bonaparte* (New York: International Publishers, 1963).

332

16 Joseph Rykwert, *The Seduction of Place: The History and Future of the City* (Oxford: Oxford University Press, 2000), 78.

17 John Burnett, ed., *Useful Toil: Autobiographies of Working People from the 1820s to the 1920s* (London: Allen Lane, 1974), cited in White, *London in the Nineteenth Century*, 106.

18 White, *London in the Nineteenth Century*, 107.

19 Ibid., 206.

20 Anthony S. Wohl, *The Eternal Slum: Housing and Social Policy in Victorian London* (New Brunswick, NJ: Transaction Publishers, 2002), 172.

21 Richard Dennis, "The Geography of Victorian Values: Philanthropic Housing in London, 1840–1900," *Journal of Historical Geography* 15, no. 1 (1989).

22 Cited in Andrew Miles, *Social Mobility in Nineteenth- and Early Twentieth-Century England* (Houndmills: Macmillan Press, 1999), 1.

23 Ibid., 23–34.

24 David Mitch, "Literacy and Occupational Mobility in Rural Versus Urban Victorian England," *Historical Methods* 38, no. 1 (2005); Jason Long, "Social Mobility within and across Generations in Britain since 1851," in *Economic History Society Conference* (Oxford: 2007).

25 Aside from the previously cited works by Andrew Miles and Jason Long, see Sara Horrell, Jane Humphries, and Hans-Joachim Voth, "Destined for Deprivation: Human Capital Formation and Intergenerational Poverty in Nineteenth-Century England," *Explorations in Economic History* 38 (2001); Kenneth Prandy and Wendy Bottero, "Social Reproduction and Mobility in Britain and Ireland in the Nineteenth and Early Twentieth Centuries," *Sociology* 34, no. 2 (2000); Paul Lambert, Kenneth Prandy, and Wendy Bottero, "By Slow Degrees: Two Centuries of Social Reproduction and Mobility in Britain," *Sociological Research Online* 12, no. 1 (2007), www.socresonline.org.uk/12/1/prandy.html.

26 Jason Long and Joseph Ferrie, "A Tale of Two Labor Markets: Intergenerational Occupational Mobility in Britain and the U.S. since 1850," ed. National Bureau of Economic Research (Cambridge, MA: 2005).

27 Leslie Page Moch, *Moving Europeans: Migration in Western Europe since 1650* (Bloomington: Indiana University Press, 2003), 149.

28 Timothy J. Hatton and Jeffrey G Williamson, "What Drove the Mass Migrations from Europe in the Late Nineteenth Century?" ed. National Bureau of Economic Research (Cambridge, MA: 1992); Dudley Baines, *Migration in a Mature Economy* (Cambridge: Cambridge University Press, 1985).

29 Cited in Richard Harris, *Unplanned Suburbs* (Baltimore: Johns Hopkins University Press, 1996), 111–25.

30 Ibid., 200–232; David G. Burley, "Review of Richard Harris, Unplanned Suburbs," *Humanities & Social Sciences Online*, March 19,1997, http://www.h-net.org/reviews/showrev.php?id=841.

31 Richard Harris, "Chicago's Other Suburbs," *The Geographical Review* 84 (1994).

32 Elaine Lewinnek, "Better Than a Bank for a Poor Man? Home Financing in Chicago, 1870–1930," in *Market Culture Colloquium at Yale* (New Haven: 2004).

6 THE DEATH AND LIFE OF A GREAT ARRIVAL CITY

1 Orhan Esen, "Self-Service City: Istanbul," *metroZones* 4 (2004), www.metrozones.info/metrobuecher/istanbul/index.html.

2 Elvan Gülöksüz, "Negotiation of Property Rights in Urban Land in Istanbul," *International Journal of Urban and Regional Research* 26, no. 2 (2002).

3 Şükrü Aslan, *1 Mayis Mahallesi* (Istanbul: Iletisim Yayinlari, 2004), translation by Belmin Soylemez.

4 Ibid., 197–218.

5 Morris Juppenlatz, cited in Lisa Peattie and Jose A. Aldrete-Haas, "'Marginal' Settlements in Developing Countries: Research, Advocacy of Policy and Evolution of Programs," *Annual Review of Sociology* 7 (1981): 158.

6 Umut Duyar-Kienast, *The Formation of Gecekondu Settlements in Turkey* (Münster: Lit Verlag Münster, 2005), 7–10, 96.

7 Tahire Erman, "The Politics of Squatter (Gecekondu) Studies in Turkey: The Changing Representations of Rural Migrants in the Academic Discourse," *Urban Studies* 38, no. 7 (2001).

8 Ozcan Koknel, quoted in Nicholas Gage, "The Violence of Extremism Grips Turkish Politics," *The New York Times*, May 7, 1978.

9 "New Turkish Rulers Give Ministry Aides Broad Civil Powers," *The New York Times*, Sept. 14, 1980.

10 John Kifner, "Ankara's Slum Dwellers Grateful for Coup," *The New York Times*, Sept. 19, 1980.

11 Amnesty International, "Turkey: Human Rights Denied" (London: Amnesty International, 1988).

12 Aslan, *1 Mayis Mahallesi*, 197–218.

13 Duyar-Kienast, *The Formation of Gecekondu Settlements in Turkey*, 9.

14 Jim Bodgener, "'We'll Halve Inflation'—Interview with Turgut Ozal," *Financial Times*, May 23, 1988.

15 Duyar-Kienast, *The Formation of Gecekondu Settlements in Turkey*, 11.

16 Gokce, cited in ibid., 88.

17 Esen, "Self-Service City: Istanbul."

18 Duyar-Kienast, *The Formation of Gecekondu Settlements in Turkey*, 123.

19 Ibid., 124.

20 Ibid., 52–53.

21 Ibid., 27.

22 Murat Cemal Yalcintan and Adem Erdem Erbas, "Impacts of 'Gecekondu' on the Electoral Geography of Istanbul," *International Labour and Working-Class History*, no. 64 (2003): 104–109.

23 Binnaz Toprak, "Religion and State in Turkey," in *Contemporary Turkey: Challenges of Change* (Istanbul: 1999), 5.

24 Ali Çarkoğlu and Binnaz Toprak, "Religion, Society and Politics in a Changing Turkey" (Istanbul: TESEV, 2006).

25 Esen, "Self-Service City: Istanbul."

26 Ayse Bugra, "The Immoral Economy of Housing in Turkey," *International Journal of Urban and Regional Research* 22, no. 2 (1998): 311.

27 Zafer Senocak, "Turkey's Corset of Moderation," *Die Welt*, July 24, 2007.

28 Esen, "Self-Service City: Istanbul."

7 WHEN THE MARGINS EXPLODE

1 Esfandiar Zebardast, "Marginalization of the Urban Poor and the Expansion of the Spontaneous Settlements on the Tehran Metropolitan Fringe," *Cities* 23, no. 6 (2006).

2 Ibid.: 39, 451.

3 Robert E. Looney, *Economic Origins of the Iranian Revolution* (Elmsford, NY: Pergamon Press, 1982), 264.

4 Ali M. Ansari, *Modern Iran since 1921* (Harlow: Longman, 2003), 147.

5 Misagh Parsa, *Social Origins of the Iranian Revolution* (Piscataway, NJ: Rutgers, 1989), 73.

6 Tahmoores Sarraf, *Cry of a Nation: The Saga of the Iranian Revolution* (New York: Peter Lang, 1990), 25.

7 Parsa, *Social Origins of the Iranian Revolution*, 78.

8 Ibid., 76–77.

9 Asef Bayat, *Street Politics: Poor People's Movements in Iran* (New York: Columbia University Press, 1997), 43.

10 Leonard Binder, "The Political Economy of the Middle East, 1973–78"

(Washington: United States Congress Joint Economic Committee, 1980), 163.

11 Ali Farazmand, *The State, Bureaucracy and Revolution in Modern Iran: Agrarian Reforms and Regime Politics* (New York: Praeger Publishers, 1989), 198–201.

12 Parsa, *Social Origins of the Iranian Revolution*, xii.

13 Bayat, *Street Politics*, 159.

14 Ibid., 99.

15 Ansari, *Modern Iran since 1921*, 221.

16 Bayat, *Street Politics*, 101.

17 Zebardast, "Marginalization of the Urban Poor and the Expansion of the Spontaneous Settlements on the Tehran Metropolitan Fringe," 451–52.

18 Amir Nikpey, *Politique et Religion en Iran Contemporarain* (Paris: L'Harmattan, 2003); Farhad Khosrokhavar, "The New Religiosity in Iran," *Social Compass* 54, no. 3 (2007).

19 Alma Guillermoprieto, "The Gambler," *The New York Review of Books*, Oct. 20, 2005.

20 Based on Venezuelan government spending figures reported at www.sisov.mpd.gob.ve and OECD population figures, and tabulated by Info Venezuela News.

21 Daniel Ortega and Francisco Rodríguez, "Freed from Illiteracy? A Closer Look at Venezuela's Misión Robinson Literacy Campaign," *Economic Development and Cultural Change* 57, no. 1 (2008).

22 Tina Rosenberg, "The Perils of Petrocracy," *New York Times Magazine*, Nov. 4, 2007.

23 Fabiola Sanchez, "Traditionally Pro-Chavez Slum Turns to Opposition," *Associated Press*, Dec. 5, 2008.

24 Francisco Rodríguez, "An Empty Revolution: The Unfulfilled Promises of Hugo Chávez," *Foreign Affairs* (Mar./Apr. 2008).

25 Indira A. R. Lakshmanan, "Critics Slam Venezuelan Oil Windfall Spending," *The Boston Globe*, Aug. 13, 2006.

26 Norman Gall, "Oil and Democracy in Venezuela," *Braudel Papers*, no. 39 (2006).

27 Sujata Patel, "The Popularity of the Shiv Sena: Urbanisation and Its Consequences," *Asian Studies Review* 19, no. 3 (1996): 44.

28 Bal Thackeray, "I Still Believe in Dictatorship," *Illustrated Weekly of India*, Feb. 19, 1984, cited in Mary Katzenstein, Uday Singh Mehta and Usha Thakkar, "The Rebirth of Shiv Sena: The Symbiosis of Discursive and Organizational Power," *The Journal of Asian Studies* 56, no. 2 (1997): 379.

29 Atreyee Sen, *Shiv Sena Women: Violence and Communalism in a Bombay Slum* (London: Hurst & Company, 2007), 26–30, 90, 180.

30 Gérard Heuzé, "Cultural Populism: The Appeal of the Shiv Sena," in *Bombay: Metaphor for Modern India*, eds. Sujata Patel and Alice Thorner (Oxford: Oxford University Press, 1995), 33–34, 219. Italics from source.

31 Cited in Kalpana Sharma, "Chronicle of a Riot Foretold," in *Bombay: Metaphor for Modern India*, 284.

32 Sikata Banerjee, *Warriors in Politics: Hindu Nationalism, Violence and the Shiv Sena in India* (Boulder: Westview Press, 2000), 54.

8 THE NEW CITY CONFRONTS THE OLD WORLD

1 Michèle Tribalat, ed., *Cent ans d'immigration, étrangers d'hier français d'aujourd'hui* (Paris: Presses Universitaires de France INED, 1991), 65–71.

2 Piotr Smolar, "L'antiterrorisme, selon le patron des R G," *Le Monde*, Nov. 11, 2005.

3 Alec G. Hargreaves, *Multi-Ethnic France: Immigration, Politics, Culture and Society* (Second Edition) (New York: Routledge, 2007), 104.

4 Several major studies have shown that second-generation African immigrants in France are fully integrated, including Michèle Tribalat, *De l'immigration à l'assimilation : Enquête sur les populations d'origine étrangère en France* (Paris: La Découverte, 1996); C. Lefèvre and A. Filhon, eds., *Histoires de familles, histoires familiales* (Paris: INED, 2005).

5 Estimate of arrival-city size derived from OECD, especially Rainer Münz et al., "What Are the Migrants' Contributions to Employment and Growth? A European Approach" (Paris: OECD, 2006).

6 Loïc Wacquant, *Urban Outcasts: A Comparative Study of Advanced Marginality* (Cambridge: Polity Press, 2008), 284. Italics in original.

7 Nicolas Sarkozy, *Testimony* (Petersfield: Harriman House Ltd, 2006), 63–65.

8 For example, see Patrick Simon, "The Mosaic Pattern: Cohabitation between Ethnic Groups in Belleville, Paris," in *Minorities in European Cities*, eds. Sophie Body-Gendrot and Marco Martiniello (Houndmills: Macmillan Press, 2000).

9 Sophie Body-Gendrot, *Police et discriminations raciales : Le tabou français* (Paris: Editions de l'Atelier, 2003); Tribalat, *De l'immigration à l'assimilation*.

10 Brice-Arsène Mankou, *Pour une France multicolore : L'exemple d'Evry* (Paris: Cultures Croisées, 2005).

11 "Zus: Les Pyramides," Délégation interministérielle à la Ville, http://sig.ville.gouv.fr/Synthese/1110040.

12 Azouz Begag, *Shantytown Kid (Le gone du Chaâba)* (Lincoln: University of Nebraska Press, 1986), 45.

13 Divorce rate: Interview with Kazim Erdogan. For other figures, see Claus Mueller, "Integrating Turkish Communities: A German Dilemma," *Population Research and Policy Review* 25, no. 5–6 (2006). For unemployment, see Berlin-Kreuzberg-Kottbusser Tor, Soziale Stadt, Deutsches Institut für Urbanistik, www.sozialestadt.de.

14 Leyla Gülçür, "A Study on Domestic Violence and Sexual Abuse in Ankara, Turkey," in *WWHR Reports* no. 4 (Istanbul: WWHR, 1999).

15 Dilek Gügö, "Germans Can Be Also Turks, Says a Berlin Author," *Turkish Daily News*, May 15, 2007; Robert Collier, "Germany Copes with Integrating Turkish Minority," *San Francisco Chronicle*, Nov. 13, 2005.

16 Şule Özüekren and Ebru Ergoz Karahan, "Residential Careers of Turkish (Im)Migrants at Home and Abroad—the Case of Istanbul and Berlin," in *ENHR International Conference* (Ljubljana: 2006).

17 Şule Özüekren and Ronald van Kempen, eds., *Turks in European Cities: Housing and Urban Segregation* (Utrecht: ERCOMER, 1997), chapters 6 and 8.

18 Kogan, "Labour Market Careers of Immigrants in Germany and the United Kingdom."

19 Roger Boyes and Dorte Huneke, "Is It Easier to Be a Turk in Berlin or a Pakistani in Bradford?" (London: Anglo-German Foundation for the Study of Industrial Society, 2004).

20 Günther Glebe, "Housing and Segregation of Turks in Germany," in *Turks in European Cities: Housing and Urban Segregation*, eds. Özüekren and van Kempen, 124.

21 Kogan, "Labour Market Careers of Immigrants in Germany and the United Kingdom," 440.

22 An excellent analysis of these problems is found in Ruth Mandel, *Cosmopolitan Anxieties: Turkish Challenges to Citizenship and Belonging in Germany* (Durham: Duke University Press, 2008), 141–54.

23 Glebe, "Housing and Segregation of Turks in Germany," 125.

24 Merih Anil, "Explaining the Naturalisation Practices of Turks in Germany in the Wake of the Citizenship Reform of 1999," *Journal of Ethnic and Migration Studies* 33, no. 8 (2007): 1366.

25 Özüekren and Karahan, "Residential Careers of Turkish (Im)Migrants at Home and Abroad—the Case of Istanbul and Berlin."

26 Francisco Javier Moreno Fuentes, "Evolution of Spanish Immigration

Policies and Their Impact on North African Migration to Spain," *Studies in Culture, Polity and Identities* 6, no. 1 (2005).

27 Niki Kitsantonis, "E.U. Systems Fail to Stem the Flow of Migrants," *International Herald Tribune*, Nov. 19, 2009.

28 Rosa Aparicio, "The Integration of the Second and 1.5 Generations of Moroccan, Dominican and Peruvian Origin in Madrid and Barcelona," *Journal of Ethnic and Migration Studies* 33, no. 7 (2007).

9 ARRIVAL'S END

1 It has become commonplace to claim that in 1996 the United Nations or one of its agencies declared Jardim Angela "the most violent place in the world." In fact, no such declaration was ever made. Rather, Brazil's crime statistics that year, which included neighborhood breakdowns for the first time, were seized upon by media, including a UNESCO newsletter, because the neighborhood's homicide rate was dramatically higher than any other place for which such rates have been recorded. The "world's deadliest" claim became a working assumption among governments and NGOs.

2 Nancy Cardia, "Urban Violence in São Paulo" (Washington: Woodrow Wilson International Center, 2000); Amnesty International, "They Come in Shooting: Policing Socially Excluded Communities" (London: Amnesty International, 2005).

3 Mota Guedes and Vieira Oliveira, "Braudel Papers 38: Democratization of Consumption: Progress and Aspirations in São Paulo's Periphery," 11.

4 Some of his analysis can be found in Bruno Paes Manso, Maryluci de Araujo Faria, and Norman Gall, "Diadema: Frontier Violence and Civilization in Sao Paulo's Periphery" (São Paulo: Fernand Braudel Institute of World Economics, 2005) and Bruno Paes Manso, *O Homem X: Uma Reportagem Sobre a Alma Do Assassino Em São Paulo* (São Paulo: Record, 2005).

5 The nature of poverty as a strategic passage rather than a permanent state is analyzed in detail in Narayan, Pritchett, and Kapoor, *Moving Out of Poverty*.

6 See, for example, the findings of the comprehensive study by Walter Russell Mead and Sherle Schwenninger, *The Bridge to a Global Middle Class: Development, Trade and International Finance* (Norwell, MA: Kluwer, 2002).

7 Steven Durlauf, "Neighborhood Feedbacks, Endogenous Stratification and Income Inequality," in *Dynamic Disequilibrium Modeling*, eds. William A. Barnett, Giancarlo Gandolfo, and Claude Hillinger (Cambridge: Cambridge University Press, 1996). For a review of the literature

demonstrating the importance of a middle class in maintaining stability and promoting democracy and prosperity, see Steven Pressman, "The Decline of the Middle Class: An International Perspective," *Journal of Economic Issues* XLI, no. 1 (2007).

8 Guedes and Oliveira, "Braudel Papers 38."

9 David Rothkopf, "Pain in the Middle," *Newsweek International*, Nov. 21, 2005.

10 Branko Milanovic, "Decomposing World Income Distribution: Does the World Have a Middle Class?" *Review of Income and Wealth* 48, no. 2 (2002).

11 Rasheeda Bhagat, "A One-Billion Middle-Class Deluge from India, China by 2020," *The Hindu Business Line*, Jun. 29, 2006. For a similar analysis using different consumer data, see Diana Farrell, Ulrich A. Gersch, and Elizabeth Stephenson, "The Value of China's Emerging Middle Class," *The McKinsey Quarterly* (2006).

12 Nancy Birdsall, Carol Graham, and Stefano Pettinato, "Stuck in the Tunnel: Is Globalization Muddling the Middle Class?" (Washington: Center on Social and Economic Dynamics, 2000), 1, 8, 14.

13 Jan Nijman, "Mumbai's Mysterious Middle Class," *International Journal of Urban and Regional Research* 30, no. 4 (2006): 758.

14 Mead and Schwenninger, *The Bridge to a Global Middle Class.*

15 Janice E. Perlman, "The Myth of Marginality Revisited: The Case of Favelas in Rio De Janeiro, 1969–2003" (Washington: The World Bank, 2005), 16, 20.

16 Mead and Schwenninger, *The Bridge to a Global Middle Class.*

17 Eduardo Zepeda et al., "Changes in Earnings in Brazil, Chile and Mexico: Disentangling the Forces Behind Pro-Poor Change in Labour Markets" (Brasilia: IPC-IG [UNDP], 2009).

18 Amartya Sen, *Development as Freedom* (Oxford: Oxford University Press, 1999).

19 A. Durand-Lasserve and L. Royston, *Holding Their Ground: Secure Land Tenure for the Urban Poor in Developing Countries* (London: Earthscan, 2002), 3.

20 Hernando de Soto, *The Other Path: The Invisible Revolution in the Third World* (New York: Harper & Row, 1989).

21 de Soto, *The Mystery of Capital: Why Capitalism Triumphs in the West and Fails Everywhere Else* (London: Black Swan, 2000), 35. A number of critics have pointed out that this number is unverifiable.

22 L. J. Alston, G. D. Libecap and B. Mueller, *Titles, Conflict and Land Use: The Development of Property Rights on the Brazilian Amazon Frontier* (Ann Arbor: Michigan University Press, 1999).

23 G. Feder and D. Feeny, "Land Tenure and Property Rights: Theory and

Implications for Development Policy," *World Bank Economic Review* 3 (1991);
O. J. Lanjouw and P. I. Levy, "Untitled: A Study of Informal and Formal
Propertry Rights in Urban Ecuador," *The Economic Journal* 112 (2002);
K. Deininger and J. Chamorro, "Investment and Equity Effects of Land
Regularisation: The Case of Nicraragua," *Agricultural Economics* 30 (2004);
E. Field, "Property Rights and Household Time Allocation in Urban
Squatter Communities: Evidence from Peru," in *Second Urban Resarch
Symposium* (Washington: World Bank, 2003).

24 Alan Gilbert, "On the Mystery of Capital and the Myths of Hernando de
Soto: What Difference Does Legal Title Make?" *International Development
Planning Review* (2002); A. M. Varley, "Private or Public: Debating the
Meaning of Tenure Legalization," *International Journal of Urban and
Regional Research* 26, no. 3 (2002); O. M. Razzaz, "Examining Property
Rights and Investment in Informal Areas: The Case of Jordan," *Land
Economics* 69, no. 4 (1993); J. M. L. Kironde, "Understanding Land Markets
in African Urban Areas: The Case of Dar Es Salaam, Tanzania," *Habitat
International* 24 (2000).

25 Robert E. Smith, "Land Tenure Reform in Africa: A Shift to the
Defensive," *Progress in Development Studies* 3, no. 3 (2003).

26 A. Antwi and J. Adams, "Economic Rationality and Informal Urban Land
Transactions in Accra, Ghana," *Journal of Property Research* 20, no. 1 (2003);
M. M. Omirin and A. Antwi, "Informality, Illegality and Market Efficiency:
A Case for Land Market Deregulation in Accra and Lagos" (London, 2004).

27 R. Home and H. Lim, *Demystifying the Mystery of Capital: Land Tenure and
Poverty in Africa and the Caribbean* (London: Glasshouse Press, 2004);
Bishwapriya Sanyal, "Intention and Outcome: Formalization and Its
Consequences," *Regional Development Dialogue* 17, no. 1 (1996).

28 Staffan Granér, "Hernando de Soto and the Mystification of Capital,"
Eurozine, no. 13 (Jan. 19, 2007): 6.

29 Donald A. Krueckenberg, "The Lessons of John Locke or Hernando de Soto:
What If Your Dreams Come True?" *Housing Policy Debate* 15, no. 1 (2004): 3.

10 ARRIVING IN STYLE

1 Gerben Helleman and Frank Wassenber, "The Renewal of What Was
Tomorrow's Idealistic City, Amsterdam's Bijlmermeer High-Rise," *Cities*
21, no. 1 (2004); Ronald Van Kempen et al., eds., *Restructuring Large Housing
Estates in Europe* (Bristol: The Policy Press, 2005).

2 Helleman and Wassenber, "The Renewal of What Was Tomorrow's Idealistic City, Amsterdam's Bijlmermeer High-Rise," 8.

3 Maurice Crul and Liesbeth Heering, eds., *The Position of the Turkish and Moroccan Second Generation in Amsterdam and Rotterdam* (Amsterdam: Amsterdam University Press, 2008), 63–85, 166.

4 Doug Saunders, "Citizen Jane," *The Globe and Mail*, Oct. 11, 1997.

5 William H. Whyte, *City: Rediscovering the Center* (New York: Doubleday, 1989); Oscar Newman, *Defensible Space: Crime Prevention through Urban Design* (New York: MacMillan, 1972).

6 Jane Jacobs, *The Death and Life of Great American Cities* (New York: Random House, 1961), 221.

7 Alice Coleman, *Utopia on Trial: Vision and Reality in Planned Housing* (London: Longwood, 1985).

8 Narayan, Pritchett and Kapoor, *Moving Out of Poverty*, 223–72.

9 Recent exposés of the failure of aid include Dambisa Moyo, *Dead Aid: Why Aid Is Not Working and How There Is Another Way for Africa* (London: Allen Lane, 2009); William Easterly, *The White Man's Burden: Why the West's Efforts to Aid the Rest Have Done So Much Ill and So Little Good* (Oxford: Oxford University Press, 2007). For a more balanced discussion of the flaws and potentials of foreign aid, see Paul Collier, *The Bottom Billion: Why the Poorest Countries Are Failing and What Can Be Done About It* (Oxford: Oxford University Press, 2007).

10 Smolka and de A. Larangeira, "Informality and Poverty in Latin American Urban Policies."

11 María Mercedes Maldonado Copello, "Operación urbanistica Nuevo Usme: provision de suelo urbanizado para vivienda social, a partir de la redistribución social de plusvilias" (Bogota: The World Bank, 2005): Lucgom, "Operación Nuevo Usme se desarrollará en 20 años megaproyecto en Usme, para frenar el crecimiento desordenado del sur," *El Tiempo*, July 21, 2009.

12 Vinit Mukhija, "Upgrading Housing Settlements in Developing Countries: The Impact of Existing Physical Conditions," *Cities* 18, no. 4 (2001).

13 Jan Nijman, "Against the Odds: Slum Rehabilitation in Neoliberal Mumbai," *Cities* 25 (2008).

14 Heather Smith and David Ley, "Even in Canada? The Multiscalar Construction and Experience of Concentrated Immigrant Poverty in Gateway Cities," *Annals of the Association of American Geographers* 98, no. 3 (2008); United Way, "Poverty by Postal Code: The Geography of

Neighborhood Poverty" (Toronto: United Way of Greater Toronto and the Canadian Council on Social Development, 2004).

15 Smith and Ley, "Even in Canada?" 708.

16 Mohammad A. Qadeer, "Ethnic Segregation in a Multicultural City," in *Desegregating the City: Ghettos, Enclaves & Inequality*, ed. David P. Varaday (Albany: SUNY Press, 2005); Kristin Good, "Patterns of Politics in Canada's Immigrant-Receiving Cities and Suburbs," *Policy Studies* 26, no. 3/4 (2005).

17 J. David Hulchanski, "The Three Cities within Toronto: Income Polarization among Toronto's Neighborhoods, 1970–2000" (Toronto: Centre for Urban & Community Studies, University of Toronto, 2007).

18 Robert E. Park, *Human Communities: The City and Human Ecology* (Glencoe, IL: The Free Press, 1952).

19 Ceri Peach, "Good Segregation, Bad Segregation," *Planning Perspectives* 11 (1996); Ludi Simpson, Vasilis Gavalas, and Nissa Finney, "Population Dynamics in Ethnically Diverse Towns: The Long-Term Implications of Immigration," *Urban Studies* 45, no. 1 (2008); Ludi Simpson, "Ghettos of the Mind: The Empirical Behaviour of Indices of Segregation and Diversity," *Journal of the Royal Statistical Society* 170, no. 2 (2006).

20 Finney and Simpson, *"Sleepwalking to Segregation"*?; Simpson, Gavalas, and Finney, "Population Dynamics in Ethnically Diverse Towns: The Long-Term Implications of Immigration," *Urban Studies* 45, no. 1 (2008).

21 Asef Bayat, *Life as Politics: How Ordinary People Change the Middle East* (Stanford: Stanford University Press, 2010), 4–5, 171–84.

22 Kwame Anthony Appiah, *Cosmopolitanism: Ethics in a World of Strangers* (London: Allen Lane, 2006), 112–13; Salman Rushdie, *Imaginary Homelands: Essays and Criticism, 1981–1991* (London: Granta, 1991), 394.

ACKNOWLEDGMENTS

This book carries my name on the cover, but its geographic breadth and topical peculiarity could only have been sustained with the encouragement, cooperation, and exhaustive assistance of a great many people. To chronicle the complexities of cityward migration across sixteen countries and thirty cities and villages in a three-year period while running a major newspaper bureau, I relied on a group of field researchers who embraced this project with an inspiring degree of enthusiasm and a level of expertise that dwarfed my own. They went to great lengths to open the obscure corners of their cities and nations to me, made important introductions and crucial criticisms, and often took the time to be generous and fascinating hosts. They are Han Yi in Shenzhen, Fan Lixin in Chongqing, Amirul Rajiv in Dhaka, Mrinmayee Ranade in Mumbai, a good friend in Tehran, Belmin Soylemez in Istanbul, Dana Wiley in Nairobi, John Zagorski in Warsaw, Naomi Buck in Berlin, Genevieve Oger in Paris, Peter Sotirakis in Madrid, Benjamin Zeitlyn in East London, Ali Rocha in São Paulo, Katia Portillo-Vali in Los Angeles, and Julia Belluz in Toronto. My main researcher in London, Joanne Shurvell, has been persistent and inventive in her mastery of the British Library, the flight schedules of two dozen airlines, the contents of numerous databases, and the fast-changing vicissitudes of publishing. A number of other people have provided invaluable help with the research and conception of this book, including Craig Saunders,

Marjan Farahbaksh, Celia Donnelly, Nahrain Al-Mousawi, Carl Wilson, Stephanie Nolen, Anna Olejarczyk, and Barbara Hui.

Years before I began researching this book in earnest, when I would bewilder people by talking vaguely of "a book about what's happening in the outskirts," one person who was always eager to listen, and often seemed to understand the project better than I did, was Michael Schellenberg, the associate publisher at Knopf Canada. He and his Random House Canada colleagues saw the potential of this project from the beginning and their efforts have turned it into something far larger and more comprehensive than I could have envisaged. I have also received exhaustive and engaging assistance throughout this book's development from Andrew Miller at Pantheon Books, in New York, and extremely useful advice and information on the book's European sections from Pieter Swinkels and Floor Oosting at De Bezige Bij, in Amsterdam. John Pearce, also an advocate of this book from the earliest stages, has been that rarest of figures, an agent willing to criticize; his quiet proddings and suggestions have encouraged me to give this book its title and its emphasis on international migration.

None of this would have been possible had I not enjoyed the fortune of working for a newspaper, the *Globe and Mail*, that sees such wide-angle explorations of global development trends as a crucial part of its mission. Foreign editor Stephen Northfield, editors-in-chief Edward Greenspon and John Stackhouse, and former Focus editor Cathrin Bradbury have all encouraged me to devote my time and their resources to the larger topics of migration, urbanization, and social mobility, to take the time I needed to write this book, and to use my newspaper column as a laboratory for the ideas and developments that seem poised to dominate the coming century. This book is in many ways a testament to the style of journalism and debate they have brought to the media.

And none of it would have been conceivable if not for the great privilege and pleasure of my lifelong partnership with Elizabeth Renzetti.

INDEX

INDEX

DATE DUE
